D1567535

HOW TO MAKE
CHEROKEE
CLOTHING

written and illustrated
by
Donald Sizemore

Cherokee Publications, Cherokee, North Carolina

Cherokee Publications, Cherokee, NC 28719
Copyrighted © 1995 by Donald Sizemore

All Rights Reserved

First Edition
Printed in the United States of America

ISBN 0-935741-18-6

Text & Illustrations by Donald Sizemore

First Printing - 1995 - 8,500

PREFACE

One might ask, "Why write a book about Cherokee Clothing?" There are few, if any, books available to the public with detailed instructions and illustrations on how to make Cherokee clothing. My purpose is to record and preserve the old way of dress in this book not leaving the subject to vague unclear memories of the past.

I have studied the Cherokee people since early childhood, read almost every book on them as a tribe, and studied sketches and paintings to get a clear image of their dress.

Years ago my father, Camie Sizemore, and uncle, John Sizemore told me many stories of our family's Cherokee ancestry arousing my deep interest in the Cherokees. I have made several trips to North Carolina, talking to Cherokee people and absorbing everything I could. After writing letters of inquiry for additional information, I began making Cherokee outfits. For years I had made items of primarily the western tribes, but at that point I narrowed my focus to the Cherokee. Now dozens of fascinating crafts decorate my home.

Many of the Southeastern tribes such as the Creek, Choctaw, and Chickasaw tribes dressed in much the same way as the Cherokee. Decorations, designs and colors were distinctive to tribal identity, but the clothes were constructed basically the same. There are still enough examples in existence to enable one to accurately produce old style Cherokee clothing.

When making Cherokee clothing, designs can be obtained from basket and pottery patterns. Shell gorgets and other articles in museums also have designs which can be utilized for accuracy and authenticity.

Colors and designs were used on clothing in harmony with their use and purpose. There are many sketches and photographs in this book designed to make it easier to make a variety of clothing versions. The Cherokee lived over a large area resulting in differences in dress within the tribe.

Old and new methods and materials can be used in making clothing. Since I had no teacher, I developed many of my own methods. There are enough examples in this book to help you get started.

This book evolves from my years spent making Cherokee crafts. I have endeavored to stick closely to the styles of the Cherokee of the Southeast. As you progress through this book, clothing styles, decorations, materials, etc. will be dealt with in sketches, photographs, instruction and further information. I hope that this book will share in a revival of the Cherokee culture helping to regain a way of life nearly lost.

ACKNOWLEDGMENTS

The inspiration for this book came from many sources such as: family, travels, reading, and my deep love for the Cherokee people.

First of all, I wish to thank my mother, Nora Sizemore, who during my childhood always kept me supplied with materials to make Native American crafts. She always admired the things I made and showed visitors my "Indian Things."

My sister, Myrtle, bought me my first Indian craft book by W. Ben Hunt. From this book I learned many of the basic ways to make Native American crafts.

I wish to thank several places in Cherokee, North Carolina for the great help I have received. First, the OCONALUFTEE INDIAN VILLAGE for the guided tours they offer the public, where several times, as part of a tour group, I learned valuable information. Secondly, the MUSEUM OF THE CHEROKEE INDIAN, where on many occasions, I learned much from their many interesting displays made available to the public. Next, the great outdoor drama, "UNTO THESE HILLS", which thrilled my soul as I watched. The costumes worn in the drama are outstanding. I wish to thank everyone involved in producing such a drama, because it teaches the public much about the Cherokee people. After watching this drama, I wondered why a movie or a mini-series has not been made of the Cherokees. Also, I would like to thank the CHEROKEE CYCLORAMA WAX MUSEUM, also located in North Carolina, which does a great job in presenting the Cherokee culture.

Rose Gwinner helped with some of the typing of this book after I lost my left hand in an accident. She kept telling me, "Don, you will type again and still be able to make Indian crafts." She was right; I can still do those things!

Ron Day of The Pineville Library has helped me over the years with my research about Native Americans.

My wife, Mable, has given me a lot of encouragement and support to keep working on this book until it was finished. The love she has for me has been my strength through many times.

I wish to thank Fred Helton and Albey Brock for their help with a craft project for this book.

DONALD SIZEMORE
PINEVILLE, KENTUCKY

CONTENTS

PHOTOGRAPHS

All of the photographs in this book were taken by the author.

MATERIALS:
TANNING LEATHER TO MAKE CHEROKEE CLOTHING

Before any in-depth treatment is presented on Cherokee clothing, the subject of the "material" from which it is made must be considered: leather!

Long ago, before cloth and wool blankets became common materials for clothing among the Cherokee, hunters had to go into the deep forests to kill bear, buffalo, deer and other animals for food and for hides. From the skins of the animals, warm clothing and robes were made.

Once the Cherokee hunter brought the hides to the camp or village, the hides had to be tanned to make clothing. Without the tanning process, fresh hides became as stiff as cardboard when they dried out. A hide in its untanned state is called rawhide.

To prepare rawhide, the skin was scraped clean of fat and muscle tissue which remained on the hide during the skinning process. A scraper made from bone, wood or stone was used to remove undesired tissue from the hides. You might want to use a dull butcher knife to scrape a hide which has been staked out on the ground or spread over a conveniently angled log.

If the hair is to be removed from the hide after is has been properly cleaned, a paste of wood ashes and water should be rubbed thickly on the hide. The hide should be folded with the hair side in and stored in a cool place, such as, a basement or a hole in the ground where it can be covered with dirt.

After two or three days, take the hide to where you have placed an angled log. Spread the hide over the log and scrape all hair from the hide. If hair still remains, use the wood-ash paste process again.

When all the hair is removed, the hide is ready to be washed in water. Lace it to a wooden frame or tack it to the side of a building to dry. You now have rawhide for drum heads, lacing, shields, and other items.

For clothing, rawhide must be tanned into leather. The Cherokee made most of their clothing from deerskin, which was called buckskin. From buckskin, they made shirts, leggings, belts, dresses, moccasins and other items. The Cherokee always kept a supply of rawhide for use as needed. If leather is to be made, further processing is required.

Leather or rawhide may be bought from a leather-craft store, or you may wish to use imitation leather or cloth to make the articles of clothing shown in this book. I will however describe the tanning process for those wishing to prepare their own leather.

When the deerskin has been prepared as described above and the hair is removed, soak the hide in water to make it soft again. While it is soaking, make a stretching frame of two uprights and two cross-pieces, as shown in the sketch. Lace the hide to the frame with leather string. Now you are ready to tan the hide.

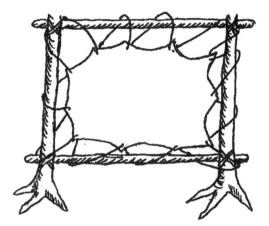

The above sketch shows a frame made of two small trees and two poles.

Use the brains and liver of a deer or hog to make the tanning solution. The brains and liver are put into a cooking container. Add lard to the mixture and put it on the stove or a fire to simmer for five or ten minutes. Stir the solution, mashing it until it becomes a paste.

Now use a smooth stone or a wooden paddle-like tool to rub the solution thoroughly into both sides of the hide. Keep applying the solution until it is used up or the hide has dried.

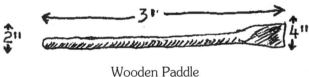

Wooden Paddle

The hide should now be put into a tub of water or into the creek and soaked again in the water. Form pockets of water in portions of the hide, squeezing the trapped water through the pores of the skin. Do the same to all parts of the hide.

The hide can be wrung out to get rid of the excess water and can be softened by pulling it back and forth around a smooth tree. If the hide is still not soft enough, repeat the tanning process.

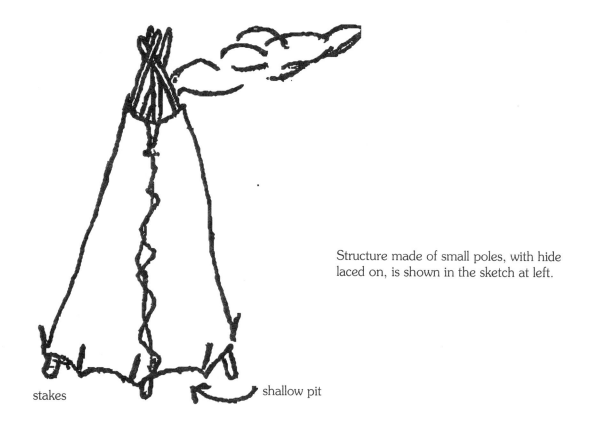

Structure made of small poles, with hide laced on, is shown in the sketch at left.

stakes   shallow pit

When a hide is to be colored or made brown or tan, it has to be smoked by lacing it to a tripod of small green trees as shown in the sketch above.

The tripod of poles and hide will look like a tee pee. First, dig a fire pit. A small smoldering fire, made of wood chips, rotted wood or moss, that produces a lot of smoke should be built at the base. Place hide over the fire. You must keep a close watch on the fire and not let it flame up. When the inside of the hide is the shade of color you desire, turn it inside out and smoke the other side until it is the desired color also.

The Cherokee sometimes dyed the buckskin black, red, yellow or just left it white, to suit the desired purpose of the garment they were making. Walnut bark, yellowroot or bloodroot were originally used for dyes. You may want to use commercial dyes.

Since leather is so costly and hard to make, I suggest you use imitation leather, tan cloth, or flannel to make your Cherokee clothing. When a fringe is needed, use chamois skin or any soft leather and sew it to the cloth.

If you desire to do your own leather tanning, books devoted to the subject are available. See your bookstore, craft store or contact the publisher of this book for available resource books to guide you in more extensive leather tanning.

TOOLS FOR CUTTING AND STITCHING LEATHER

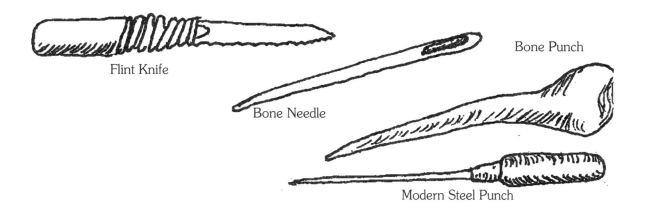

Flint Knife

Bone Needle

Bone Punch

Modern Steel Punch

Shown in the sketches above are some of the main tools that were used for cutting and sewing Cherokee clothes. Also pictured is a modern metal punch that was used later on. A sharp flint knife was used to cut leather into pieces for shirts, leggings, dresses, strings, fringes and other items.

Since early Cherokee had no steel needles until the coming of white traders, bone needles were used. Needles of bone broke very easily when using them to sew. Thread made of fiber, such as, hemp or stinging nettle, was used. Leather strings were also used to lace pieces together. Another source for thread was sinew made from the tendons of animals, such as deer. The sinew was made the desired thickness, then when it was ready for use, it was soaked in water or held in the mouth to be softened.

When making a garment, the bone or steel punch is used to push the sinew or thread through a series of holes made in the leather. Refer to sketches below.

The punch is pushed through the leather to make holes for the thread or sinew.

The punch is also used to push the thread or sinew through the holes as shown.

There is no need for further description of the old way of using the punch as a sewing tool because steel needles, punches and thread are more suitable, and you will probably want to use scissors, instead of a flint knife, to cut leather. The sewing machine can also be used when working with cloth or imitation leather. It is my hope that my instructions will enable you to use either the ancient method or more modern method to make your clothing items, according to your choosing.

Finished seams are usually hidden by turning the garment inside out, as is true when making modern clothes. When sewing seams together, there are two stitching methods that can be used.

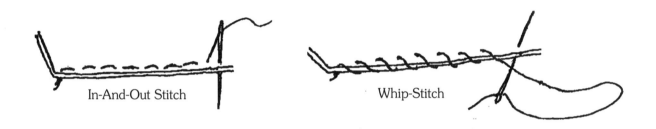

In-And-Out Stitch   Whip-Stitch

The first stitch is called the in-and-out stitch. Refer to the sketch above on the left. The other stitch is a whip-stitch shown in the sketch above at the right. Always stitch at least $1/4$ " back from the edge of the material.

Most of the Cherokee clothes I have made are sewn totally by hand. Since I lost my left hand in an accident in 1989, I now sometimes use a sewing machine. Though I sew by hand less now, I still find that I can sew, or even do beadwork, like I use to do.

As you can see, I am still determined to make clothes of the Cherokee, and I enjoy it. You must likewise be determined to spend hours at making craft projects to get the desired end product. Later you can sit back and admire the beauty of what you have made.

CHEROKEE CLOTHING

The Cherokee woman was trained from her early childhood in the art of making clothes for her family. The sewing was considered a woman's task. The men did sew some things, however, such as war or ceremonial items.

Depicted in early paintings and drawings, clothing styles among the Cherokee varied from one section of their country to another. Their contact with white explorers and settlers, as well as contact with other tribes, had a great impact on their way of dress as they adapted new materials and styles to that of their own.

Three uses for clothing among the Cherokee were:

1. Plain clothing for everyday use
2. War clothing
3. Ceremonial clothing used during rituals and dancing

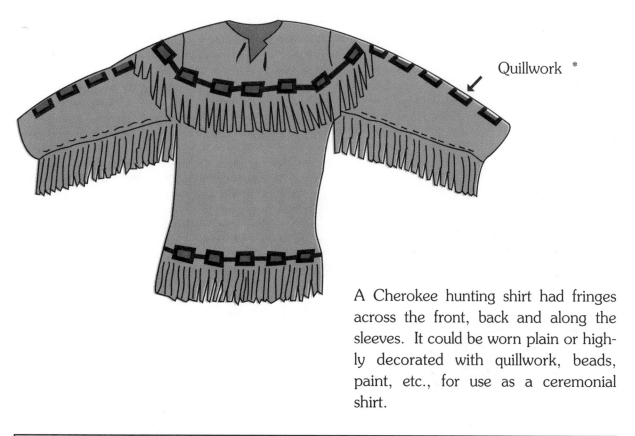

Quillwork *

A Cherokee hunting shirt had fringes across the front, back and along the sleeves. It could be worn plain or highly decorated with quillwork, beads, paint, etc., for use as a ceremonial shirt.

---

* Imitation quillwork is described later in this book. For use of actual quills, further reference books should be consulted.

Garters made of leather or yarn were worn below the knees by both men and women.

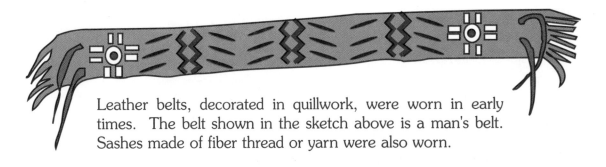

Leather belts, decorated in quillwork, were worn in early times. The belt shown in the sketch above is a man's belt. Sashes made of fiber thread or yarn were also worn.

Decorations for moccasins also varied.

Moccasins and boots were made of deerskin or bearskin.

Boots were sometimes decorated with beads and feathers, quillwork, paint, seed beads, ribbon-work, claws, etc.

In the winter months the boots and moccasins were made with the fur left on the inside for added warmth.

Some men among the Cherokee wore fur hats and robes of animal skins. Tassels made of fur also decorated breech-clouts, leggings, etc.

Old styles of the Cherokee shirt were loose fitting, bulky and long, reaching almost to the knees.

Lighter robes known as mantles were made of turkey feathers and worn during cool times.

They made blankets and robes of bearskin and buffalo hide with the fur left on for warmth.

These robes and blankets were wrapped around the body as shown in the sketch at the left.

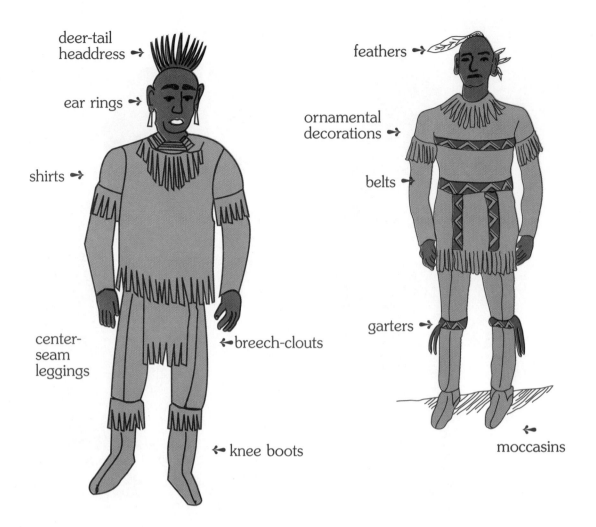

deer-tail
headdress →

ear rings →

shirts →

center-
seam
leggings

← breech-clouts

← knee boots

feathers →

ornamental
decorations →

belts →

garters →

← moccasins

Cherokee men dressed in the skins of animals, as pictured above. The two Cherokee men in the sketches depict clothing made of deer-skin worn during the winter months.

The ears were deformed by cutting the outer rim and lobe to separate it from the rest of the ear. Ornaments were added when the ear was healed.

Turkey feathers decorated with seed beads, tin cones and fluffs were worn in the hair.

Silver or tin cones and beads, as well as glass and shell beads, were used as ear rings. Nose rings were also worn by the men.

The women wore wrap-around skirts, and sometimes they did not wear a top at all. They wore leggings under their skirts which were fastened with garters just below the knees.

The customary short skirt, leggings and a brief jacket of deerskin were worn during the cold months. It might also be noted that the slip or shirt-waist, as it was called in those days, worn underneath the dress was made of cotton calico.

When it came to footwear, women and young girls usually went barefooted during the summer. Of course, when cold weather arrived, center-seam moccasins were worn.

CHEROKEE SHIRTS

The Cherokee, like all Native Americans in the Southeast, wore some kind of shirt. Those of the Cherokee in early times were bulky and had loose fitting sleeves. These shirts were long, reaching to just a few inches above the knees. Old paintings show Cherokees in their turbans and long shirts. The more recent style of shirt, made of cloth, is a carry-over version of the earlier deerskin shirts. It is interesting to note that whenever the Cherokee obtained items from the white traders, they usually converted them to a Native American look.

HUNTING SHIRT

After contact with the nearby white people, there emerged a style of shirt that seemed to have been patterned after the cloth shirts of the white man. This shirt was called a "hunting shirt." The hunting shirt of the Native American became very familiar to the white people of the historic period. It was worn for its warmth and protective qualities.

Any Cherokee man could wear the hunting shirt. Being an everyday shirt it would have had little, if any, decoration on it.

Note: The neck opening can be fringed or made with a split down the front.

When decorations of symbols and designs were desired on a shirt, they were applied by painting or quilll-work. All such designs and decorations had great meaning to the one who wore the shirt, bringing protection and power. A highly decorated shirt was a ceremonial shirt and worn only for special events.

Some war shirts and ceremonial shirts were lavishly done in quillwork, embroidery, beadwork, shells, fur or hair tassels, tin cones, etc. They would have been decorated according to things seen in visions and dreams. Certain symbols or other shirt adornments showed one's status in the tribe.

The old men of the tribe, wore the most elaborately decorated shirts because of the many honors they had earned through the years of warfare and service to the tribe. A young warrior was not allowed to wear a shirt decorated like that of a chief or of a great warrior.

The shirt was not usually worn on the warpath unless the weather was cold. The breechclout, leggings and moccasins were the most common war uniform. Leggings were not always worn either.

It usually required two or three deer skins to make a shirt, but we can use cloth instead of leather. Leather substitutes include tan flannel, imitation leather, dyed muslin, or even an old leather coat.

When you need Cherokee designs to go on your shirt, perhaps a pottery or basket design can be used. Finger-woven sashes, shell gorgets and museum pieces are rich sources of designs also.

You may have to rely on your spiritual powers to help guide you on designs and decorations for the shirt. There are endless ways to decorate a shirt to make it beautiful. Do not feel limited to my designs when making shirts or any other item in this book but rather design your own.

The instructions given on the following pages should be all you will need to get started.

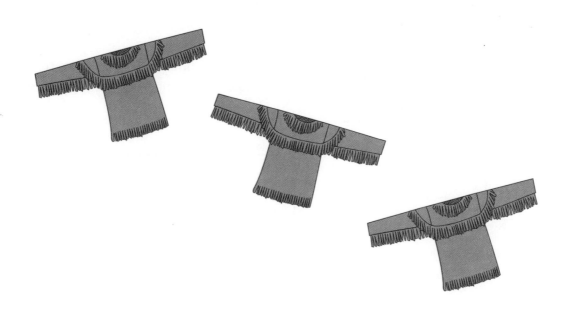

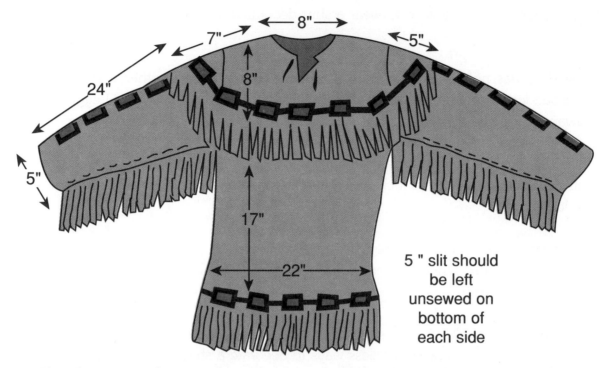

The above is a hunting shirt. It was made of deerskin in the old days. When on a hunt, it could be worn plain with no decorations. The same style shirt could also be worn during ceremonies or as a war shirt and decorated with quillwork, beads, paint or embroidery. Symbols on the shirt indicated one's power.

I might also bring to your attention that this type shirt would have been commonly worn during the cold months. It was seldom worn during hot weather.

When making a hunting shirt, keep in mind that it was loose fitting. Adjust above measurements if necessary for a proper, loose fit. For designs, try to find authentic symbols of the Cherokees.

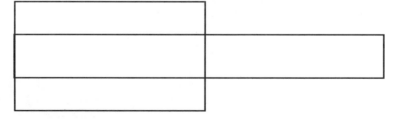

Actual size of design used above

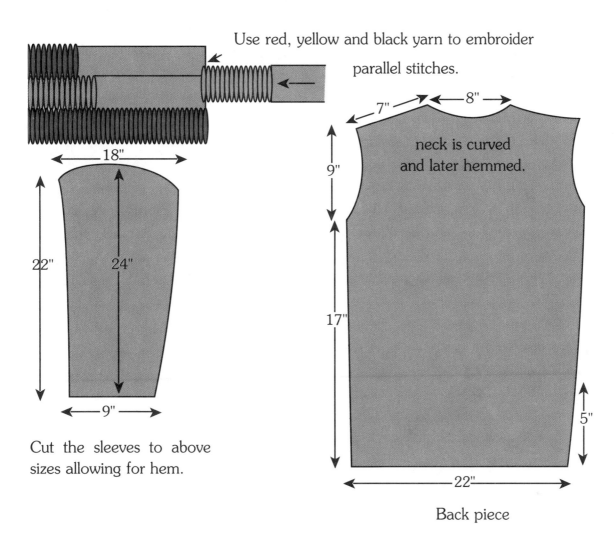

Use red, yellow and black yarn to embroider parallel stitches.

18"

22" 24"

9"

Cut the sleeves to above sizes allowing for hem.

7" 8"

9"

neck is curved and later hemmed.

17"

5"

22"

Back piece

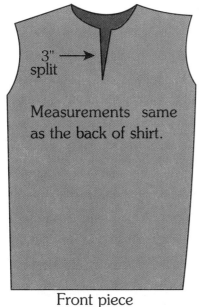

3" split

Measurements same as the back of shirt.

Front piece

Cut front and back of the neck opening as shown in sketch at left. The front has a 3" split.

Fit the front and back pieces together and sew the side and shoulder seams. Next sew on the sleeves.

Draw your embroidery pattern on the shirt with a pencil. Use an embroidery hoop as much as possible when doing the designs.

When designs are finished, sew on 4" soft leather strips where the fringe should be. Use scissors to cut the fringe $3/8$" wide.

MEDICINE MAN'S SHIRT - THE OPEN SLEEVE TYPE

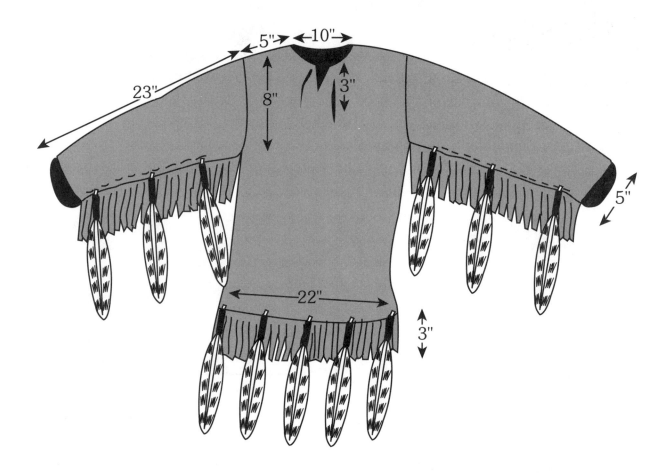

The sleeves are left open from the armpits down to the ends of the sleeves. The sleeves could be fastened together with tie thongs. Many of the old-style Cherokee shirts had open sleeves and were probably worn when the weather started to turn cool.

The sleeves and bottom of the shirt have three-inch fringes sewn to them. Three hawk feathers per sleeve are attached with thread. Ten feathers are fastened around the bottom at intervals as shown in the sketch of the shirt above.

NOTE: *Many birds are protected by law and the use of their feathers forbidden.*
Check the laws, both federal and state before using bird feathers in your projects.

When selecting feathers for the ornaments, try to get ones that are 5-6 inches long. Feathers much longer than that seem to take away from the effect and get in the way. Red flannel is used to wrap the ends of the feathers. See instructions given elsewhere in this book for preparing feathers the old way.

The owl was an emblem of what Cherokees called the "Night-goer" and had to do with witches and medicine men. Owl feathers were often used on this shirt and gave it a mystical power, known only to the Medicine Man or the one who wore it.

Hawk feathers have a power also, and Hawks were spoken about in old Cherokee mythology such as Tla-na-nu.

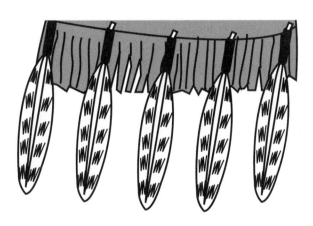

Note: *I do not encourage you to hunt owl, hawk or eagle for feathers. These birds are protected by Federal Laws. This shirt will look just as good if you use small or short turkey feathers.*

THE EMBROIDERED OR QUILLED SHIRT

The shirt shown above is of the 1780-1830 period. It displays the early characteristics of the shirts worn by some Cherokee. The long tapered fringes, the quill work, and the loose fitting sleeves are traits of Cherokee shirts.

To make this shirt as it was originally made you will need deerskin. If deerskin is hard to get, make it from tan cloth or imitation leather.

When I made the shirt, I had only a tan colored suede coat which I took apart and reworked to get the shape of the shirt I was making.

Instead of doing quillwork, I used red yarn to imitate it.

Some of the things needed to make certain Native American crafts, like quills and leather, are hard to obtain. Search for a material that will serve the same purpose.

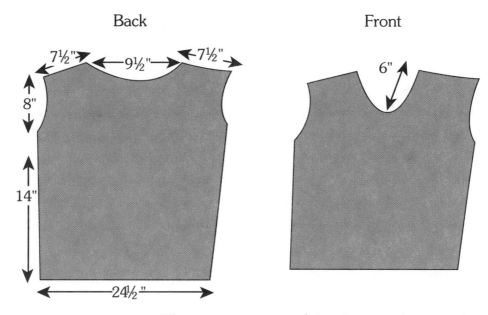

Back Front

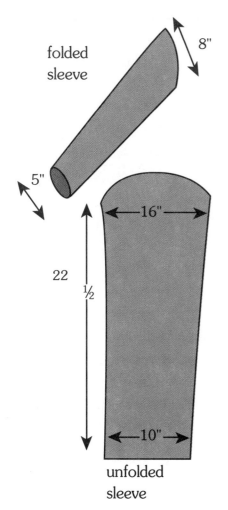

folded sleeve

unfolded sleeve

The measurements of the shirt are shown in the sketches on this page. You may have to alter the measurements to fit your size. This shirt should fit very loose.

A quick way to make this shirt without doing a lot of measuring is to double the material you are going to use. Lay the material on a flat surface, then put a large shirt or coat on top of the material for a pattern.

Straighten out the shirt or coat as a pattern; mark around the shirt or coat pattern onto the doubled material making the outline of the shirt. (Use a pencil or pen to do the marking and allow for 1/4" extra for the hemming.)

Now cut out the parts with scissors, and you are ready to start sewing. Sew the front and back parts up the sides and across the shoulders. Use the in-and-out stitch.

The neckline of the back part is rounded somewhat and the front neckline is rounded even more.

To get the proper sleeve size, use the sleeves of the coat or shirt as a pattern also.

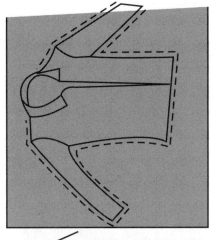

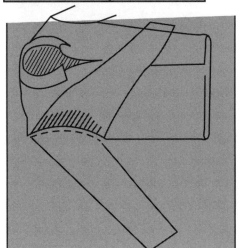

If you are using a shirt as a pattern on doubled material, fold the shirt back at it's seams along the shoulders and armpits. Mark the material with pencil or pen.

Note:
In the old days when a Cherokee woman made a new shirt, she sometimes used an old one to get the proper fit.

Allow $1/4$" extra for hemming.

Cup the shoulder seam, as shown at left in the sketch. Mark the rounded part of shoulder seam.

Once you have all of the parts cut out, begin sewing the shirt together.

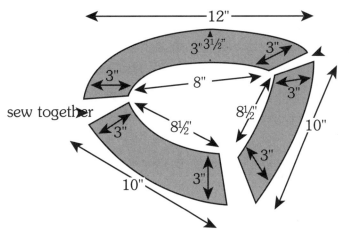

sew together

After the collar pieces are sewn together, sew the collar to the neckline of the shirt.

Preadjust measurements to fit your own size.

Keep the shirt form basically like the shape shown in the photographs and sketches.

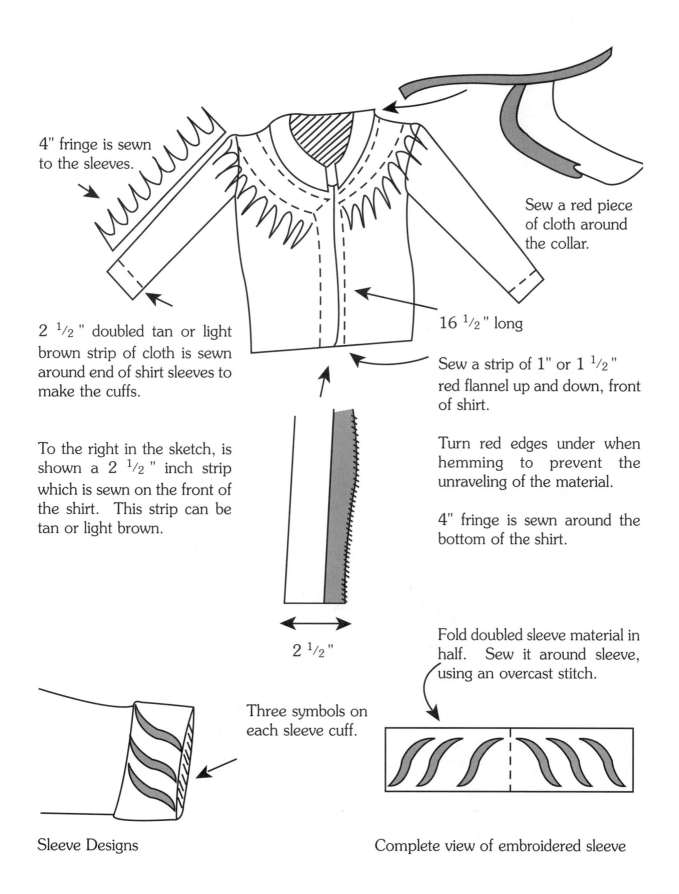

4" fringe is sewn to the sleeves.

2 $\frac{1}{2}$" doubled tan or light brown strip of cloth is sewn around end of shirt sleeves to make the cuffs.

To the right in the sketch, is shown a 2 $\frac{1}{2}$" inch strip which is sewn on the front of the shirt. This strip can be tan or light brown.

Sew a red piece of cloth around the collar.

16 $\frac{1}{2}$" long

Sew a strip of 1" or 1 $\frac{1}{2}$" red flannel up and down, front of shirt.

Turn red edges under when hemming to prevent the unraveling of the material.

4" fringe is sewn around the bottom of the shirt.

2 $\frac{1}{2}$"

Fold doubled sleeve material in half. Sew it around sleeve, using an overcast stitch.

Three symbols on each sleeve cuff.

Sleeve Designs

Complete view of embroidered sleeve

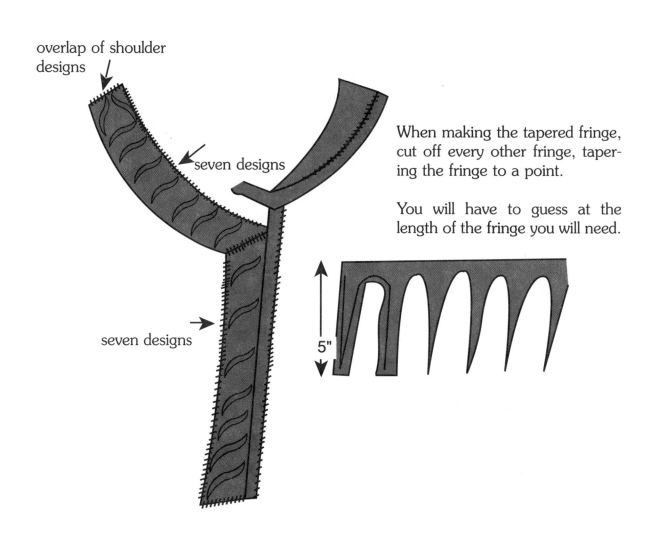

overlap of shoulder designs

seven designs

seven designs

When making the tapered fringe, cut off every other fringe, tapering the fringe to a point.

You will have to guess at the length of the fringe you will need.

5"

The photograph below shows the back side of the shirt.

The sketches below show designs that you may wish to use on your shirt. Designs can be chosen from many designs and patterns of the Cherokee.

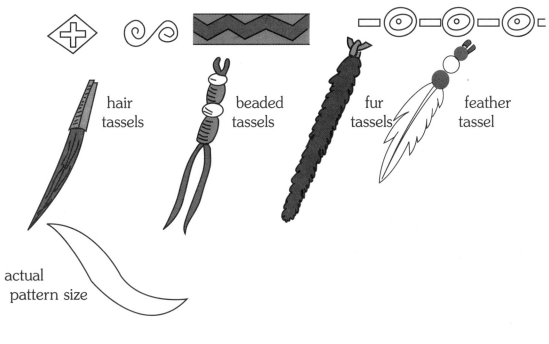

hair tassels

beaded tassels

fur tassels

feather tassel

actual pattern size

When making this shirt, be creative and give it your personal touch in order to feel its power and beauty.

Adjust the pattern to a length that suits you.

EMBROIDERY

Sometimes embroidery is used to imitate quillwork. If you cannot obtain quills, or choose not to use them, the following instruction will help you to obtain the "quill-look" through embroidery techniques.

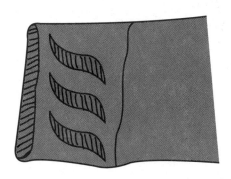

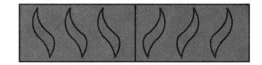

As shown in the above sketch, the designs are drawn out in pencil on the cuffs. Three designs are on the left and three designs are on the right of the cuff.

In the above sketch, four strands of red yarn are put on the embroidery needle. Straight side by side stitches are used to imitate quill work.

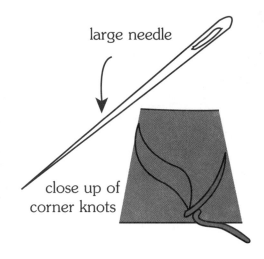

large needle

close up of corner knots

Use a large-eyed needle and follow the instructions which are given.

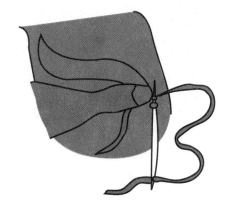

Lay about a half inch of thread across corner of the design. Hold the thread down with the thumb, then insert point of needle through the corner of the design. Pull the thread through.

Do not pull the thread too tight as to shrink the design while embroidering.

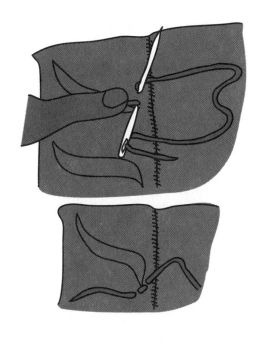

Pass the needle again through the same thread holes and pull thread through again.

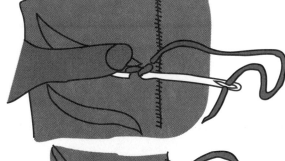

The corner knot is now formed and should look the same as that pictured in the sketch at left.

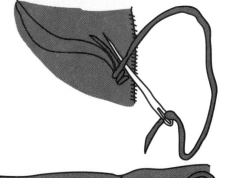

Now make a stitch back to the left.

Insert the needle in and out of cloth at the top left of the prior stitch. Pull the thread through.

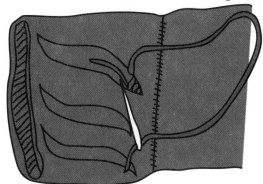

Then insert needle again at the left of prior stitch. Pull the thread through, inserting the needle at the top of design, next the bottom of design.

Repeat the same process over and over until the design is finished to the other corner. Form a corner knot and conceal cut thread under the embroidery.

Keep the rows of stitches close together, as shown in the sketch at left.

You can see in the sketch at left how a stitch looks when being formed.

Another stitch is being made in the drawing at the left.

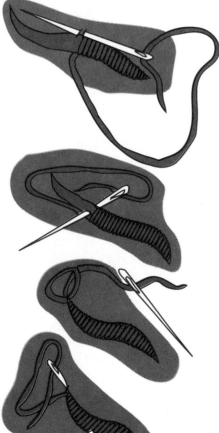

The sketch to the left shows another way of making quick stitches.

The left corner stitch is being made in these two drawings. Pull the thread taut to form the knot. Go under stitches (ten stitches), bring the needle up, pulling out slack. Cut off excess thread.

The drawings above are to give you further details for doing embroidery. Once you have learned this method you should be able to embroider any design you want on your Cherokee clothing.

CHEROKEE WAR SHIRT

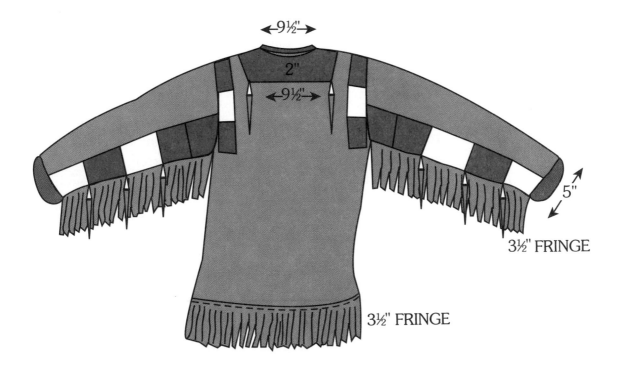

The above shirt was originally made from tan colored deerskin, but you can make it from tan flannel or imitation leather if deerskin is unavailable. If possible use a suitable soft leather.

Lay your material on a flat surface; double it. Place a shirt which is two sizes too large for you on top of the material. Then with a pencil, mark out your material allowing about $1/2$" extra along the edges where the shirt is to be sewn together.

The shirt should be measured to reach just above the knees. Most shirts were made to fit loose.

White and red flannel can be used to form the designs on the sleeves as well as the part around the collar. The red rectangles are patch-worked onto a white strip on each sleeve. Turn all edges of the cloth under on the designs to prevent the edges from unraveling. Use an over-cast stitch on the patchwork.

The tassels are made of human hair and tin cones. You will need 10 tassels for this craft project. If hair cannot be obtained, then you might use black yarn, imitation hair, horse hair, or even dyed unraveled hemp rope as a substitute.

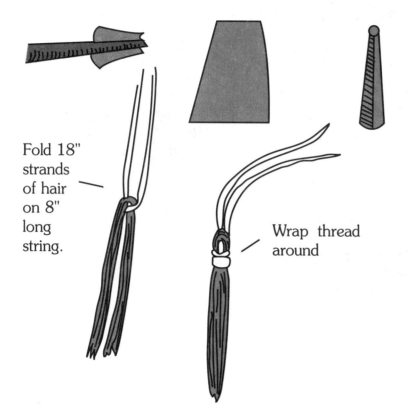

Cut ten pieces of tin to the size shown in the sketch at the left. You can use a tin can. Cut it with scissors, being careful not to cut yourself.

Fold 18" strands of hair on 8" long string.

Wrap thread around

Once the tin pieces are cut to the proper shape, use a tapered pencil or artist brush as a mold. Bend the tin slightly around the tapered end. Finish rounding the tin cone with a pair of wire pliers.

When the cone is properly rounded, the cone will look like the one in the sketch above.

To make hair tassels, fold strands of hair in half on a string. Wrap a string around the top portion of the tassel several times and tie the thread, as shown above.

Hair tassels with tin cones are made by threading the strings of the tassel onto a needle then pulling the string through the tin cone. Put a little glue on the tied end of the hair tassel where the cone is positioned.

One at a time, as each tassel is made, anchor the tassels with needled thread at the proper locations, using the sketch of the shirt as a guideline. Knot the ends of the thread several times on the inside of the shirt. There are two hair tassels on the back of the shirt.

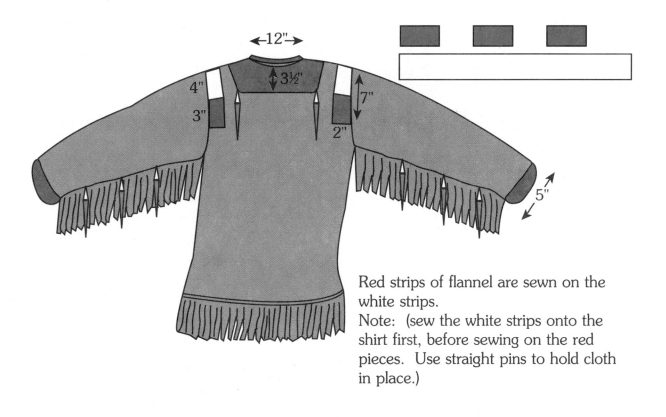

Red strips of flannel are sewn on the white strips.

Note: (sew the white strips onto the shirt first, before sewing on the red pieces. Use straight pins to hold cloth in place.)

The above photo shows a back view of the same shirt.

When the Cherokee obtained trade cloth and blankets, they began making long, loose fitting shirts from the material.

Some shirts had elbow length sleeves and others had sleeves reaching to the wrists. These shirts were long, reaching almost to the knees.

Ruffles were later added to the collar and sleeves.

The above two shirts have ribbon-work, a method sometimes used by the Cherokee to put designs on their clothing

Below is a sketch of a deerskin shirt with bead or quillwork.

THE CHEROKEE CHIEF'S CLOAK

This particular cloak or mantle (incomplete when photographed above) is made of burlap with the tail feathers of the brown turkey sewn onto the cloak in overlapping rows. The red and black fluffs on the shoulders stand for war and death.

The brown tail feathers probably represented the spread tail of the turkey when it felt threatened. Also, anger is depicted by the color red, since the turkey gobbler's comb turns red when the enemy is near. Much meaning can be read into all parts and designs of the cloak.

Since the turkey gobbler meant much to the Cherokee, the Chief, who wore such a cloak believed he took on the powers of such a bird. Engravings on shell gorgets from the early mound builder era depict humans dressed to look like birds .

As the above photograph shows, the inside of the cloak or mantle is done in patchwork designs using red flannel. The design is called "Road to Soco".

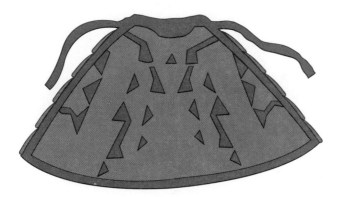

The designs in the sketch at the left are similar to ones in the Museum of the Cherokee in Cherokee, North Carolina.

The photograph above shows the backside of the cloak or mantle.

When war was over and the War Chief vacated his office, the Peace Chief came into power wearing a cloak or mantle like that of the War Chief except the shoulders of his cloak had yellow feathers.

Once the Peace Chief had been installed with a proper ceremony he wore his cloak with white feathers about the shoulders .

Sketches on the next pages will give you a better idea of how the cloaks should look.

The tie straps of the cloak were long enough to be criss-crossed on the chest, crossed at the back and brought around the waist to form a figure eight.

The cloak above with the yellow feathers is the initiation cloak of the peace chief.

Once the peace chief was initiated he wore the cloak with white feathers when conducting business.

According to a tour guide at the Oconaluftee village in North Carolina, the lining for this cloak was made of a net-like material. The feathers were attached to the lining during the weaving process. Another old way of making a base for the feathers was by sewing the feathers to strips of mulberry bark. The strips of bark and feathers were then sewn in overlapping layers, until enough rows were completed to make the cape or cloak.

Using burlap material instead of bark, nettle or hemp serves the purpose better and lasts longer.

The original designs and straps would have been made of leather patchwork dyed the proper color. Cloth, such as flannel, is a good substitute for leather in making the designs.

44

MAKING A CHIEF'S CLOAK OR MANTLE

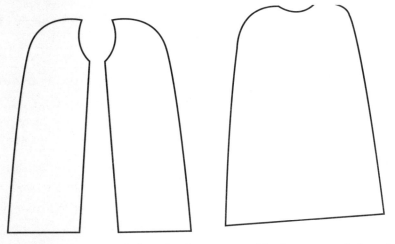

The two front pieces of the cloak   Back piece of the cloak

Sew the two front pieces to the back piece by stitching up the sides and shoulders. Sew the straps on, as in the sketch below.

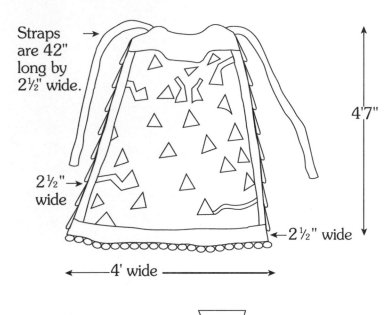

Straps are 42" long by 2½" wide.

2½" wide

←2½" wide

4' wide

4'7"

Make the shoulders of the cloak wide enough to go around your back and to meet at the center of the chest. A woman's shawl might be used as a pattern.

Cut out the designs in cloth and sew them to the inside of the cloak. Turn the edges of the cloth under as you whip-stitch the patchwork. (Use a paper pattern.)

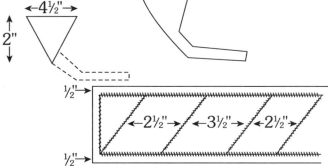

←4½"→

2"

½"

←2½"→ ←3½"→ ←2½"→

½"

The measurements of the tie straps are shown in the sketch at the left. Straps are sewn into place at the front of the cape.

Back View Of The Cloak Or Mantle

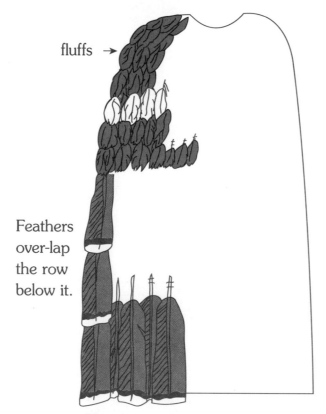

fluffs →

Feathers over-lap the row below it.

Shown in the sketch at left is how the colored black and red fluffs are sewn onto the War Chief's cloak.

You must begin at the bottom of the cloak to sew on the first row of tail feathers and work upward with the rows. I sewed on seven rows of tail feathers, since seven is a sacred number to the Cherokee.

Once the seven rows of tail feathers are sewn on, begin sewing on rows of overlapping fluffs on the shoulders and chest part of the cape.

Close-up of how the needle is pushed through the side of the quill as it is sewn to the burlap liner of the cloak

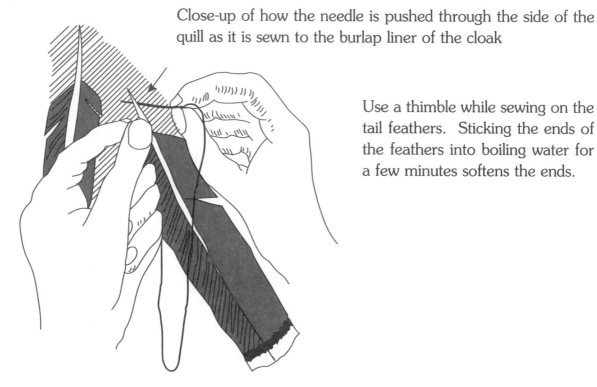

Use a thimble while sewing on the tail feathers. Sticking the ends of the feathers into boiling water for a few minutes softens the ends.

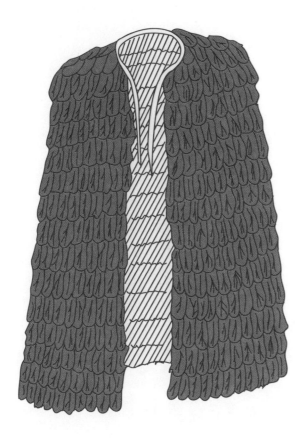

Feathered cloaks or mantles were also made from the breast feathers and smaller fluffs of the turkey.

The cloak at left would have been well suited for an important man of status in the tribe.

Other long feathered cloaks were made to be worn by men, but feathers other than those of the turkey were used.

The feathered short cloak at left would have been made of the breast feathers of the turkey. Such a cloak could be worn by a "Beloved Woman" who served in the Cherokee government.

Since these women held such an honored position, the cloak may have been trimmed in yellow fluffs for her initiation, trimmed in white fluffs as she performed her duties during peace, and trimmed in red fluffs when she was involved in war.

Ordinary women made their feathered skirts and cloaks out of other kinds of feathers for warmth and beauty.

FEATHERED SKIRTS OF THE "BELOVED WOMEN"

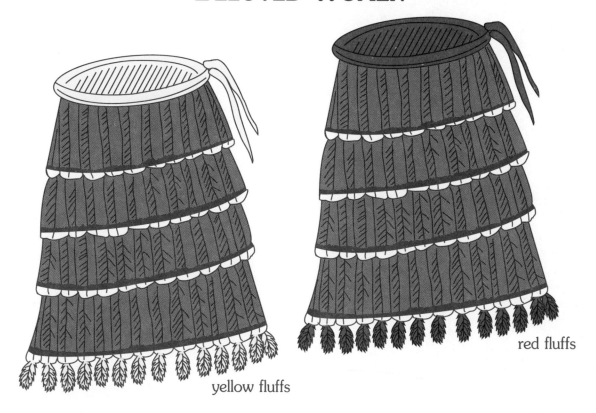

yellow fluffs

red fluffs

Above is an initiation skirt worn on the first day the peace woman took office.

The above skirt trimmed in red feathers was worn by the Beloved Woman when she became War Woman during a declared war.

The above skirt is a wrap-around skirt and covered with turkey breast feathers. White fluffs are used to represent the Peace Woman.

It is only appropriate to present the feathered skirts of the Beloved Women at this place since they were made very similar to the way the Chief's cloaks were constructed.

Turkey tail feathers or breast feathers were sewn in rows which overlapped. The lining can be burlap dyed the proper color. Trim the bottom with fluffs of the appropriate color representing the office of the Beloved Woman.

CHEROKEE FUR CAPE

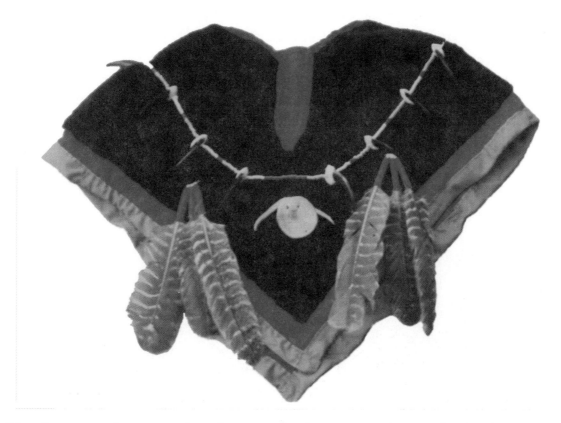

The fur cape shown in the photograph above is similar to the kind worn in the Southeast in early times. Capes were beaded, quilled and decorated in many ways. Usually the cape was made of leather with or without the fur. Later, when white traders came and brought cloth to trade to the Cherokee, capes were made of cloth.

The fur cape was made of buffalo, bear or any other suitable kind of fur.

The purpose of the cape was, first of all, for warmth. The cape was also worn for its beauty and for the symbolism behind the items that adorned it.

Many of the old paintings or drawings of the Cherokee and other southeastern Native Americans of the 1820-30 era include shirts resembling these capes.

When making a cape for yourself, you may want to make it of plain leather, use a fur-like material, make it of velvet, or use some other kind of suitable cloth.

Regardless of the material that you use, make a paper pattern before you cut out your material. An old coat or large size shirt can also be used as a pattern.

HOW TO MAKE A FUR CAPE

Since I could not kill a bear to make the cape shown in the photograph, I used imitation black fur. You might want to use the fur from an old fur coat to make the cape.

To get started, having the desired materials before you, stretch out a doubled piece of the fur on a flat surface. If you want the cape to fit well, line up the doubled fur on a shirt or pattern and cut it to the shape shown in the sketch below. Cut around the shoulders, using the shirt as a guide.

Fold the fur, as seen above.

A. Fold black fur inside.

B. Use a shirt or coat as shown in the sketch at left.

C. Now cut the fur about ½ inch bigger around the shoulders than the shirt or coat you are using as a pattern.

D. Now with scissors, trim out or cut out the back and front neckline. The front neckline has a split.

E. Next, lay a doubled piece of red flannel down on a flat surface. Lay your imitation black fur pieces on top of the red flannel. Cut the red flannel just like the two fur pieces except 2" longer (Refer to sketch at left.)

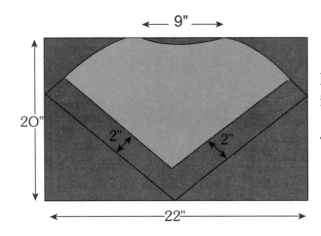

Doubled red flannel is cut two inches longer in the front and back than the black fur.

The neckline is nine inches across.

One piece of the red flannel and one piece of black fur should have a 5-6 inch split down the front.

The front split should be slightly rounded. The red flannel shown at the left is the lining. It could be made out of a red shirt.

Place the fur on the inside (fur to fur) on top of red flannel as shown.

When the shoulders have been sewn, flip over the piece of fur shown at left. Use a whip-stitch to sew it down at the edges.

$\frac{1}{4}$" seam

Use stick pins to hold things in place.

Hem the neck of cape to make it look better.

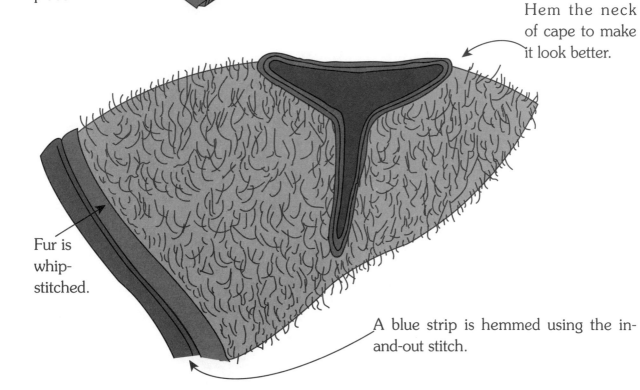

Fur is whip-stitched.

A blue strip is hemmed using the in-and-out stitch.

LACING ON THE CLAWS AND BEADS

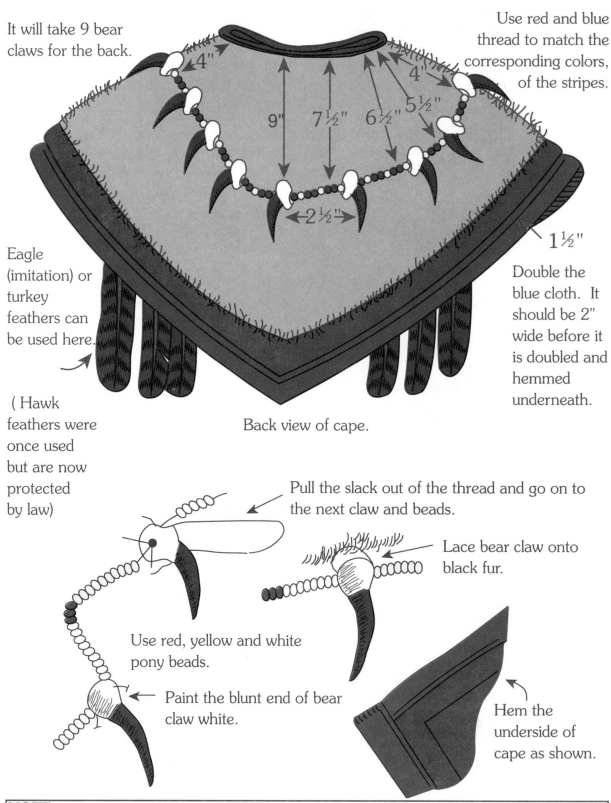

It will take 9 bear claws for the back.

Use red and blue thread to match the corresponding colors, of the stripes.

4"

4"

9" 7½" 6½" 5½"

←2½"→

1½"

Double the blue cloth. It should be 2" wide before it is doubled and hemmed underneath.

Eagle (imitation) or turkey feathers can be used here.

(Hawk feathers were once used but are now protected by law)

Back view of cape.

Pull the slack out of the thread and go on to the next claw and beads.

Lace bear claw onto black fur.

Use red, yellow and white pony beads.

Paint the blunt end of bear claw white.

Hem the underside of cape as shown.

NOTE: *It is illegal to use real bear claws in some states, because the bear is protected.*
Imitation claws are available from some craft supply stores. See list in back.
Some people carve their claws from wood.

FEATHERS FOR THE CAPE

When selecting feathers for the cape, you will need three feathers that curve to the left and three feathers that curve to the right. Feathers were used to decorate capes, skirts of the "Beloved Woman," the Chief's mantle, headdresses, ornaments, etc.

A Cherokee who wore this cape exhibted that he had been a good bear hunter and had been endued with powers. The hawk feathers also had special meaning. This cape would have been ideal for a medicine man to wear.

In the early days many kinds of capes were worn to show one's status and personal power.

Eagle or hawk feathers were used on this cape. Due to the law protecting these birds, artificial feathers or turkey feathers should be used.

To get turkey feathers, ask a hunter or check with a turkey farm. The feathers on this cape are 10-11 inches long.

I attached the feathers on this cape with fishing line. Twine can also be used. A very large needle may be used on the thread when lacing feathers

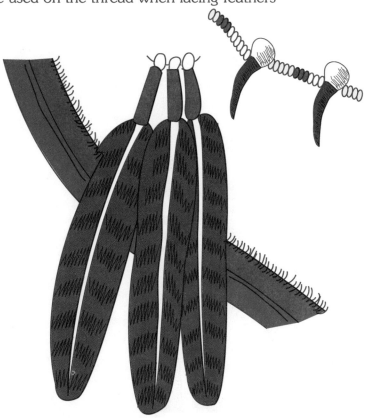

AN OLD WAY OF PREPARING FEATHERS FOR USE

10"

Soak the ends of the feathers in boiling water to soften the points.

Use a utility knife to cut a gash near the point, about $1/2$" back. The gash is $1 \, 1/2$" long and curved.

Next, flatten the point and put a little glue inside the hollow quill part.

Turn the flattened point back and insert into quill. Leave a small loop for the stringing process.

If further decoration is desired, follow the examples in the sketches below.

Put glue on the feather and a little on the red, blue and yellow cloths cut for this purpose.

Roll the cloth piece around the feather being careful that the seam ends up on the backside of the feather.

Whip-stitch the seam with thread that matches the cloth color

How To Make The Shell Gorget For The Cape

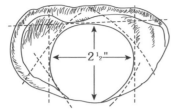

First make a visit to the shoals of a river and get a mussel shell.

Draw in pencil a 2 1/2 inch disk, as shown in the sketch.

Cut it out as shown in the above sketch, using a hacksaw.

Use wire-pliers to break off pieces around the edge to get a rough circle look.

Next, hold the edge of the gorget to an electric grinder sanding it to a better shape. Sand the back of the gorget.

As shown in the sketch below, the design on the gorget is drawn out and engraved into the shell with an engraver.

Use a drill to bore two holes 3/4 of an inch apart near the top of gorget.

engraver

Use a utility knife to cut small slots in the cape for the gorget as shown.

Once the design has been engraved, hold a flame (a burning match will do) under the design and burn it. This darkens the design and makes it look old.

When I first made a gorget, I used a stone to chip off pieces of the shell to get a disk. It sometimes broke the wrong way. Later I learned that it was better to use pliers and a hack-saw.

Before my dad gave me an electric grinder, I spent hours sanding the shell round using a sand stone rock or a file.

Use a leather thong to fasten the gorget to the cape.

As with any Native American craft, try the old methods but do not discount using modern things if the same result is accomplished.

THE WHITE FURRED CAPE

The above cape would have been considered very powerful medicine to the one who wore it. White fur and eagle feathers were always sacred to the Cherokee. The eagle feathers may have stood for the Great Man Above. Eagle claws are for strength and the white fur for sacredness.

It would seem that the red stripe is for the Red Man of the east, the yellow stripe for the Yellow Man of the south and the blue stripe for the Blue Man of the north.

You can use imitation white fur, eagle claws and eagle feathers obtained from a craft store. Yellow wooden round beads are used and red wooden beads. The blue beads are plastic crow beads. I used red, yellow and navy blue cotton cloth on the rest of the cape when making it.

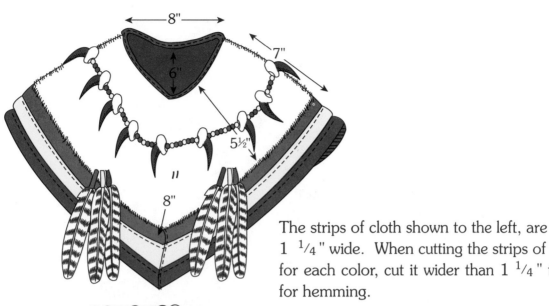

The strips of cloth shown to the left, are 1 ¼ " wide. When cutting the strips of cloth for each color, cut it wider than 1 ¼ " to allow for hemming.

order of bead color

Taper the neck opening when recutting the collar.

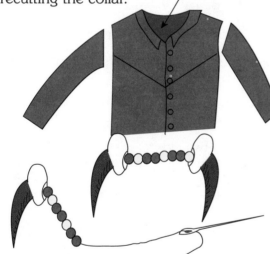

The sketch at left shows how you can use a red shirt by taking it apart to use as the lining for the cape.

The collar and sleeves have to be removed. The shirt is buttoned up and sewn shut at the front. Remove the buttons.

Cut the whole thing in a tapered fashion on the front and back as shown by the dotted lines in the sketch.

Refer to the instructions given on the "Black Fur" cape when lacing on the beads and claws.

It takes 12-13 eagle claws and strong twine to make the necklace on this cape.

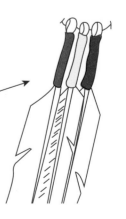

Make the ends of the red, yellow and blue tipped feathers the same way as instructed on the "Black Fur Cape." You may also want to look at the photograph of this cape when making it.

For quicker construction of this cape, use new cloth instead of a shirt.

THE FRINGED CAPE

The deerskin cape pictured above features a fringe along the edges. Red cloth is sewn along the upper part of the fringe.

The designs on the left of the cape and around the backside are embroidered in yarn or quilled. Bone hair-pipes are put between the red wooden beads. Use strong thread or twine to string the beads and bone hair-pipes onto the cape. Sew them down to secure each bead in place.

Since I could not get real quills for the white decoration on the cape, I used white plastic tubing from a window shade. I cut the material the lengths I desired. Then after sewing each plastic tube in place, side by side, I flattened each of them. This gave it a quill-work look without the quills.

Since deerskin was not available for this project, I used tan cloth. The red curved designs are drawn in pencil before being embroidered.

NOTE:
See page 50 and 51 as well as the following pages for guidance in making this cape.

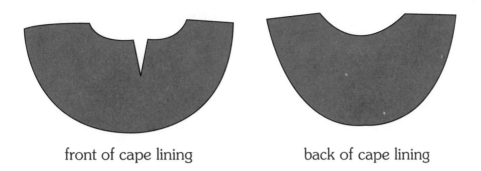

front of cape lining   back of cape lining

Note: The lining is red or maroon cloth and has the same dimensions as the outside of cape.

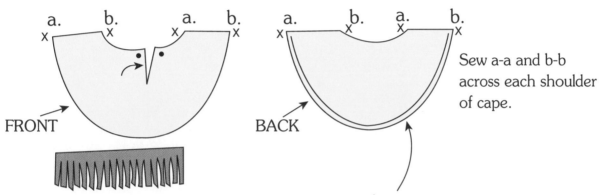

FRONT

BACK

Sew a-a and b-b across each shoulder of cape.

The fringe is 4 inches wide and long enough to go all around the cape.

Sew $1/2$" back from the edge when sewing on the fringe. You can use chamois skin for the fringe.

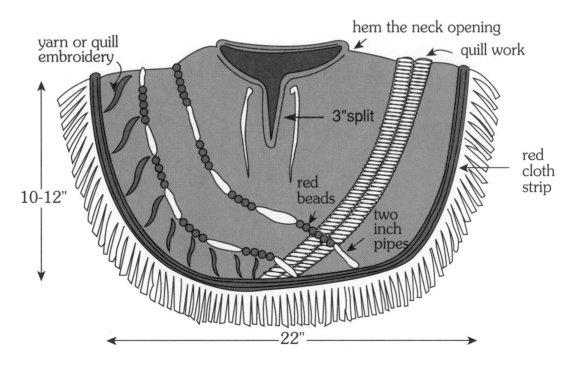

yarn or quill embroidery

hem the neck opening

quill work

3"split

red beads

two inch pipes

red cloth strip

10-12"

22"

Once the cape pieces have been sewn together, measure and cut a four inch strip of chamois skin, soft leather or cloth long enough to be sewn all around the edge of the cape. Use the in-and-out stitch.

Turn up the edge of the strip under (behind) the fringe strip as you sew it down or you will have problems with the thread getting tangled into the fringe.

After the fringe strip has been sewn on, cut a red strip of cloth 1 $\frac{1}{4}$ " wide and long enough to go around the cape. Allow extra width to the red strip for the hemming. Red ribbon or bias tape can be used. Use the in-and-out stitch.

Most of the imitation quill work on the white design starts at $\frac{5}{8}$ " wide and narrows with the design.

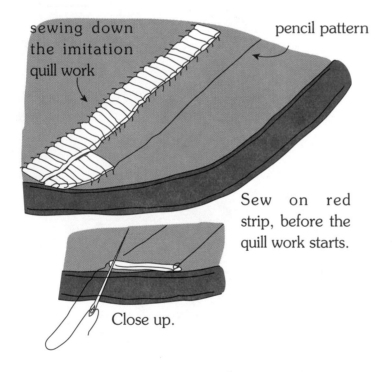

sewing down the imitation quill work

pencil pattern

Sew on red strip, before the quill work starts.

Close up.

a. Once you have a suitable number of white quills cut to the desired size of 5/8" for the first row, you are ready to begin sewing them.

b. Attach the thread into the material at the edge of drawn out design. Go through the quill to the other side of the design then go down into the cloth with the needle.

c. Now, using your needle, string on another imitation quill. Go through the quill with the needle and attach thread to cloth. Repeat the same process over and over until the rows are finished from front to back.

d. Mash each imitation quill with your fingers as you sew them on, or when completed.

e. Cut quills to size to fit the design as you work.

ATTACHING BONE HAIR-PIPES AND RED WOODEN BEADS

First, attach the thread on the right side of the quill work on the front of the cape. (Refer often to the sketch or photo of cape.)

Pass thread and needle through the hair-pipe and a red bead. Next, go down into the cloth with the needle, then back up through the cloth at the other end of red bead, pulling the thread tight.

Now pass the thread and needle back through the red wooden bead. String on another red bead and repeat the process from one bead to the next. There should be four red beads between each hair-pipe.

You will need two packs of red wooden beads and two packs of the two-inch hair-pipes for this project. If leather is used to make the cape, real quills can be used.

Close up.

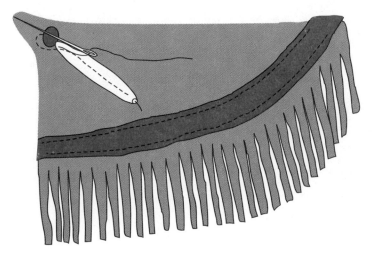

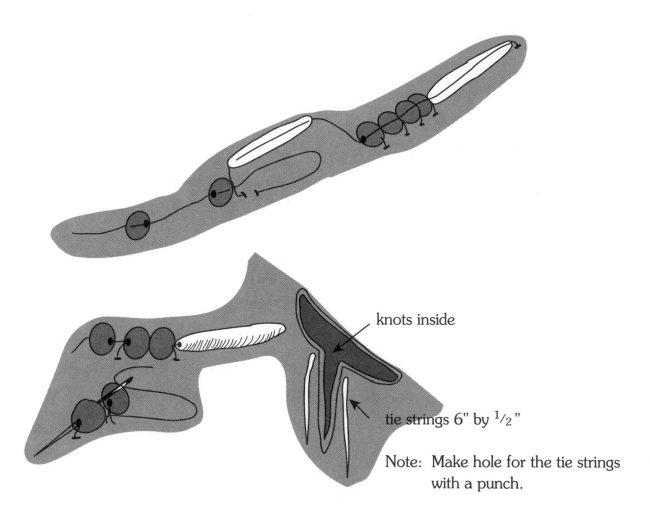

knots inside

tie strings 6" by $^1\!/_2$"

Note: Make hole for the tie strings
with a punch.

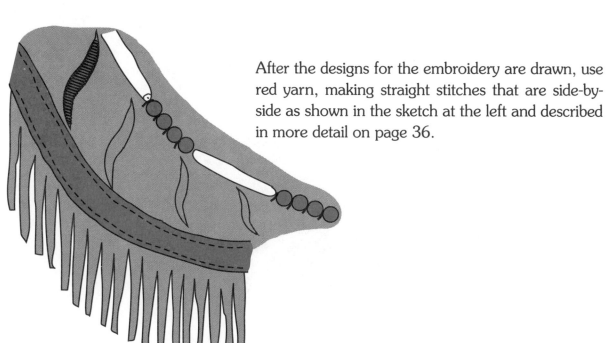

After the designs for the embroidery are drawn, use red yarn, making straight stitches that are side-by-side as shown in the sketch at the left and described in more detail on page 36.

BEADED AND QUILLED CAPE

The above cape is made of soft deerskin with seed beads of black, red, and blue. The quill work is done in white. A shell gorget decorates the lower part. Tin cones with black hair tassels adorn the collar portion of the cape.

This particular cape is made of two identical pieces of leather sewn together at the shoulders with no lining required.

A TYPICAL CLOTH CAPE

The above cape, made in 1986 by the author, took approximately ten hours to make. It is made of red flannel and black cotton cloth. The designs are done in white pony beads. The lining can be made of any kind of cloth that is available.

This cape could be worn by any Cherokee and did not require any special rank or status to wear it. In the old days such a cape would have been made of deerskin dyed red or black. In those days, leather capes had no lining.

To get a good fit in making this cape, as in the case of the other capes of this book, lay a shirt of your own size on the material as a pattern. Mark around the shirt pattern onto the cloth to get the general shape, marking the front and back. Cut the parts out allowing for the seam.

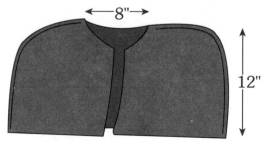

Round out the neckline on the back part about one inch in a tapered fashion as shown in the sketch at left.

Cut the front neckline as shown in the sketch. The front of the cape is open down the front.

Cut the lining for the inside the same size as the two red outside pieces.

Now lay the red pieces under the two inside lining pieces evenly. (back piece to back piece)

Pin them in place around the seam. Check the parts to the cape, the lining parts and red flannel parts that you have pinned together, making sure that they are in order. If, when the cape is turned inside out, the red flannel parts are on the outside, you are ready to sew the cape around the seams as shown above left.

pencil
line

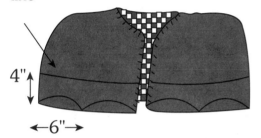

4"

←6"→

Using a pencil, mark the pattern shown in the above sketch.

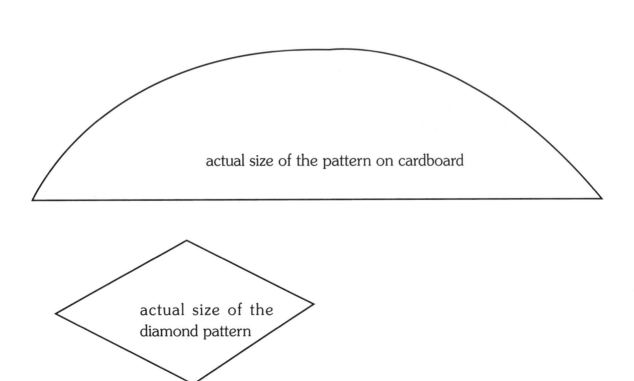

Sew around the collar and the front, as shown in the sketch, turning the edges under as you hem.

actual size of the pattern on cardboard

actual size of the
diamond pattern

Next, cut the two strips of black material 5" wide and long enough to go around the bottom of the cape. Line one strip of the black material with the line on the outside of the cape, and line up the other strip on the inside of the cape. Use straight pins to hold the black strips in place as you sew along the pencil line.

Next, use the cardboard pattern that is half-moon shape. Lay the pattern on the black strip and use a yellow lead pencil to mark the pattern onto the black cloth.

You can now cut out the bottom shape of the cape as shown in the sketch below. Hem the bottom, turning the edges under. Hem the front edges into cape.

Mark the diamond patterns and bead them.

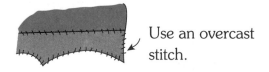 Use an overcast stitch.

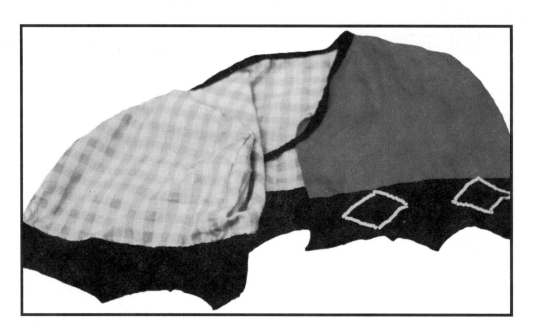

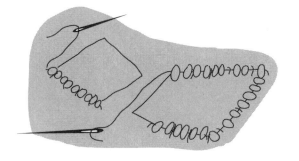 Beadwork as shown in the sketch at left is called "spot beading". Use pony beads and sew down every two or three beads until the beads have been strung around the entire design.

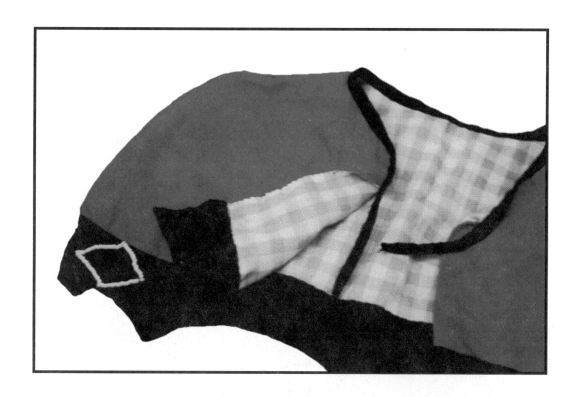

You will need to cut a strip of black cloth for the tie string about 2" wide and long enough to go around the collar. There has to be enough extra to be used as the string parts. Two and a half feet should be enough.

Tie Strings

Sew the tie string for 7 $\frac{1}{2}$ " as shown and sew the next few inches to the collar of the cape as shown in the photo, then sew the remaining part for the other tie string.

fold in → middle

As shown in the above sketch, a piece of black cloth cut into a strip is folded in the middle. Part of the black strip goes around the collar, evenly centered and whip-stitched into place, allowing for the tie strings on front.

Your cape should now be finished and ready to wear!

CHEROKEE EMBROIDERED VEST

Many of the Cherokee clothing styles gradually changed to look like that of the white man, as shown in the vest photograph above. Beautiful floral designs decorate the pockets and collar panels. Black buttons are sewn to the front. The inside of the vest is lined with white cloth.

The vest is made of soft tan leather, but imitation leather or cloth that has a leather look can be used. Use a suit vest for a pattern and cut it to the shape shown in the photograph.

Instructions for embroidery work are described elsewhere in this book (*see page 125*).

NOTE: *The vest photograph above is used by permission of Mr. Edds of Virginia (now deceased) who had it in his collection and estimated it to be over 100 years old dating back to between 1800 and 1850, the period when embroidery was first introduced. His friendship and cooperation were invaluable to me in my study of Cherokee clothing.*

The sketches below show measurements that can be used when making the vest. You may have to alter the measurements to fit your own size.

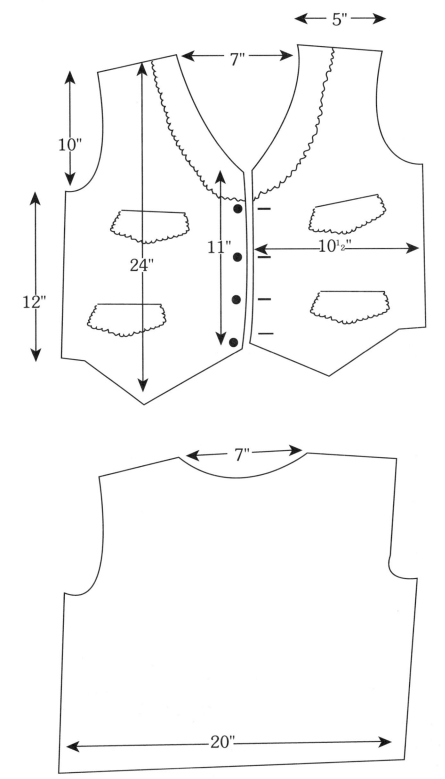

A short cut to use when making this vest is to choose a vest that is already made and re-cut the shape somewhat. Then cut the leather to the shape you want using the photo as a guide then sew the leather to the front of the vest.

Of course, the embroidered panels will still have to be done as instructed earlier.

This vest and will give you something to wear that bridges the old culture with the new!

Below are sketches of the floral designs for the collar and pocket panels of the vest. Remember, when doing embroidery, draw out the designs on the material, placing it in an embroidery hoop to embroider the designs.

When the embroidery is finished use pinking shears (scissors with a jagged edge) to cut out the shape of the pocket and collar panels. They are then sewed to the vest.

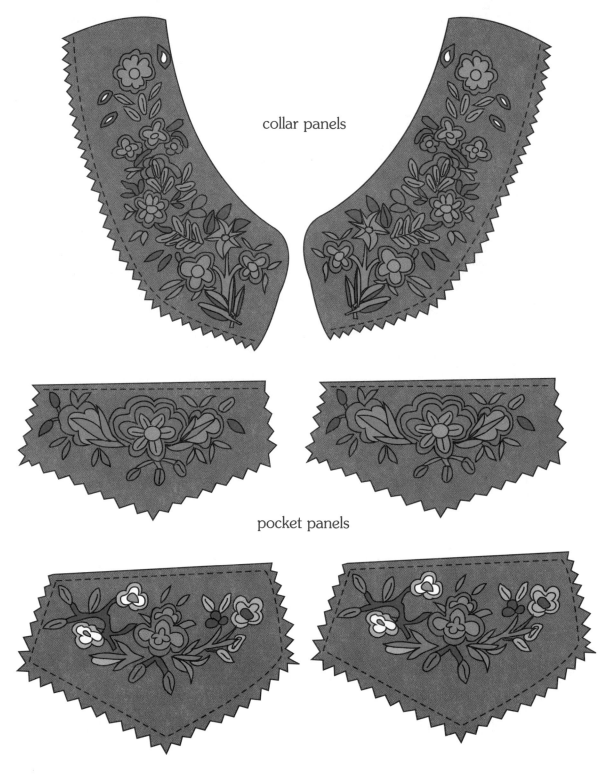

collar panels

pocket panels

THE MODERN CHEROKEE CAPE

The cape shown above depicts how the Cherokee men of the 1830-40 period blended the ancient way of dress with the new style adopted from the white man's clothing.

Glass beads, bone hair-pipes and fringe are mixed with ruffles and various colors of cloth. Even the cloth turban with feathers reflects the old style hat worn by the Cherokee in earlier times.

FUR ROBES AND BLANKETS

In the ancient days of the Cherokee domain bear and mountain buffalo were in abundance. The Cherokee made robes from the furs of such animals to wear for warmth during the cold winter months. These robes were large and could be used for blankets when traveling and sleeping outside on the ground.

Cherokee men and women were fond of sitting around the campfire talking among themselves or conducting business in the council house. During such times, the fur robes and blankets were used as wraparounds for both warmth and appearance.

These robes were wrapped around the body, sometimes the long way, as pictured above. One arm was left free to grasp the blanket or robe, helping to hold it in place. Sometimes it was worn over the shoulders but tied with a belt or sash at the waist. This manner of wearing the blanket or robe allowed the upper part of blanket to fall, allowing use (or movement) of both arms.

When the weather was very cold or raining, the robe was draped over the head with only the face showing. Old men often left their right arm free and held the ends together with the other arm and hand. Most of these robes reached to the knees or below.

For winter robes, the fur was left on and worn on the inside. Summer leather robes had the hair removed and were usually decorated with painted designs of black, red, and yellow.

Quilled designs were also used on robes in the old days. After the coming of the white man, cloth blankets were decorated with ribbon-work and colored strips of cloth.

Other robes or mantles, which reached to or below the knees, were made of turkey breast feathers, turkey tail feathers, feathers of the red bird, bluejay and other small birds.

Such light-weight mantles or robes were ideal for the cool summer nights. The women were fond of the light-weight robes. Feathers were fastened to a net-like base woven from the fibers of the nettle, hemp and other plants. In our time, burlap is the best replacement for the net or bark material usually used for the base.

Rabbit fur was also used to make warm blankets by cutting the fur in strips to make a large roll of fur. When enough of the rabbit skins had been saved, the fur was strung back and forth on an upright loom or frame and woven into a blanket.

For sleeping purposes, robes were spread on the bed or ground, and the sleeper laid on one end of the blanket or robe. He folded the robe or blanket over himself and placed the rest under him. The bottom of this bed blanket was folded underneath the legs. Extra robes were used as needed to provide layers of warmth during cold weather.

The blankets obtained from the white traders who came to the Cherokee were in colors of black, red, and navy blue. If you want to make a decorated blanket, silk ribbons, cloth strips, beads, embroidery, jinglers, tassels, etc. can be used.

THE MAKING OF A MEDICINE MAN'S BEAR ROBE

The bear robe was part of the medicine man's uniform, identifying him as such. This bear robe was believed to give great power to the one who wore it.

It is thought that long ago, there was another Clan called the Bear Clan or the "Ani'-Tsa'guhi." (I refer you to James Mooney's book, *Myths of the Cherokee and Sacred Formulas of the Cherokee*, pages 264, 325-329. Read about, *"Origin of the Bear,"* and *"The Bear Man."*)*

Among the Cherokee, both men and women could practice medicine.

Bears, in many ways, act like people. They stand upright, eat many of the same foods as humans eat and have many human-like mannerisms.

The Cherokee once had Bear Dances to honor the bear.

The above Bear Robe is patterned from one in the Museum of the Cherokee in North Carolina. Carol Sizemore, my twin sister, is the model in this photograph. All of the clothes she is wearing are ones I made as copies of Cherokee clothing.

* Mooney, James, 1891 "Sacred Formulas of the Cherokees," *Burreau of American Ethnology*, Seventh Annual Report, and 1900a "Myths of the Cherokee" *Bureau of American Ethnology*, Nineteenth Annual Report.

NOTE: These two books have been republished in a single volume available from the publisher of this book.

Since the black bear is rare in most parts of the country and can be seen primarily in the old part of the Cherokee country, the Great Smoky Mountains, you will probably be unable to obtain a real bear hide for this project. If you are able to get it, use a good tanned bearskin. A stiff untanned bearskin will not be suitable for this project. You may want to use an old fur coat or imitation bear fur. Use black if possible.

After you have the fur ready to be used, you must make an immitation bear head. It will take several hours to make a bear head for this project.

Papier-mache' proved to be a usable method. Newspapers should be cut into long strips and dipped into a glue made from flour and water. You may want to use a commercially prepared paste. For the frame of the bear head, a cap cut to the shape shown in the sketch below works nicely.

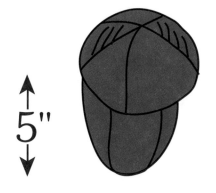

Cut the bill of an old cap to 3 or 4 inches wide, using scissors.

When gluing the paper strips onto the cap, you may want to use a picture of a bear head or even a teddy bear, as a model, in shaping the head.

When the glue and paper strips are ready, begin gluing layers of paper strips all over the cap and under the bill of the cap. Add more and more layers of paper length-wise, cross-wise and overlapping until the rough shape of the head is made.

Use black marbles for the eyes. The ears are glued on last.

Once the head is made, allow it to dry. Paint it all over with a light brown paint. Use black paint to shade in dark areas in hair-like patterns.

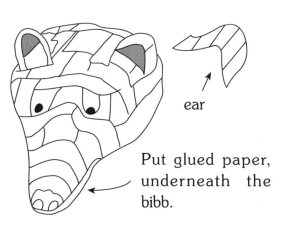

ear

Put glued paper, underneath the bibb.

A mask carved from a wood, such as buckeye, would also be a possibility for your bear head.

The photograph at the left illustrates old style bone and bead necklace with Bear Robe. A pottery drum and drumstick are held.

The Bear Robe is attached to the head in the correct manner.

Tie thongs also help to hold it in place when one is moving around.

Remember while wearing your Bear Robe that the Medicine Man took on the spirit of the bear. It is no wonder that people had a respectful fear of the Medicine Man!

After the bear mask is finished, cut and trim a piece of fur to glue over the forehead, the sides of the head, over the ears, etc., as shown in the sketch below.

Allow for extra fur at the bottom edges of the mask, for sewing it into position on the robe.

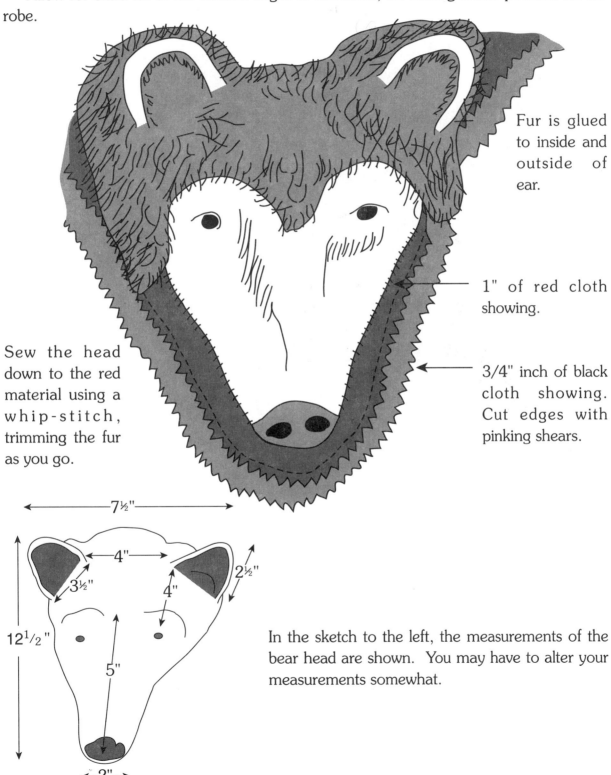

Fur is glued to inside and outside of ear.

1" of red cloth showing.

Sew the head down to the red material using a whip-stitch, trimming the fur as you go.

3/4" inch of black cloth showing. Cut edges with pinking shears.

In the sketch to the left, the measurements of the bear head are shown. You may have to alter your measurements somewhat.

To make the lining for the fur you will need black cotton cloth, seven feet and two inches long by seven feet wide. The piece of red cloth should be the same shape as the black but 3/4" shorter all around .

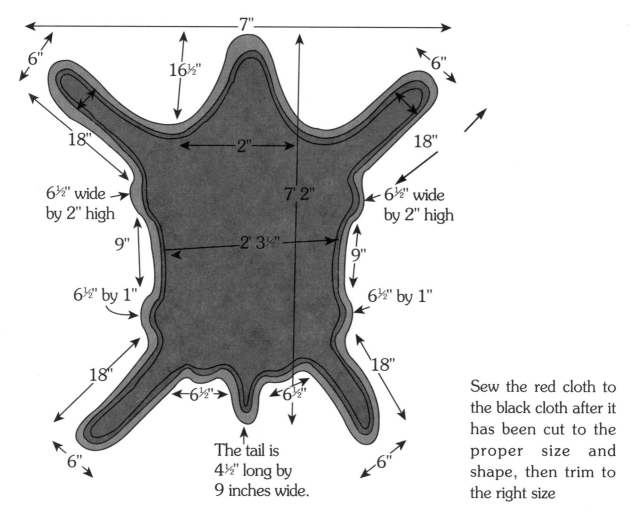

7"

6"

6"

16½"

18"

18"

2"

6½" wide
by 2" high

7' 2"

6½" wide
by 2" high

9"

2' 3½"

9"

6½" by 1"

6½" by 1"

18"

18"

6½"

6½"

The tail is
4½" long by
9 inches wide.

6"

6"

Sew the red cloth to the black cloth after it has been cut to the proper size and shape, then trim to the right size

After you have the red and black cloth cut and sewn together, cut the black fur piece the same shape as the red cloth except 1 inch shorter all around.

Use a utility knife to cut the fur. Always cut fur on the backside. Use straight pins to hold the fur in place as you whip stitch the edges of the fur to the red cloth. When sewing fur down, keep the hair pushed back as you sew so it will not get tangled in the thread. A trick to cutting the fur to shape is to put it in place on the cloth and then fold the edge back as you cut the fur-shape free hand. I took a fur coat apart and pieced it together in order to get enough fur to make this robe.

A front pose of the robe (Carol Sizemore, modeling).

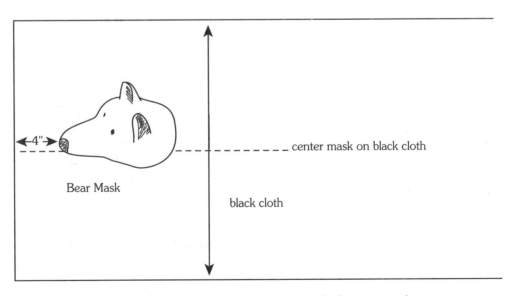

The sketch above shows how to center mask on cloth to get the measurements and shape of the robe.

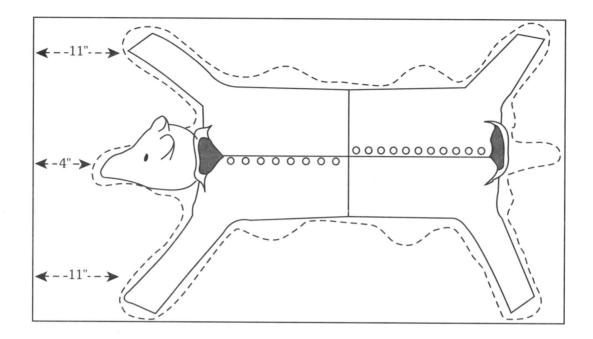

Above is shown a short-cut to getting the shape of the black cloth. The head is centered 4 inches back from front edge of cloth, then two shirts are lined up on the cloth as shown. Next use a yellow leaded pencil to draw out the shape around the shirts and bear head.

Once the outline has been marked on the cloth, re-adjust outline marks to those of the sketch on an earlier page of this project. Enlarge the whole pattern by 1 $1/2$ " all around the outline.

Use pinking shears (scissors that make a jagged cut) to get the finished look shown in the photographs and sketches. The red cloth can be cut the same size as the black cloth then reduced in size.

The sketch above shows how fur is sewn together when piecing fur.

Always cut fur on the back side.

Cut and sew pieces on the slits for the ear openings.

Sew the fur down around the edges.

Use stick pins to hold the fur in place while sewing.

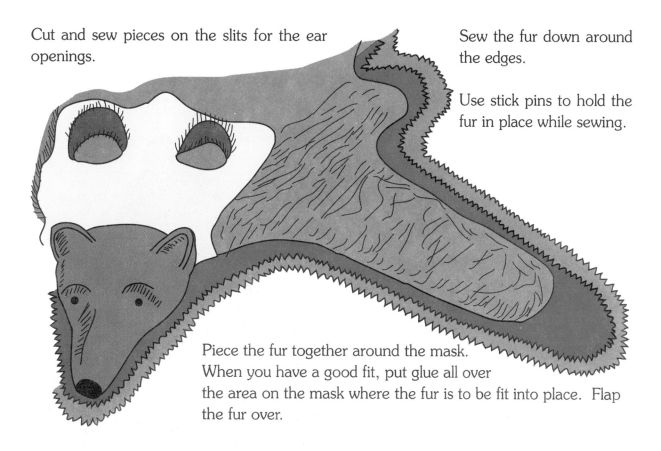

Piece the fur together around the mask. When you have a good fit, put glue all over the area on the mask where the fur is to be fit into place. Flap the fur over.

Sew fur edges down around bear head. (Use Elmer's or a similar type of glue.)

The head should look like the one in the photograph below when the fur has been glued down and sewn at the edges.

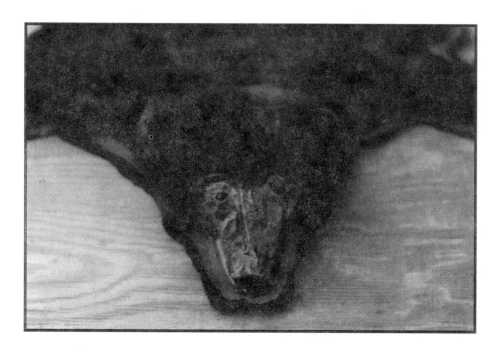

CUTTING THE UNDERSIDE OF THE BEAR HEAD FOR THE LINING

Using scissors, cut an opening on the underside of the bear head as shown in the sketch below.

Be careful not to cut all the way to the stitches holding the bear head in place on the robe.

The photograph at the right shows how the cutting should look when the opening is finished.

The sketch below depicts the pre-cutting of the cloth underneath the bear head showing how it is done.

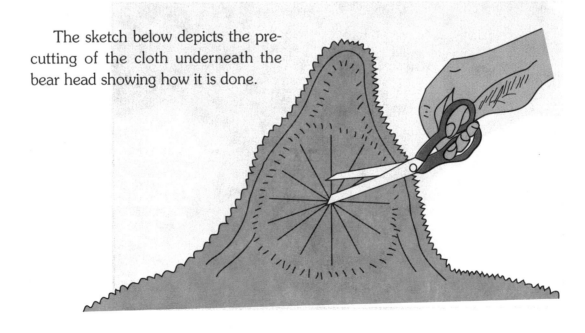

STEPS IN MAKING THE LINING FOR THE BEAR HEAD

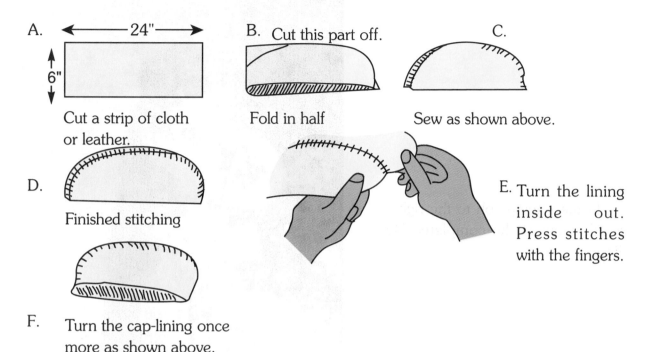

A. ← 24" →

6"

Cut a strip of cloth or leather.

B. Cut this part off.

Fold in half

C.

Sew as shown above.

D.

Finished stitching

E. Turn the lining inside out. Press stitches with the fingers.

F. Turn the cap-lining once more as shown above.

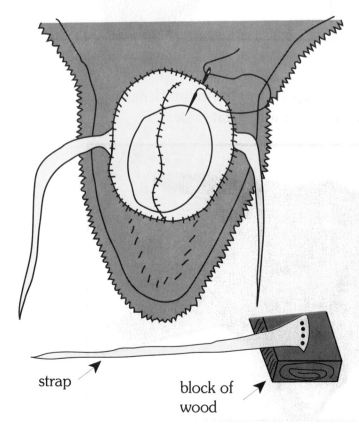

strap

block of wood

Sew the cap lining into the opening.

As shown in the sketch below cut two straps of leather 22 inches long. The wide end of the strap is 1 3/4 " wide, tapered down to a point. (See sketches at left.)

Place the wide ends of the straps on a wooden block. Use a nail to make the sewing holes. You can now easily sew the straps to the sides of the hat as shown in the sketch at the left.

In the photograph to the right, is a side view of the completed Bear Robe.

The photograph below shows a top view of the entire Bear Robe. Such a robe can be worn with great pride!

BREECHCLOUTS AND APRONS

The breechclout, worn by the Cherokee men, was a long piece of deerskin about 10 to 12 inches wide and about 6 feet long. Men wore the breechclout by passing it between their legs and securing it with the sash or belt in the front and back allowing it to flap over. (See sketch below.)

Most breechclouts were more heavily decorated on the front flap than the back one, because one would be sitting down on the back decorations. Breechclouts were attractive and often had decorations of quillwork, embroidery, ribbon work, painted designs, shells, beads, tassels, bones, etc. The decorative breechclouts were usually worn for ceremonies, rituals, and other important events. The plain breechclouts were worn for everyday use.

Breechclouts were later made of blanket cloth, but these were decorated, too. Several layers could be used when wearing a cloth breechclout to provide sufficient warmth. The leather breechclout worn during the winter would have had the hair left on the inside to provide warmth.

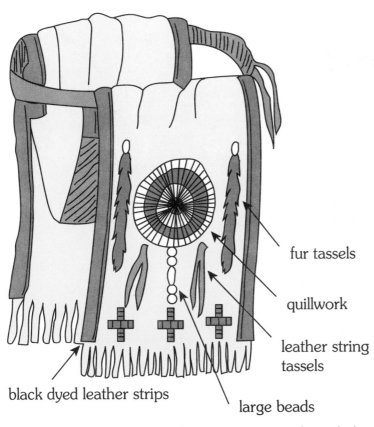

fur tassels

quillwork

leather string tassels

black dyed leather strips

large beads

It was the custom in those days for men and boys to wear only a breechclout with or without moccasins and leggings, the weather permitting.

A belt or a leather string, was usually tied around the waist of very young boys to accustom them to wearing clothes. Young boys usually went naked around home during the warm months.

Around 1790, the Cherokees rapidly turned to the ways of the white settlers.

During this period, wearing of the breechclout by the Cherokee was seldom seen as they began to

The above sketch shows the way to wear a breechclout dress more like the whites. from a belt.

Breechclouts, made from the trade blankets of the white man, were in colors of red, blue, black and other colors. The wool breechclout was lined with cotton cloth to prevent skin irritation. The ornaments on this new kind of breechclout consisted of ribbons, silver broaches, glass beads, tinkling brass or tin, etc., also reflecting trade items.

When you make your own breechclout, determine the length of it by holding the material for use from your feet to the top of your head. Many breechclouts hung down to the middle of the upper leg. Other breechclouts were longer, reaching to the knees or lower. I like making my own breechclouts 14 inches wide and about 6 feet long.

Flannel, thick cloth of different kinds, suede, velvet, tan-colored cloth, real or imitation leather can be used when making a breechclout.

The following examples of breechclouts and aprons show a variety of designs. You may want to make a breechclout created in Cherokee fashion using your own personal touch.

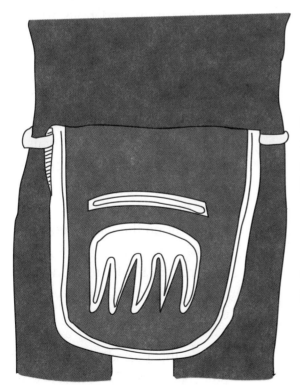

The breechclout in the sketch at left can be worn by a warrior. A design of a bear claw can be seen on the front flap, denoting strength and valor. The stripe is for a war honor.

This particular breechclout can be made of soft brown leather or cloth with patchwork designs sewn onto the material.

The breechclout at right has an eagle design painted on soft deerskin. The design can be patch-worked on with red flannel.

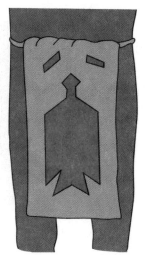

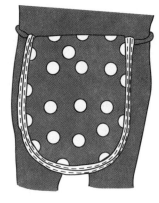

The breechclout at left is made of brown leather or cloth, with white dots painted on and hemmed with white cloth. A similar breechclout was sometimes worn during stick ball play.

Worn during ball play, this breechclout design appears to be that of the grapevine signifying strength.

This breechclout is made of leather with a painted design and trimmed with cloth.

The design at the right was once worn during the Eagle Dance in Cherokee, North Carolina.

The designs appeared to be painted on cloth. Dance bells were sewn around the belt.

bells

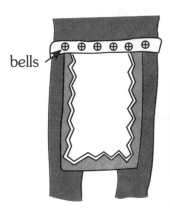

To the left is a leather fringed breechclout with a beaded belt. Any number of designs can be painted on this breechclout.

cowrie shells

The breechclout at the right is made of brown leather trimmed in yellow cloth. The bird design is made of bones. I used chicken wing and leg bones. A hack-saw is used to cut the bones to the proper length. I saw a dancer wear the design during the "Harvest Dance."

The breechclout at the left is made of deerskin or cloth and trimmed with red flannel. This would be an ideal breechclout for a warrior.

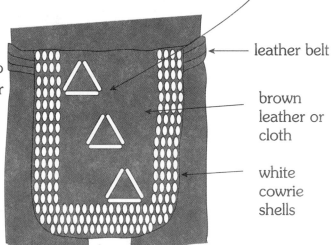

bones (wing or leg bones of the chicken or turkey)

leather belt

brown leather or cloth

white cowrie shells

The breechclout at the right is similar to one I saw worn by a chief in the outdoor drama in Cherokee, North Carolina.

To left is shown a breechclout made of blue cloth with red trimmed edges.

The above apron-type breechclout depicts the style the Cherokee started making after they obtained seed beads and cloth.

This style is worn today by Cherokee men for demonstration and ceremony. The apron is easy to put on by tying the strings at the sides.

Aprons made of cloth, such as velvet, are usually in dark colors. Black seems to be one of the favorites. When using velvet or any other cloth to make an apron, hem around the edges.

The apron pictured above is beaded in floral patterns with white and light green seed beads.

Remember, the apron is a replacement by modern Native Americans, made to imitate the old breechclout worn with leggings. The apron is not worn by those who wish to be be dressed in authentic, pre-white Cherokee dress.

When wearing the apron-type breechclout, regular trousers must be worn underneath.

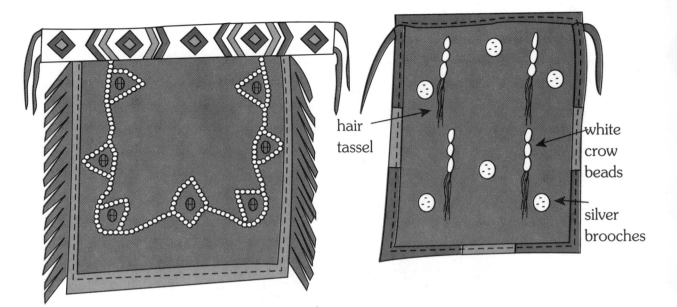

hair tassel

white crow beads

silver brooches

The apron above is made of brown leather with a black cloth edge. White pony beads are sewn on it. The belt is made of seed beads.

The apron above is made of brown cloth with the edges in red and black.

Apron above is made of red flannel, black cloth, with the edge trimmed in blue. Pony beads hang down loosely in horse shoe shapes. The other designs are done with seed beads.

The apron in the above sketch is also made of red flannel, with red and black edges. White pony beads and cowrie shells hang on the flap. Seed beads form the diamond designs. A beaded belt is also worn with the apron.

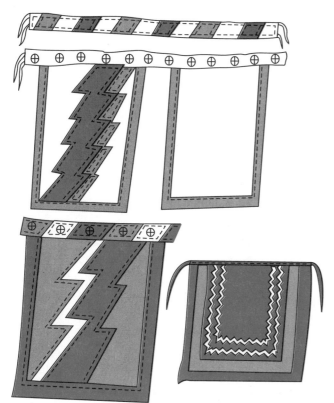

The apron-type breechclout is made of cloth and done in patchwork. The designs are done in much the same way as Native Americans used to do ribbon work, by cutting and folding cloth or ribbons, then sewing the material down to hold the designs in place.

The breechclout shown to the left, is similar to the Eagle Dancers' breechclout aprons worn in the outdoor drama in North Carolina.

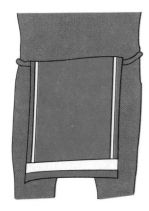

This is a cloth or trade blanket breech clout. From a study of old paintings, the older breechclouts of the southeast appear to be shorter and narrower.

The breechclout to the left is made of brown leather, but can be made of cloth. It is trimmed in red flannel. Such a breechclout would be good to wear during war time.

At the left is a breechclout made from a trade blanket, with embroidered designs and green ribbon stripes.

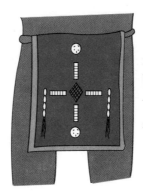

This breechclout is made of cloth and has beads, red hair tassels, brooches, and seed bead designs.

THE LEAD EAGLE DANCER'S BREECHCLOUT

The above picture shows the breechclout of the lead dancer of the Eagle Dance. It was made using patchwork.

On the following pages are the step-by-step instructions for making the breechclout.

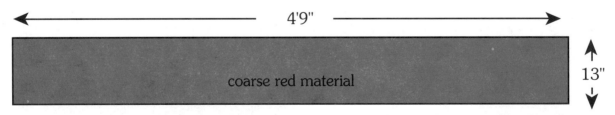

First, you will need a length of cloth cut to the size shown in the sketch above. Red flannel cloth will be perfect. If it is not available use any thick red cloth that does not stretch.

Turn left edge and top edge under and whip-stitch.

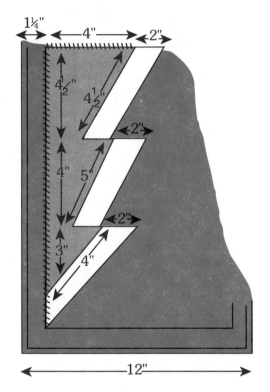

A. The black material should be laid over pencil designs made on the cloth, the cloth held in place and scissors used to cut the black material, folding it back along the pencil markings on the cloth. Allow $1/4$" extra when cutting the black lightning design. Turn the extra under for the hem.

B. Use straight pins to hold the material in place. Use black thread to sew the black cloth.

Note: Allow an extra inch in width and length so the breechclout can be hemmed.

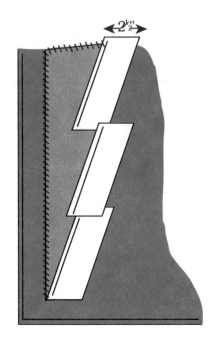

A. Cut 3 2 $1/2$" wide strips of white cloth, similar to the sizes in the sketch at the left. Use your own best guess in judging the sizes when cutting the material for the patch work.

B. Align the three pieces of white cloth in their proper places and pin them in place. Turn the edges under as you sew, using the whip-stitch. Sew all around each white piece. Use white thread on the white pieces.

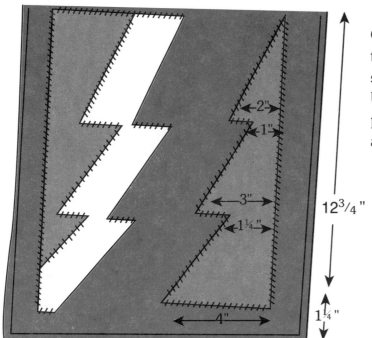

Cut the black thunder design for the right side of breechclout as shown in the sketch at the left. Use straight pins to hold it in place. Turn $1/4$" extra edge under and whip stitch.

Draw the designs onto the belt as seen in the sketch below.

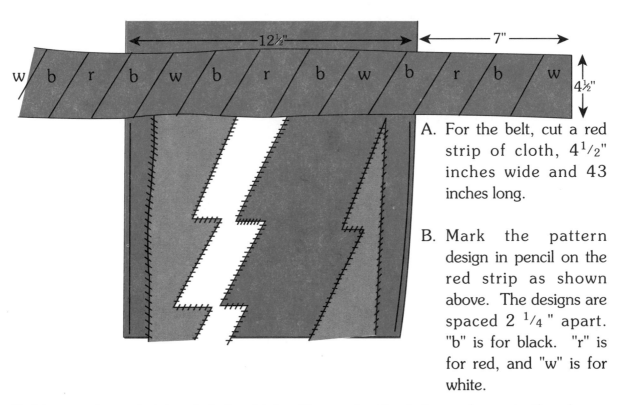

A. For the belt, cut a red strip of cloth, $4^1/2$" inches wide and 43 inches long.

B. Mark the pattern design in pencil on the red strip as shown above. The designs are spaced $2 \ 1/4$" apart. "b" is for black. "r" is for red, and "w" is for white.

C. Line up the red strip of cloth which will soon be the belt, as shown in the above sketch. Use the lightning and thunder designs as guides for alignment. Hold the belt in place, turning edges of the belt under, and pin in place.

D. Cut one long white piece and pin over the stripes marked "b - w - b" (as marked in illustration on page 94) , just above the red lightning design and under the two top black pieces as shown below.

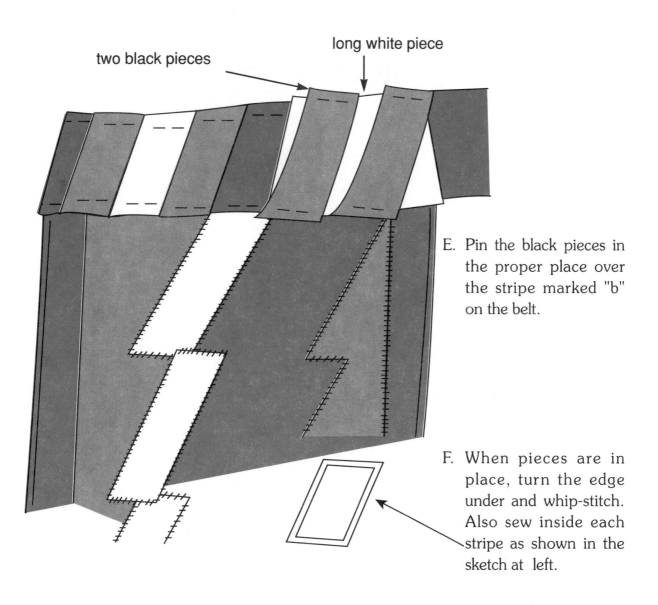

two black pieces

long white piece

E. Pin the black pieces in the proper place over the stripe marked "b" on the belt.

F. When pieces are in place, turn the edge under and whip-stitch. Also sew inside each stripe as shown in the sketch at left.

Note:
  You will have to lift the pieces from time to time to make sure the alignment is correct.

Above is pictured the back view of the breech clout.

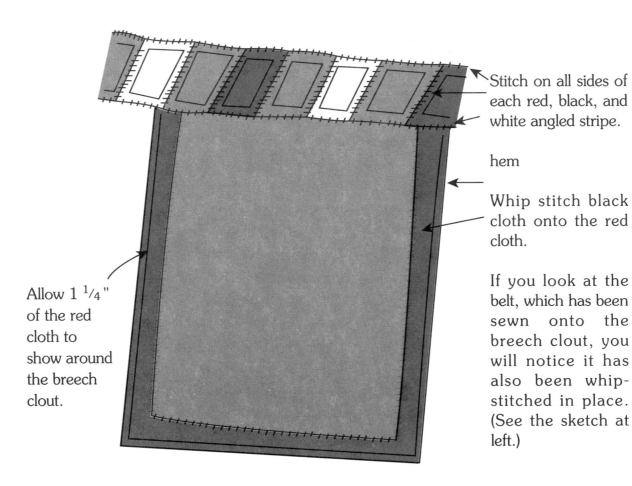

Stitch on all sides of each red, black, and white angled stripe.

hem

Whip stitch black cloth onto the red cloth.

If you look at the belt, which has been sewn onto the breech clout, you will notice it has also been whip-stitched in place. (See the sketch at left.)

Allow 1 1/4 " of the red cloth to show around the breech clout.

When the front of the breechclout has been aligned with the belt and whip-stitched into place, put the breechclout on and align the back flap. Fit it properly to your own size. Holding the back flap in place pin it securely. Now whip-stitch the back flap to the belt as you did the front flap. Be sure to get a snug fit, because this breechclout is worn without any underwear.

A small bell for each strip is sewn into position, as shown in the sketch above. Do not sew bells on the stripes where the belt over-laps. You can use safety pins or tie strings to hold the two ends of the belt together when the breechclout is worn.

This is a modern version of the breechclout where it is already attached to the belt. In the old days the breechclout and belt were two separate parts but worn together.

THE FEATHERED HAT OF THE WAR CHIEF

The war chief wore a feathered hat similar to the one shown above. The base of the hat was probably made of otter skin. Red and black fluffs were put all over it. Crane or heron feathers, dyed black, stood up and curved round about the hat. When making a hat like this, rooster tail feathers can be used as a substitute.

The red feathers sticking up on the top of the hat can be made of dyed turkey feathers with much of the feather stripped from the quill. Some of these red upright feathers have all of the feathers stripped from the quill.

Copper or brass-colored sun-disks are attached to the leather band. Cherokee used some copper in the old days and sometimes gold. Later, with the coming of the white traders, they obtained brass and other metals for their use.

The feathers on top of the hat represented the "Great Thunder Bird" or some other war emblem. Mystical power gave wisdom to the war chief when he wore this hat to lead his people in battle.

The photograph above shows my first attempt at making a War Chief's Hat.

THE MAKING OF THE WAR CHIEF'S HAT

In the photograph is an example of a War Chief's hat. Having no instructions to go by, I leaned heavily on my knowledge of other Native American hats and their construction.

While making this hat, some of its meaning seemed to flood my being as I thought of its symbolism. The hat, in its entirety, represents a great war bird. The chief takes on the powers of this bird when the hat is worn.

The four striped feathers on top of the hat may have stood for the four directions in which warfare might take the chief. The black curved feathers stand for the tail of the war bird. Red and black fluffs are the symbols of war and death to the enemy at the hands of the war chief. The round disks are for the power of the Sun and Spirit to guide the chief.

Black rooster tail feathers work well as the curved feathers for this hat. To make the feathers longer, dye turkey wing feathers black, then trim them to the same width as the rooster tail feathers. Next glue the rooster tail feathers onto the tip of the trimmed turkey feathers. Sew them down just a bit with black thread.
Refer to the sketch below:

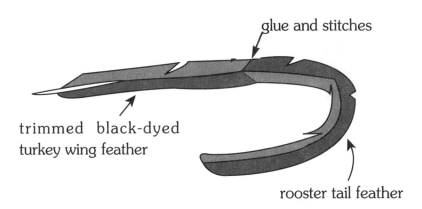

glue and stitches

trimmed black-dyed
turkey wing feather

rooster tail feather

You will need red and black fluffs which can be purchased from craft stores. A soft black belt or a strip of black leather will be needed for the band. Silver or metal buttons for the disks can also be obtained from a craft store or you can make them yourself

To make the sun disks yourself:

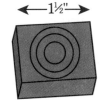

←—1½"—→

Mark the disk pattern of circles on a block of wood, as shown in the sketch at left. Whittle ¼" down into each circle creating a rounded out form. You can use a round file. You now have a mold.

Once your mold is made, press wood filler or wood putty into the mold and while the wood filler is still soft, insert a semi-stiff bent piece of wire into the soft wood filler as shown in the sketches to the left. (Shape the wire in advance.) Cover up the ends of the wire with the wood filler to conceal the ends. Let the disk dry, then remove it from the mold.

Make as many of the sun disks as needed to go around the band. Sand the disks, apply glue, then cover them with aluminum foil.

Note: The lid of a tin can, which has the indented circle pattern of the sun disks would also serve as a mold.

To make an imitation of the otter skin leather hat on which to mount the feathers, you will need soft brown leather. Split cowhide leather is fine, or a felt hat can be used.

If you are making the hat of leather, first make a paper pattern, then select a bowl that fits your head. Tape paper around the bowl to form a hat pattern. Fold the paper on the bowl toward the center of bowl as shown in the sketches below. Then remove it from the bowl by cutting it into four sections.

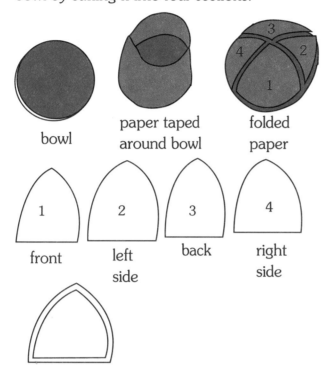

bowl

paper taped
around bowl

folded
paper

1
front

2
left
side

3
back

4
right
side

Number the paper patterns in the order they are removed from the bowl.

Use the paper pattern parts by laying them on the leather and marking around the patterns with a pen or pencil.

After the leather parts are cut out, punch holes around the edges of each part as shown in the sketch at the left.

Sew the parts together. Sew 1 to 2, starting at the bottom and sewing upward. Then sew 2 to 3 from the bottom up, then 3 to 4 and lastly 4 to 1. Turn the cap inside out and press all stitches with your fingers.

Note: The rough side of the leather should be the outside of the hat. Also, once the hat is sewn together, trim it around the bottom to make it even.

Sew the black leather band around the bottom of the hat using a whip-stitch, as shown in the sketch below.

The black band should be 2 inches wide. Sew the sun disks to the leather band.

Space the disks about 2 $\frac{1}{2}$" apart. Every other disk is attached above an imaginary center line, and the alternate disks just below center. The positions of the disk stand for the rising and setting sun.

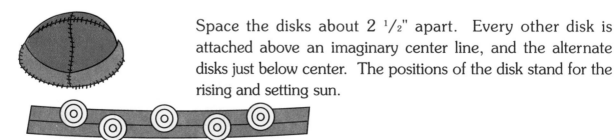

The above photograph depicts an old Native American way of mounting several feathers on the hat. It is unclear whether this is the way the Cherokee did the mounting on this particular hat, but this way works.

There are two other ways of mounting feathers, as shown in the sketches below. Perhaps the fan method could be used as in the "eagle fan" construction.

The sketches above show how the holes for the feathers can be drilled into small blocks of wood.

The feathers are glued into the holes. Small holes are drilled on angles along the side of the wood blocks for sewing the blocks to the hat.

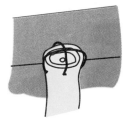

The sketches to the left show a socket for the feather, made from bone or river cane.

Use a hack-saw to cut each socket 1 inch long. Use a small drill bit to bore 4 needle size holes $1/4$" from the bottom of the socket.

The holes should be so drilled that the threads cross each other under the base of the hat.

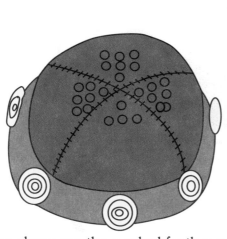

Shown above are the marked feather positions.

The four top sockets are sewn on first for the top red feathers as shown.

Once the four top sockets are sewn into place, mark the positions of the other sockets and sew them into place.

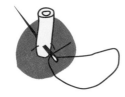

Take the needle straight through to the other side, then go down with the needle into the leather beside the socket. Come back up with the needle at a position beside another hole in the socket. A socket is sewn on about the same way you would sew on a button.

Knot the end of the thread when the stitching on a socket is finished, as shown.

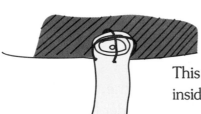

This sketch shows how the underside of the socket looks from inside the hat.

Note: A total of 25 sockets are shown for this hat. You may wish to add more sockets.

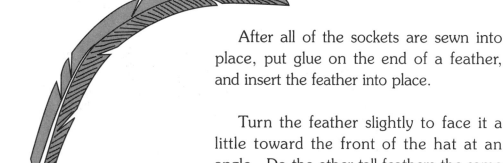

After all of the sockets are sewn into place, put glue on the end of a feather, and insert the feather into place.

Turn the feather slightly to face it a little toward the front of the hat at an angle. Do the other tall feathers the same way. There are left and right feathers, so be sure the lefts go on the left and the rights go on the right of the hat.

When all of the tall curved feathers are in place, glue red fluffs and black fluffs onto the hat in an overlapping fashion, as shown in the photograph on a prior page. Make sure the quill-ends of the fluffs at the black band are concealed behind the band.

Note: Start gluing feathers at the top part of the leather hat, covering all spaces between the sockets.

fluffs are overlapped

Glue the feathers on in rows, going downward and over-lapping the prior row of fluffs.

Once all of the fluffs are glued on, the hat is finished and ready to wear!

Note: If the hat fits too loosely when worn, sew an extra band of cloth inside the hat.

The peace chief's hat is made of white feathers, and the ordination hat is made with yellow feathers.

THE WAR CHIEF'S CLOTHING

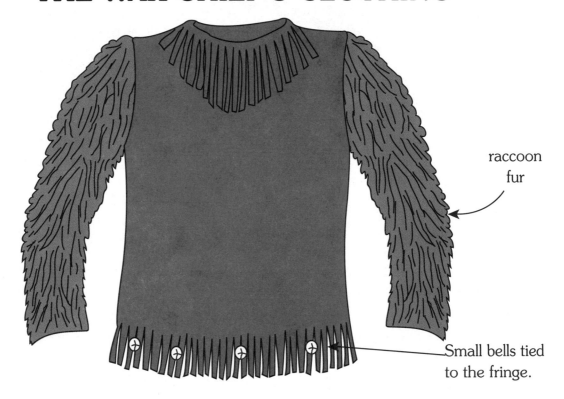

raccoon
fur

Small bells tied
to the fringe.

The war chief wore a deerskin shirt that was dyed red. This shirt was long enough to reach below the hips, or longer. As far as can be determined, the sleeves of this shirt were made of raccoon fur. Such a shirt, without a doubt, was worn during the cold months.

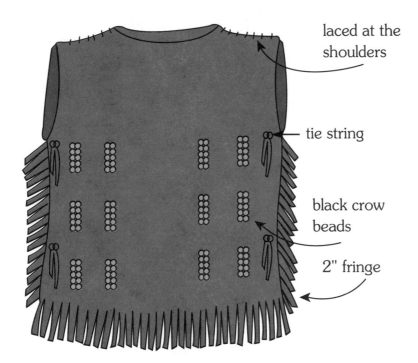

laced at the
shoulders

tie string

black crow
beads

2" fringe

During the warm months, if a shirt was worn at all, it would have been a sleeveless shirt.

It was also made of red-dyed deerskin. Sometimes shirts were open at the sides and fastened with tie strings.

To make the shirt shown in the sketch at the left, I used heavy red cloth and black crow beads.

THE WAR CHIEF'S LEGGINGS

The war chief's leggings were made of deerskin dyed red. The leggings to the left are the center-seam type, which Cherokee men wore in the old days. Fringes were often sewn to the side of the legging, but were sometimes made without them.

I believe the leggings were decorated in a style to honor the chief and were not plain and dull. The designs could be patch-worked on in black leather.

The leggings in the photograph above are made of cloth (see page 121 for details).

THE WAR CHIEF'S BREECHCLOUT

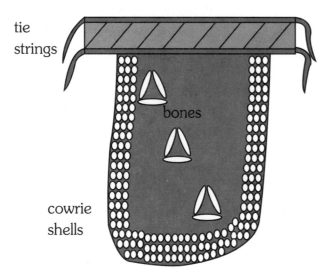

tie
strings

bones

cowrie
shells

The war chief's breechclout was made of deerskin dyed red. It tied on the sides and was probably made the way the breechclout for the lead "eagle dancer" was made as shown earlier in this book.

The breechclouts shown at left and below are examples of ones seen in North Carolina.

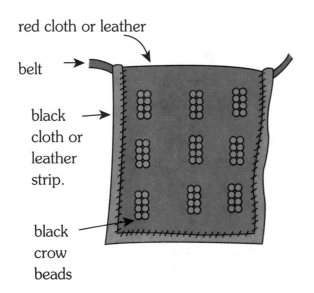

red cloth or leather

belt

black
cloth or
leather
strip.

black
crow
beads

The sketch at the left is another version of the war chief's breechclout.

THE WAR CHIEF'S BELT

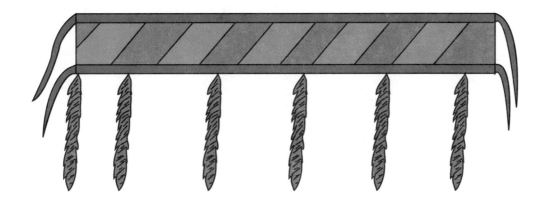

Shown above is a version of the war chief's belt made of red, orange and black dyed deerskin. The stripes on the belt are a symbol for warfare.

The belt can be made by patch-working the designs with leather or by painting the designs. The fur tassels, which hung from the belt, were probably otter tails. You can make tassels of black fur by cutting strips of fur, then folding the fur in half. The fur should be on the inside of the tassel as you sew it up the side. When the sewing of the tassel is finished, turn it right side out. It is now ready to be sewn to the belt. The number of tassels is up to you. Seven and fourteen are Cherokee good-luck numbers thought to help the belt wearer during warfare.

A less desirable but quicker method of sewing the tassel is to fold a strip of fur with the the fur on the outside and stitch the seams. This leaves the seam more likely to show but but avoids the difficulty of turning a small tassel right side out.

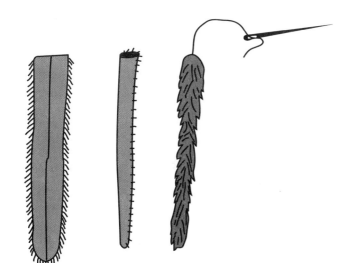

It is illustrated in the sketches to the left how fur can be cut, folded, sewed and turned right side out to form a tassel. Needle and thread are used to sew the end of the tassel to the belt.

The belts for the peace-time chief can be made the same way. The colors of the materials used should be white and yellow.

OTHER ITEMS WORN BY THE CHIEF

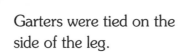

Garters were tied on the side of the leg.

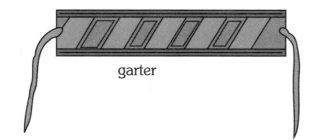

garter

leather pouch

center-seam war moccasin

Finger-woven garters were worn below the knees. They were once made of plant fibers or fur made into string dyed, and then woven. Later, yarn from the white man was used.

The sketch to the left shows a leather or cloth garter. The designs can be painted on or patch-worked.

The War Chief had a leather or woven pouch attached to his belt. Tobacco and small items for war could be carried in this pouch.

Small bells were attached to his moccasins. Red stripes were painted, quilled or beaded across the toe of the moccasins.

Deer hoofs on strings were worn around the War Chief's ankles.

The necklace in the sketch to the left is a version of the necklace worn by an actor playing a Cherokee War Chief in the outdoor drama, "Unto These Hills", shown in Cherokee, North Carolina.

The War Chief wore a necklace made of a mussel shell, which had been stained or engraved with his war emblems, as shown in the sketch to the left.

The War Chief also carried a wand or fan made of swan feathers. These feathers would have been dyed red and black.

Dyed turkey wing feathers can be used. Fluffs dyed black are also used on the fan.

These two sketches show versions of the fan or wand he held.

Above is a sketch of a red and black painted war club.

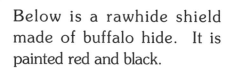

Below is a rawhide shield made of buffalo hide. It is painted red and black.

The red bowl and the black one hold the substance mixed with grease to make war paint.

Shown to the left is an arrow painted red with black stripes.

Some Cherokee bows were made from the wood of a locust tree.

A red deerskin arrow case was worn by the war chief as shown in the sketch to the right.

THE RAVEN SKIN NECKLACE

When the war chief was in office, he was called, "The Raven." People of the tribe referred to him as the "Great Honored Man."

At one time, the war chief wore a raven skin about his neck. The head of the raven was at the front of the chief's neck and the wings spread out over either shoulder. This bird necklace tied behind the neck.

The raven skin necklace was worn with great honor and brought the chief respect.

THE CHIEF'S DEER-HOOF ANKLETS

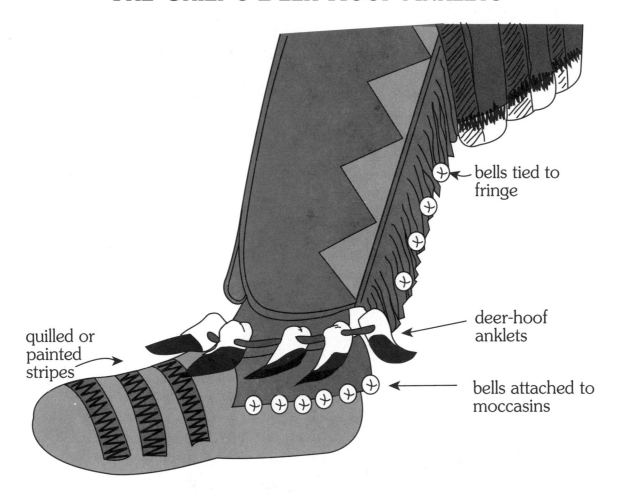

bells tied to fringe

deer-hoof anklets

quilled or painted stripes

bells attached to moccasins

The chief of a Cherokee village had great influence over the people. He was true to his culture and office of power. The chief dressed in such a way that he was recognized by all who saw him.

The chief also wore deer-hoof anklets. Deer-hoof anklets were made of deer-hoofs on leather strings as shown. An anklet of deer-hoofs was worn on each ankle like bracelets. The anklets made a clatter as the chief walked.

The wearing of deer-hoofs in this fashion was thought to give the chief strength in his legs. The deer was known for swiftness and flight. Also, the deer could detect an intruder or an enemy nearby.

The deer was also associated with the "Upper World" in Cherokee mythology and came down to live in this world. It is no wonder the chief desired such powerful traits as that of the deer.

There are stories handed down among the Cherokee, about a man named "Kanati." He was a great hunter who kept all the deer in a cave, killing them as needed for food. Much to the father's dismay, his son let the deer out of the cave making it necessary to hunt for food.

The Chief of all the Deers decided to punish mankind with rheumatism if man killed a deer without saying the hunter's prayer.

Deer-hoof anklets were worn as a powerful charm. Deer symbols were sometimes put on the chief's clothing as magic emblems and were associated with war decorations, done in beadwork, quillwork, embroidery, and painted designs.

The above photograph shows a pair of deer-hoof anklets.

MAKING DEER-HOOF ANKLETS

If you are able to obtain deer-hoofs for the anklets, try making a set of these ankle bracelets as part of a chief's attire. Hunters cut the legs off a slain deer and usually discard them. They would probably be glad to save them for such use.

To prepare the hoofs for use, cut through the part that bends just above the hoof. You will need a handsaw and knife.

A deer-hoof has two prongs or parts to it. Use a knife to cut them apart as shown in the sketches below.

Cut here with a knife.

left hoof

severed joint

right hoof

It will take the hoofs of two deers to have six to eight hoof-halves. Once they have been cleaned, put salt on the exposed bone of each hoof section. Now they must be put away somewhere in a dry place and cured for a few days. Make sure the hoof sections are stored where dogs or cats cannot get them.

When the hoof sections are ready to use, you will notice an odor. To cover up this smell, brush clear varnish over the bone part of each hoof section and allow a day for drying.

After the varnished hoof-sections are dry, use a $1/8$th inch drill bit to drill a hole through the side of the top part of each hoof section, as shown in the sketches below.

Center the drill bit on the hoof - section and bore the hole.

The dew-claws, also can be used for necklaces. Drill the holes the same way.

Once the dew claws have been cleaned, sand them a little on the bone part. They will need to be varnished, just as the deer-hoofs. Dew claws can be used on necklaces.

Put the deer-hoof sections on a thong which is $^1/_4$" wide and 29" long. Do the same thing to another leather thong. You may need a utility knife or scissors to cut the strings.

When you have three left hoof parts and three right hoof parts on a thong, as shown in the sketch below, you are ready to make another one of the pair.

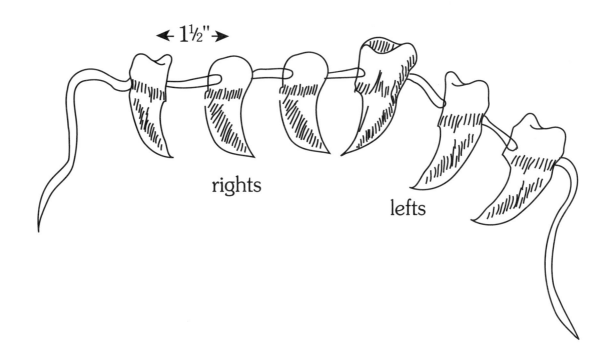

The anklets are tied behind each ankle. There seems to be a mystical power with you when wearing the anklets. No wonder the chief walked the earth proudly.

FEATHERED HATS OF THE PEACE TIME CHIEF

The hat to the left was worn only at the ordination of the peace time chief. At this particular time most of his garments, including the hat, were yellow.

White fur was dyed to get the yellow look. Yellow Root, a wild plant that grew abundantly in Great Smoky Mountains, was a source of natural yellow dye for the Cherokee. You may chose to use a commercial dye.

After the peace time chief's ordination in yellow, he wore a white feathered hat and white deerskin clothing.

The fur for the hat was usually the white deer fur from the deer's tail and the band was made from swan skin with its fine white feathers.

The author used white rabbit skin (more readily available) for the hat and for the band.

One must remember that the costume of the principle chief who was at the Cherokee empire capitol in Echota varied somewhat from the chiefs in the villages scattered throughout the Cherokee territory.

NOTE: A good resource for the chief's clothing is: Mails, Thomas, **THE CHEROKEE PEOPLE , The Story Of The Cherokees From Earliest Origins To Contemporary Times**, 1992, Council Oak Books, Tulsa, Oklahoma.

THE PEACE TIME CHIEF'S CLOTHING

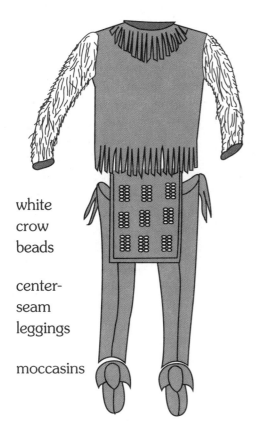

white
crow
beads

center-
seam
leggings

moccasins

The ordination shirt of the peace time chief is shown in these two sketches. They are made the same as the war chief's except the color is yellow. The sleeves of the long sleeve shirt were probably white fur instead of brown fur.

This yellow outfit is worn only on the day the peace chief is reinstated.

Both warm and cold weather styles are pictured.

sleeveless shirt or waistcoat

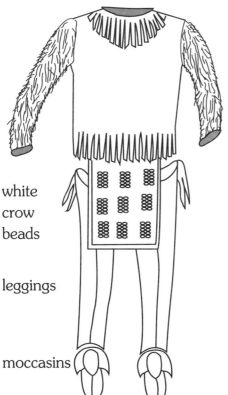

white
crow
beads

leggings

moccasins

The clothing of the peace chief, after he takes office, is entirely white.

These outfits can be quilled, embroidered, beaded, etc. with the clan symbol of the chief who wears it. If it is a war outfit, the decorations or symbols refer to war and the chief's honors. If the outfit is for a peace chief, the clan symbol can also be used, as well as peace symbols, etc.

CENTER-SEAM LEGGINGS

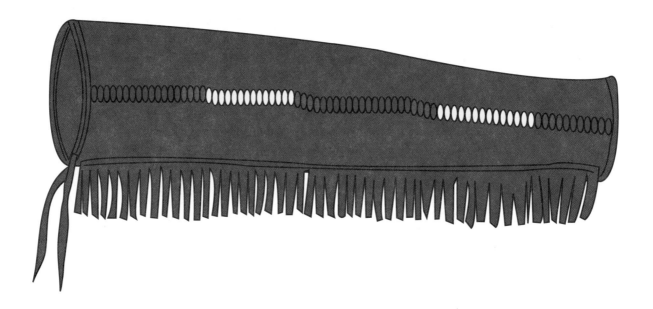

A study of old drawings or paintings of Cherokee men show their legging styles.

One style I will attempt to describe, is shown above. The seam is not down the side as in the making of the white man's trousers, but rather up and down the front of the legging. This center-seam was left plain or embroidered with quills, beads, or yarn. Others decorated the seam or either side with silver disks, buttons, tassels of fur, tin cones and other things. Most leggings of this style, worn by the Cherokee, had no fringe. In some cases leggings had fringes sewn up the side.

This style of leggings reached to just above the knees and attached to the belt with long tie strings. Later, when trade blankets were used for leggings, the leggings reached to the top of the thigh and were made to fit more loosely than old tight-fitting leather leggings. During hot weather, if leggings had to be worn for protection, the shorter style was cooler. As the weather got colder, the longer leggings were worn to provide warmth as well as protection.

The center-seam legging can be made to fit tightly and the cuff of the legging can be worn either inside or outside of the moccasin.

HOW TO MAKE A CENTER-SEAM LEGGING

One way to get a good personal fit without a pattern is to wrap the material, such as deerskin or blanket cloth, around the leg, trimming it as you sew the seam up the front. The other method, that most people use, is to have a pattern made of paper. I find it best to use an old pair of well-fitting pants for a pattern.

Use soft deerskin or imitation leather to get the old time look. If using cloth, a blanket material or other thick material may be used in colors of black, red, navy blue, or green. You can reconstruct a pair of your own pants by cutting off the legs and resewing them into center-seam leggings.

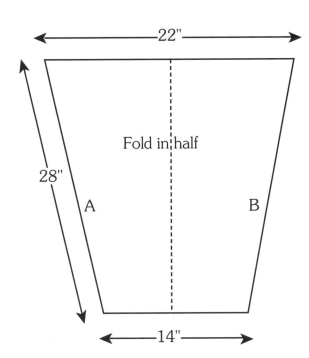

I used my dimensions on this pair of leggings. You may have to alter the size to fit you.

Measure the width and length of a leg of your own pants to determine your size. (Allow an inch for the hemming.)

Now that you have cut your two pieces of material for the leggings, fold each piece in half, bringing A to B. Sew from top to bottom.

The legging may then be turned inside out and embroidered with yarn from one end of the center-seam to the other end.

tie strings

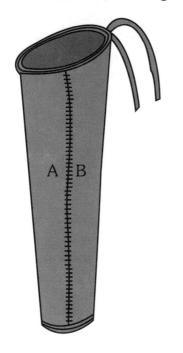

The straps for the strings are $\frac{1}{2}$ inch wide and 24 inches long, folded in half, then sewn to the side of the legging at the top, as shown in the sketch to the left.

The tie strings are attached to the belt just above the hip.

The two leggings shown below depict decorations that can be used on the center-seam style.

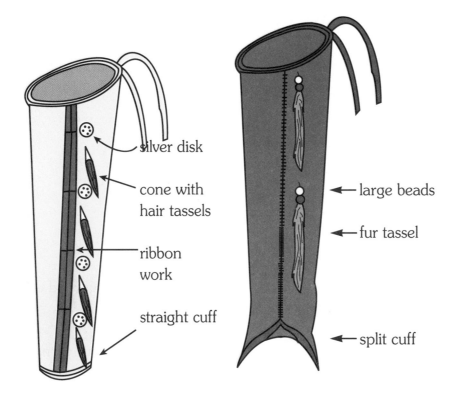

silver disk

cone with hair tassels

ribbon work

straight cuff

large beads

fur tassel

split cuff

My Own Version Of Making The Center-Seam Legging

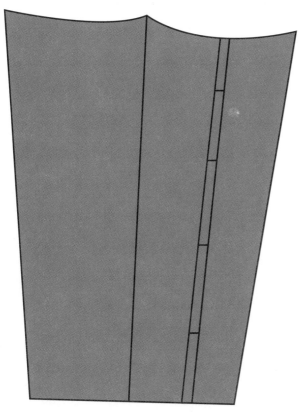

left legging

The instructions presented on the following pages are my own version of Center-Seam leggings using the legs from a pair of pants.

This version looks like the Center-Seam type, but in reality, they are the "side seam" type.

First, cut the legs off a tan pair of pants that fit you. Cut the legs to the shape shown in the sketch to the left.

Once the two leggings are cut, draw the design with a pencil up and down on what will be the front of the legging, as shown in the above sketch. The design should be centered.

In this version, it is best to embroider the center-seam before sewing the legging up the side and adding the fringe. You must also remember that there is a right legging and left legging, in order to get the designs in the proper place.

right legging

Note where the design goes on each legging.

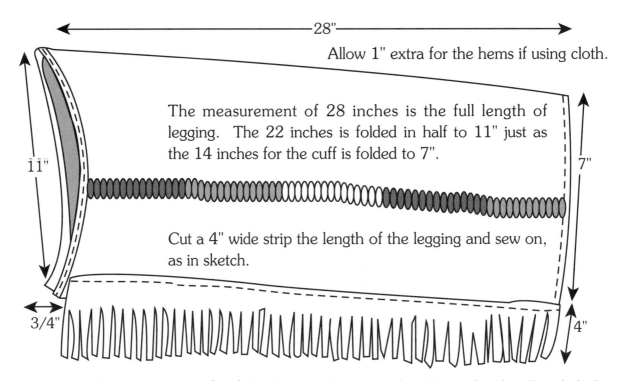

The measurement of 28 inches is the full length of legging. The 22 inches is folded in half to 11" just as the 14 inches for the cuff is folded to 7".

Cut a 4" wide strip the length of the legging and sew on, as in sketch.

Cut a four-inch strip of soft leather, as shown in the above sketch. Punch holes along the upper side of the strip After the holes are punched, sew the strip on the legging about $^3/_4$ inch from the edge, as shown above.

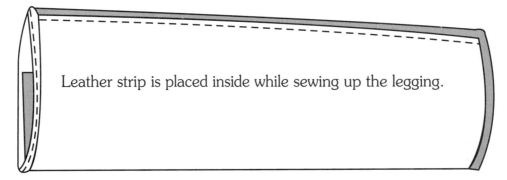

Leather strip

Do the other legging the same way, remembering which is the right and left legging, so when the fringe is cut, it will be on the correct side of the legging. The fringed strip is optional.

Fold the legging inside out, making sure the uncut fringed strip is folded back. Sew the side of the legging together.

Leather strip is placed inside while sewing up the legging.

Once the legging is sewn together, turn the legging inside out, then cut the leather strip into fringe.

EMBROIDERING THE CENTER-SEAM LEGGINGS

Hem the top and bottom of leggings.

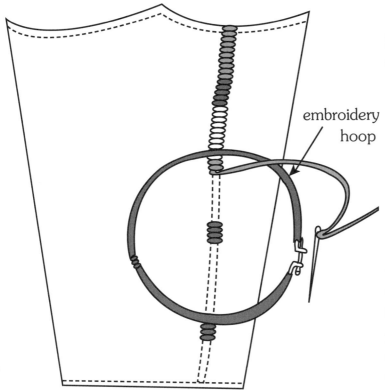

The Cherokee used quills or dyed thread to cover the seam.

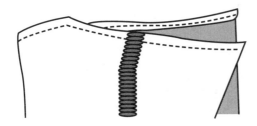

Do the hemming first before you begin the embroidering.

I used blue, red and yellow yarn to do the embroidery work. A large needle was also used.

embroidery hoop

Start embroidering with the blue yarn. Knot one end of the yarn. Come up through he bottom of the material with the needle at the edge of the design. Cross over to the other side of the design. Go back up beside the stitch.

Begin the next stitch and continue, changing to the red yarn, then the yellow yarn, etc.

The stitches are parallel (side by side) and close.

BLANKET CLOTH LEGGINGS

The type of leggings shown in the photograph below are made of the trade blankets similar to ones obtained from traders around the 1760 period.

Deerskin was quickly replaced with trade cloth and blanket material to make leggings. Other types of cloth were used also.

If blanket cloth is not available, a thick grade of cloth from the fabric store will work or use an old pair of trousers.

The white designs on these leggings can be made with seed beads, yarn or a strip of white corduroy material. The strips are cut 1 $1/2$ inch wide and as long as needed to make the design. Cut the corduroy so the ridges run cross-ways on the strip. When sewing the strip of white cloth down, turn the edges under and put the stitches between the ridges.

The above photograph shows a front and back view of my leggings.

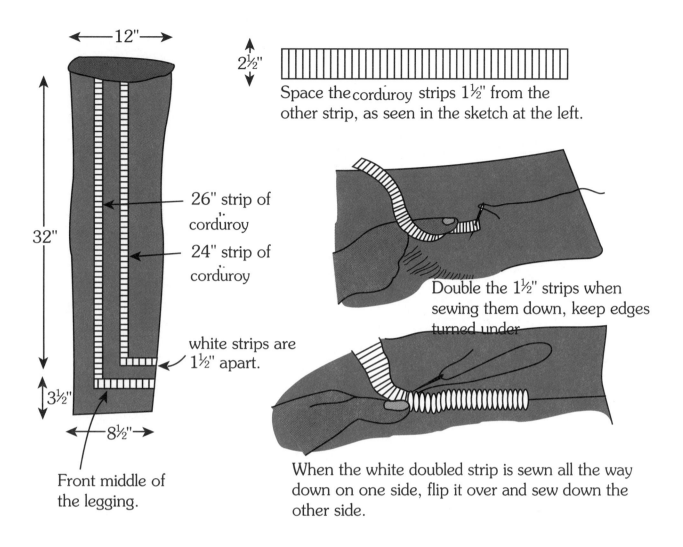

← 12" →

2½"

Space the corduroy strips 1½" from the other strip, as seen in the sketch at the left.

32"

26" strip of corduroy

24" strip of corduroy

white strips are 1½" apart.

3½"

← 8½" →

Front middle of the legging.

Double the 1½" strips when sewing them down, keep edges turned under.

When the white doubled strip is sewn all the way down on one side, flip it over and sew down the other side.

This photo pictures the finished left legging.

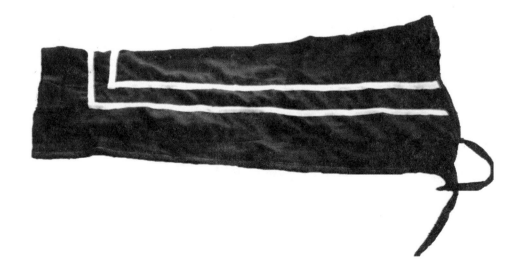

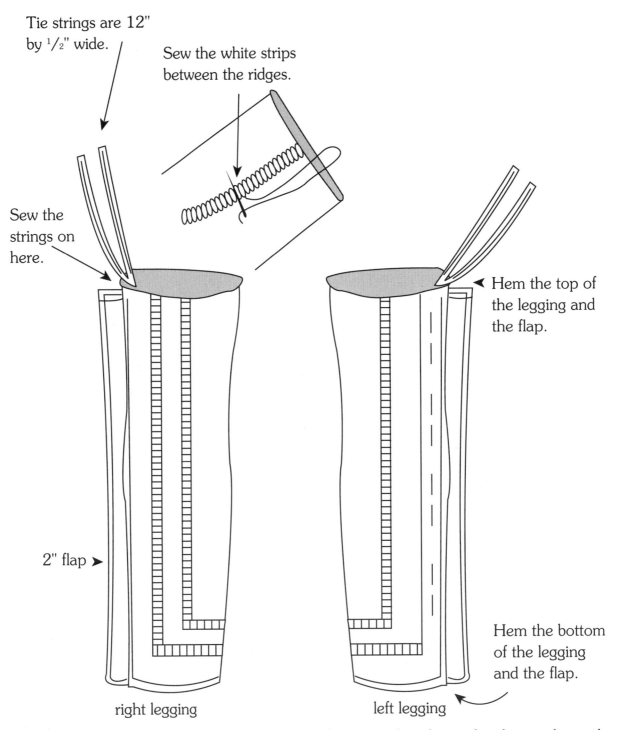

Tie strings are 12" by $\frac{1}{2}$" wide.

Sew the white strips between the ridges.

Sew the strings on here.

2" flap ➤

right legging

Hem the top of the legging and the flap.

Hem the bottom of the legging and the flap.

left legging

Draw pencil lines on the leggings as shown in the above sketches to keep the corduroy strips running straight as you sew.

When the white strips have been sewn on, fold and hold the legging the way it goes using straight pins to hold the seam in place. The legging should be loose enough to get the foot easily through the cuff when all sewing is finished. The seam, indicated by straight pins above, should be sewn up and down twice for strength.

128

HOW TO MAKE THE WAR CHIEF'S LEGGINGS - MY WAY

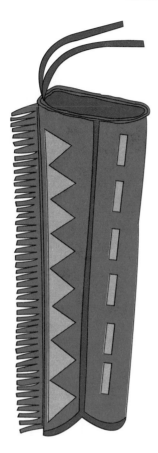

The war chief's leggings were made of red dyed deerskin. Designs on these leggings can be made of black dyed deerskin.

Shown in the sketch to the left, are the center-seam leggings with added fringe along the side and a split cuff.

If you are going to use leather for the leggings, the designs can be quilled, beaded, painted or patch-worked onto the legging.

The legs from an old pair of pants can be reworked into center-seam leggings.

The half-diamond or mountain designs and broken-line or trail designs on the leggings are done with black patch-worked cloth. These designs represent the many paths of war over the mountains and through the valleys where the chief leads his warriors.

There were other style leggings worn by the Cherokee, but the center-seam style was the most common. Most of the center-seam leggings had straight cuffs, but some had split cuffs. The split-cuffed legging was probably worn by the most important men of the tribe to show rank. The straight cuffed legging could be worn by any male or common warrior of the tribe. For the Native American, certain clothes and their special adornments indicated one's position in the tribe.

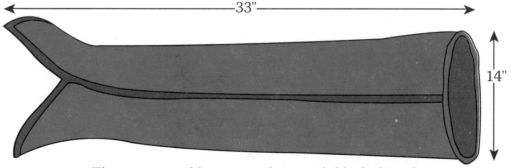

The seams and hems are done with black thread.

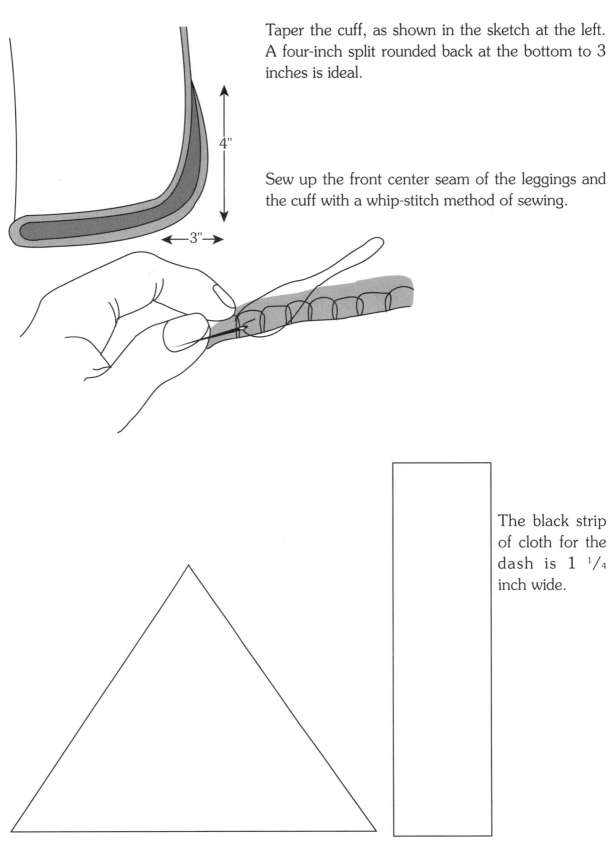

Taper the cuff, as shown in the sketch at the left. A four-inch split rounded back at the bottom to 3 inches is ideal.

4"

←3"→

Sew up the front center seam of the leggings and the cuff with a whip-stitch method of sewing.

The black strip of cloth for the dash is 1 $\frac{1}{4}$ inch wide.

Above are the actual sizes of the paper patterns to be used for the mountain and the trail designs for the leggings.

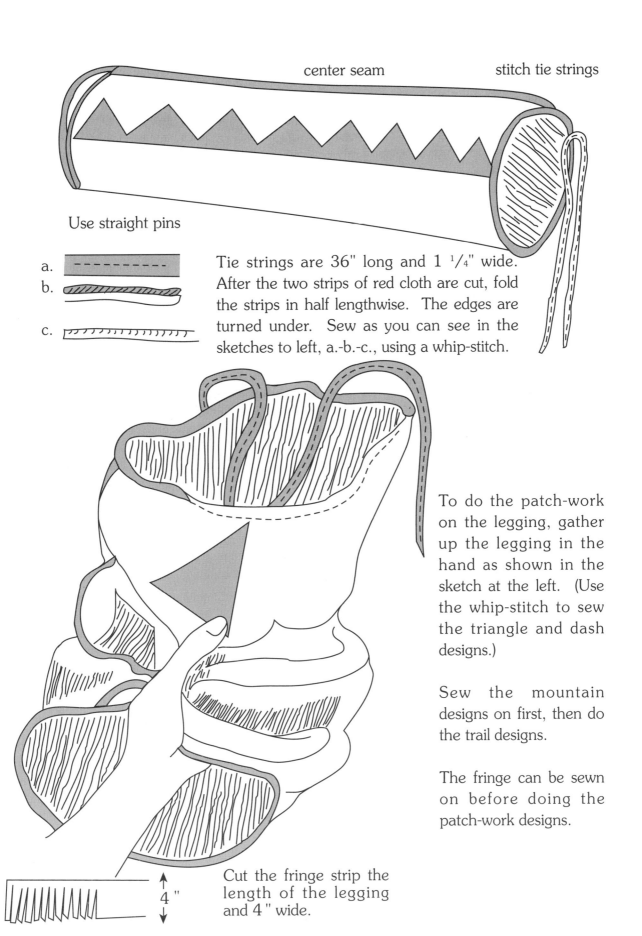

center seam   stitch tie strings

Use straight pins

a.

b.

c.

Tie strings are 36" long and 1 ¹/₄" wide. After the two strips of red cloth are cut, fold the strips in half lengthwise. The edges are turned under. Sew as you can see in the sketches to left, a.-b.-c., using a whip-stitch.

To do the patch-work on the legging, gather up the legging in the hand as shown in the sketch at the left. (Use the whip-stitch to sew the triangle and dash designs.)

Sew the mountain designs on first, then do the trail designs.

The fringe can be sewn on before doing the patch-work designs.

4"

Cut the fringe strip the length of the legging and 4" wide.

131

right legging   left legging

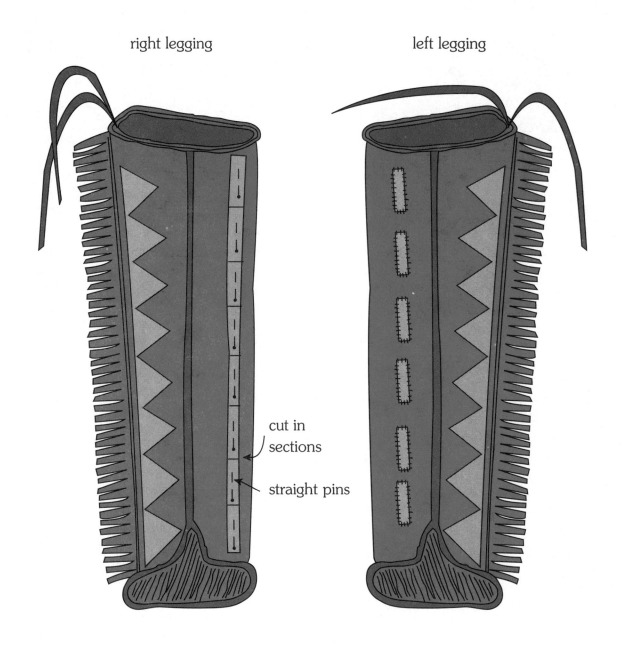

cut in
sections

straight pins

Cut the black strip for the trail designs, as shown above in the sketch.

Then cut the strip in sections at even distances apart; turn the edges under and whip-stitch as shown in the sketch above on the right. It is always helpful to use straight pins to hold things in place.

Once all patch-work is finished and the fringe sewed on, the leggings are finished.

Try the leggings on and see what it is like to wear the leggings of a War Chief.

Shown in the examples on this page are center-seam leggings, decorated and worn in various styles to suit one's own personal taste.

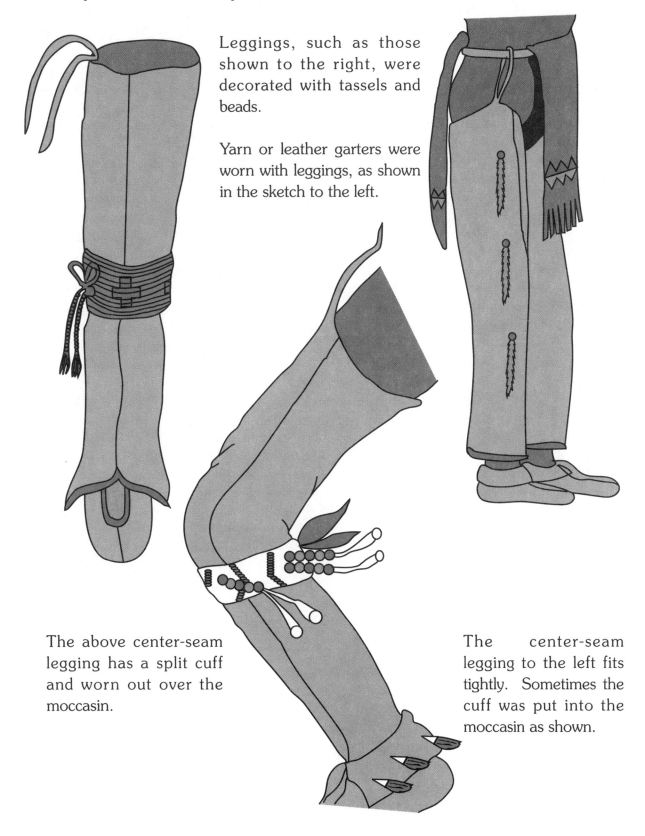

Leggings, such as those shown to the right, were decorated with tassels and beads.

Yarn or leather garters were worn with leggings, as shown in the sketch to the left.

The above center-seam legging has a split cuff and worn out over the moccasin.

The center-seam legging to the left fits tightly. Sometimes the cuff was put into the moccasin as shown.

THE SIDE-SEAM LEGGING

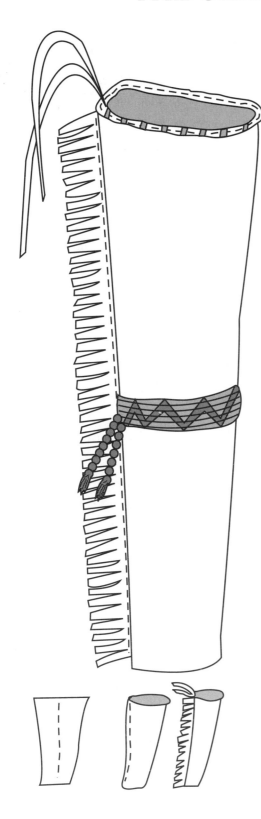

This style of legging was worn by some Cherokees as well as neighboring tribes.

As long as you stick to the basic structure of the legging and decorate them with the designs known to be Cherokee, you can consider your leggings to be a true Cherokee type.

When looking for a design, a pattern from Cherokee pottery or a basket can be used.

Fringe is very common for the side of this style of legging, with decorations of any type put along the area next to the fringe.

For decorations on this style, you can use things like tassels, beads, quill or ribbon work, fur, dew-claws, shells, patch-work, etc., as used on the center-seam leggings.

As indicated by the sketches to the left, this style legging is simple. Cut the leather or cloth, as seen in the sketch, to fit your leg. Fold the leather, sew it up the side, adding fringe and tie strings.

MODERN CHEROKEE BREECHES
AND LEGGINGS

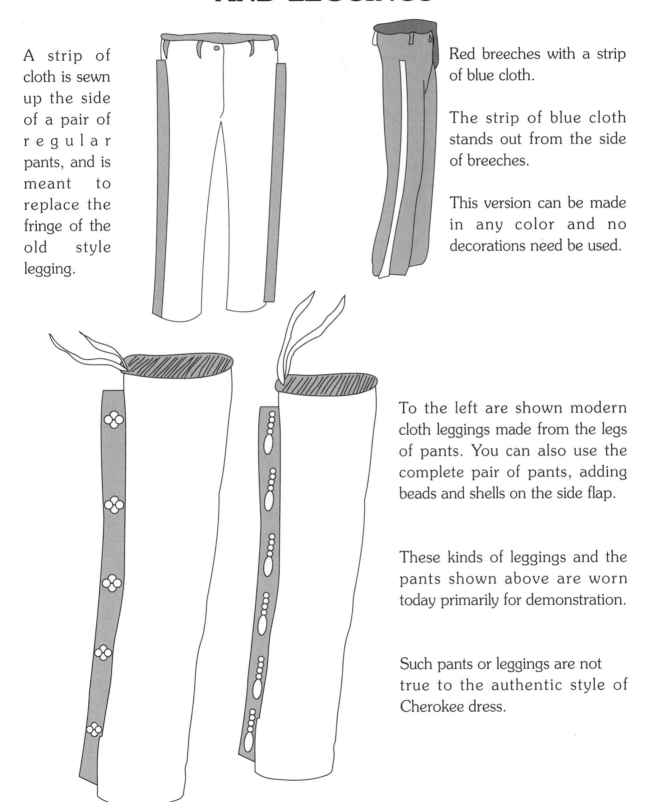

A strip of cloth is sewn up the side of a pair of r e g u l a r pants, and is meant to replace the fringe of the old style legging.

Red breeches with a strip of blue cloth.

The strip of blue cloth stands out from the side of breeches.

This version can be made in any color and no decorations need be used.

To the left are shown modern cloth leggings made from the legs of pants. You can also use the complete pair of pants, adding beads and shells on the side flap.

These kinds of leggings and the pants shown above are worn today primarily for demonstration.

Such pants or leggings are not true to the authentic style of Cherokee dress.

KNEE-HIGH LEGGINGS

Knee-high leggings were popular among both the Cherokee men and women. Such leggings protected the lower legs when walking through brush or thickets. This need for protecting the legs led to half-leggings becoming a part of their everday clothing.

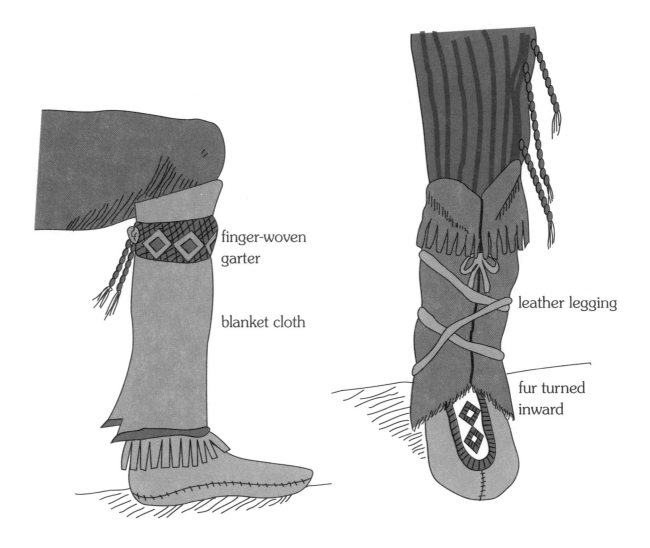

finger-woven garter

blanket cloth

leather legging

fur turned inward

Leggings of this kind were tied just below the knee with garters or tie strings. Some of the knee-high leggings were held in place by criss-crossing a leather strap, as shown in the sketch above on the right.

Pictured here are leggings with the fur turned in for warmth during cooler weather.

The half-legging shown above is an old style version of the center-seam type, made of deerskin. Note the split cuff and the way the legging is tied on the side.

Shown in the sketch to the right is a legging made of deer or bear skin. The fur is on the inside of this legging also. It is worn over the top of the moccasin, has a split middle-seam and is wrapped with leather strings to hold it in place. A garter is tied in place at the top of the legging.

The knee-high legging, shown in the sketch above, is made of blanket material. It is decorated with seed beads of yellow, red, blue and white. Tin cone jinglers are also a part of the decoration.

Above is another version of a legging made of blanket cloth. Seed beads form the designs. Designs can also be done with ribbon or embroidery.

As shown in the sketches to the left, Cherokee women wore short leggings made much the same way as the men's. They tied their leggings with garters.

The women decorated their leggings in a variety of ways, such as ribbon, bead and embroidery work. Silver brooches were also used on their leggings and dresses.

THE OPEN KNEE-HIGH LEGGING

The knee-high leggings appear to be only for looks and open in the front.

These open front short leggings are worn with trousers or over regular leggings and have tie strings. They should be made from heavy black cloth, such as velvet or other suitable cloth. A short-cut when making these leggings is to cut off the legs of a black pair of pants, and redesign them a little.

To get the length of the legging, measure from just below the knee to the top of the ankle. The legging should be cut to the shape indicated in the photograph below.

The photograph above shows some beadwork in progress on the leggings.

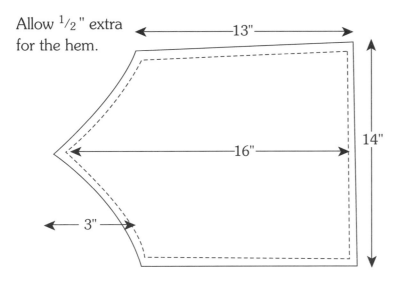

Allow ½" extra for the hem.

13"

16"

14"

3"

The sketch to the left shows my measurements for the open-front legging.

Cut a back lining, ½" larger than the front panel. Put the parts together, turn the edges under and whip-stitch all around the hem.

(If you prefer, sew the lining on when the beadwork is finished.)

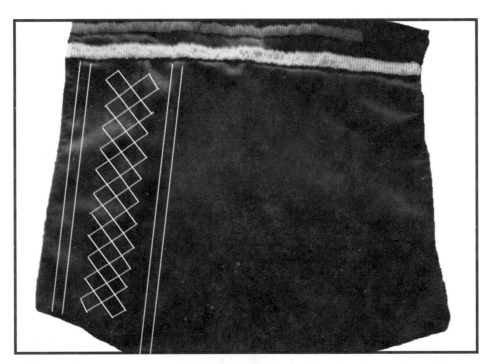

Draw the patterns on the cloth using a yellow-lead pencil as shown in the photograph above.

Once the cloth has been cut and the designs marked on it, you are ready for the beadwork. The yellow and red strips are lazy-stitched onto the leggings. A loom can be used to make the strips, then the beaded strips transferred to the legging. The diamond designs are spot-beaded. When doing the beadwork, keep in mind that the vertical beadwork goes on the outside or side of the legging.

When drawing the designs on the cloth, use a ruler on the vertical strips. On the diamond designs, use a $1/2$" paper square to mark out the design.

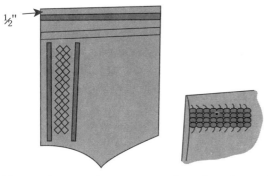

Sew on a 14" loom-beaded strip or lazy-stitch the strip of red beads across the legging. This strip should be six beads wide.

Sew down the outer edge of each row if using a loom-beaded strip.

The red vertical strips are four beads wide.

On the following pages various methods for doing beadwork are shown.

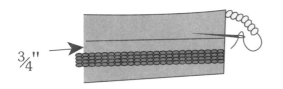

Knot the end of the thread and attach it as shown in the sketch to the left. String on 9 yellow beads and begin doing the yellow strip the same way as the red strip if using the lazy stitch method. You can also use a loom to make the yellow strip.

The yellow strip is 14" long. There is a $3/4$" space between the red and yellow strip of beadwork.

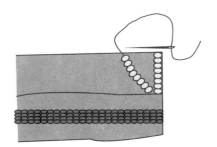

The next row of yellow beads are put on the thread, as shown in the sketch to the left. It is then sewn down at the other end of the beaded strip. Continue doing the other rows of beads the same way until the whole strip is finished.

Note: If you are going to use the lazy-stitch method, after you have done a few rows of beads go back to the first row and start sewing down every third bead in a row. This makes your work look neater.

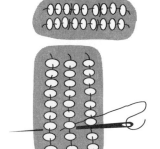

As shown in the sketch to the left, every third bead is sewn down.

The sketch shows the needle being pushed down into the cloth on the right side of the row of beads. Go back up with the needle on the left side of the next row of beads. Pull the slack out of the thread and do the same to the next row of beads. Continue the same process all across the beaded strip row by row.

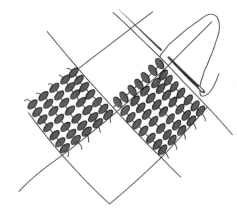

The diamond designs are done about the same way as the beaded strips. At the corner of the design that is drawn on the cloth, come up with the needle, underneath the cloth, stringing the desired number of beads on the thread.

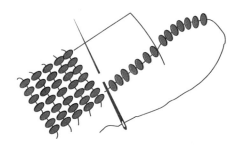

Now that you have the right amount of beads to form a row, go back down with the needle into the cloth at the end of the row of beads. Pull out the slack in the thread as you come back up through the cloth beside the row. You are now ready to begin another row. Refer to the two sketches to the left.

In the sketch above, you can see how the second row of beads is started to form the blue diamonds. Every third bead is sewn down in the rows of each diamond. Use ten beads per row and make the diamond seven beads wide, or to fit the drawn design.

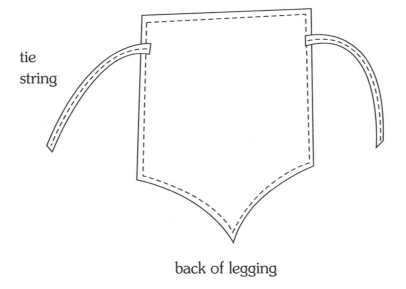

tie
string

back of legging

When both leggings have been hemmed, as shown in the above sketch, cut four 10" by $1/2$" straps. Sew on two straps per legging as in the sketch. For added strength, the tie-strings should always be double material and hemmed.

The leggings are now finished and ready for wear. The other leggings, similar to this pair, can be made about the same way. Designs can vary but should be true to Cherokee culture.

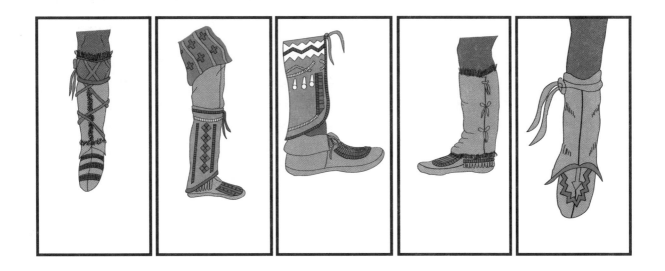

EMBROIDERED GARTERS

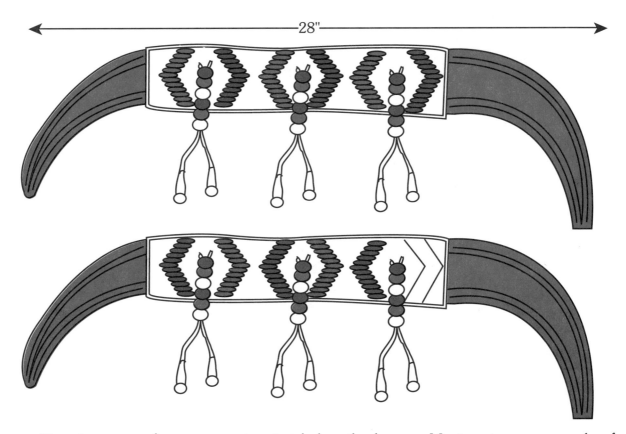

28"

Cherokee men often wore garters just below the knees. Most garters were made of yarn during the historic period. They were made by the finger weaving process. Yarn was unraveled from trade blankets and dyed the desired colors.

Earlier, garters were made of leather or from fiber turned into weaving material. Natural, native dyes were used to get the colors needed to form the designs.

The garters in the sketch above were made by using cloth, imitation leather, red and blue yarn for the diamond designs, blue, red and white crow beads and tin cone jinglers on leather strings.

I embroidered the diamond designs in yarn, with side by side stitches, to give a quill effect. You can use yarn to embroider the designs on any kind of garters. On the following pages are instructions for making garters.

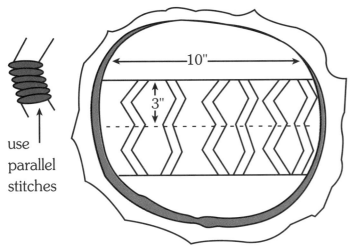

use parallel stitches

To make the garters, shown in the prior sketch, put a piece of soft leather or imitation leather on an embroidery hoop.

Use a ruler to draw the designs shown in the sketch at the left.

Next, use blue yarn for half of a design and red yarn for the other half of the design (see embroidered strips sketch below).

When the designs are complete, remove the embroidered leather from the hoop and cut the garter strips off as shown below.

embroidered strips

Cut two red or maroon strips of cloth 5" wide by 28" long. Sew the leather pieces onto the cloth strips, centering them. The edges should be hemmed as you sew and the tie-string part of the garters narrowed down, as shown in the sketch below.

Once all sewing is finished, cut a set of slots in the center of each diamond design, as shown in the sketch above to the left.

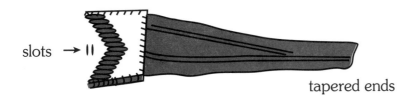

slots →

tapered ends

Cut six leather strings 16 inches long by ¼ inch wide. Insert a leather string into the slots in the center of a diamond, as shown in the sketch to the left. You now have the leather string folded, making 2 dangling strings.

The red, blue and white crow beads are now put on the leather strings.

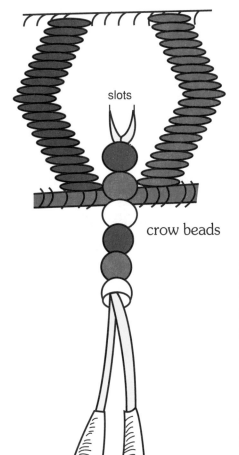

slots

crow beads

Make tin cones and put them on the ends of each leather string. Push each tin cone up the string a little and tie a knot on the end. Push the cone back down over the knot.

Note: This book includes instructions for making tin cones. See page 38.

This completes the garter project. Now the garters can be worn with a pair of the leggings described in previous projects.

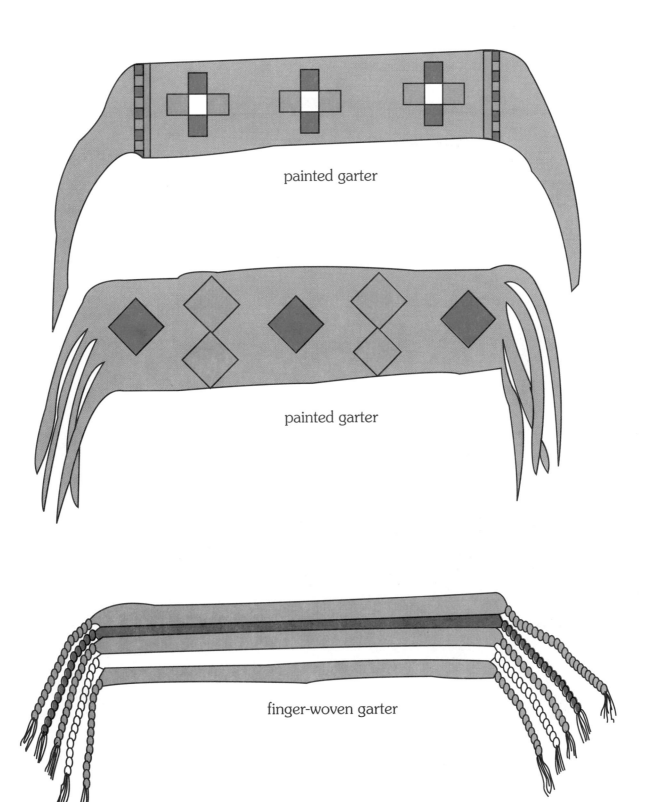

painted garter

painted garter

finger-woven garter

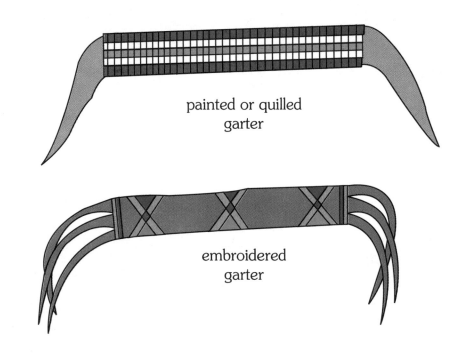

painted or quilled
garter

embroidered
garter

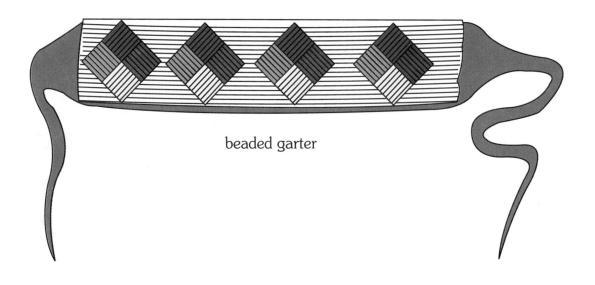

beaded garter

BELTS OF THE CHEROKEE

The Cherokee, like many of the Native Americans, wore a belt of some type. Belts were used to hold the breechclout in place or a knife, a pouch, or even to gird a garment around the waist.

Breechclout belts were often plain, but some belts, like the one in the sketch below, were highly decorated. The decorated belts were worn during special events, with the plain belt holding the breachclout, underneath and concealed.

Belts were decorated with beautiful designs of quillwork, seed beads, embroidery, shells, paint, and etc., sewn on to leather backing. Woven belts, made of threads from hemp, nettle, hair or yarn, were also worn. The finger-woven belts of yarn are still made today by skilled Cherokee women.

When the Cherokee first obtained blankets, yarn threads were unraveled from the blankets and dyed the colors needed to form the desired designs.

Decorated leather belts tied in the back, not on the side or front as the white man's belt. Of course, the sash belts of the finger-woven type, tied on the side of the waist. Some Cherokee men liked wearing a long sash belt that went around the waist, over one shoulder and angled at the back, then to the side where it was tied.

Old paintings and sketches give a clear idea of how the sash was worn.

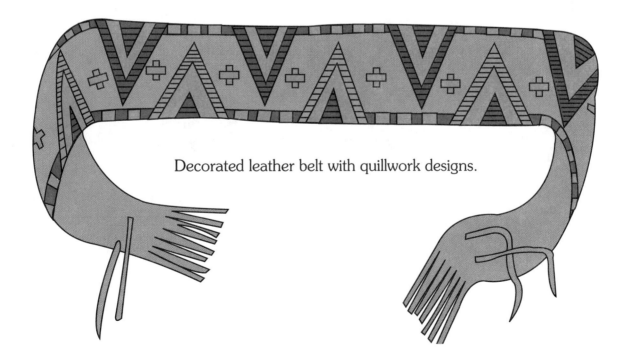

Decorated leather belt with quillwork designs.

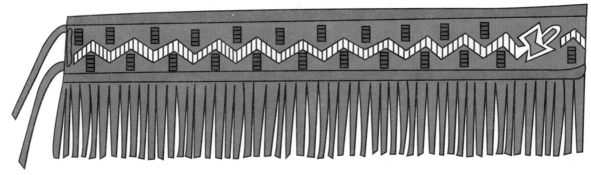

The above belt is made of leather and trimmed with fringe and a red cloth edging. Seed beads are used to make the blue and white designs.

This belt can be done with quillwork, seed beads or embroidery.

The quillwork on this belt is done only at certain spots. Designs can also be done in bead or quillwork.

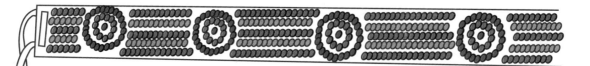

Quill or embroidery work can be used to make this belt.

THE LOOM-BEADED BELT

After the Cherokee started trading with the white man, small glass beads, like the seed bead, were obtained. Soon these small beads were used in many ways on their clothing. Shell beads became a thing of the past. The old style quilled belts were now decorated with seed beads of various colors. Seed beads of that time were a little larger than the modern seed beads.

If a beaded strip was desired for a leather belt, it was made on a loom. Strings were stretched on the loom and beads put between the strings using a needle and thread.

A loom can be made with boards as shown below or may be purchased from craft suppliers. Once you have a loom you can make beaded belts with numerous designs.

Beadwork Loom

grooves

Protruding nails hold ends of strings as you work

The beaded strip, once it has been removed from the loom and the ends taped, can be sewn, using a whip-stitch, to a strip of leather as shown in the sketch below.

When Cherokee women in North Carolina make beaded strips they do not always use a loom. However, we will give instructions here on using the loom

Loom Beaded Belt

NOTE: Detailed methods of loom beading are described in many books. Check with your bookstore, crafts store, library or contact the publisher of this book.

Shown in the photo above is the completed beaded strip and belt.

The above beaded belt is 43" long by 2 ³/₄" wide. The fringe is 4" long. The beaded strip was made on a loom. It is 36 beads wide and 21" long. Black and red beads form a checker-board design. To form the design use four black beads, then four red beads, over and over from one side of the loom strings to the other side in a row. Do the next two rows the same. The first set of check designs are now complete. Alternate the checks, as shown in the photograph above, until the whole strip of bead work is long enough.

When the beaded strip is finished, tape each end of the beaded strip on the strings. Cut the strip from the loom. Whip-stitch the beaded strip to the leather strip, turning the taped ends underneath. If you think the leather will be difficult to push the needle through, make holes around the edges of the leather in advance for the needle and thread to pass through as shown in the sketch.

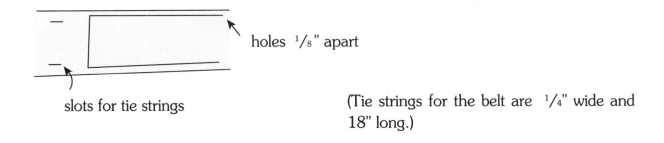

holes ¹/₈" apart

slots for tie strings

(Tie strings for the belt are ¹/₄" wide and 18" long.)

Shown in the above photo is a beaded strip in progress on a loom.

In the photo below is a close-up of beadwork.

Shown below are some belt designs like ones seen in Cherokee, North Carolina, using seed beads and pony beads. Such designs can be drawn first on graph paper to get a more exact pattern.

You may prefer to find your own designs from Cherokee baskets, pottery, artifacts, etc. Determining which designs were exclusively Cherokee is very hard since there was much exchange between Native American tribes even before the influence of the white explorers, traders and settlers.

THE EMBROIDERED BELT

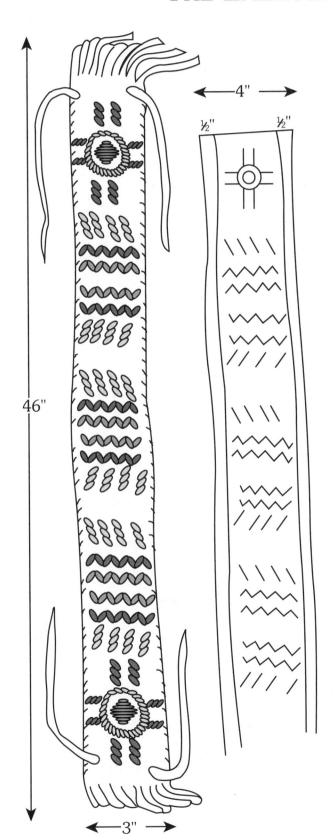

This belt is made of soft white deerskin and is embroidered with red, blue and black yarn. The belt is backed with red flannel.

First cut a strip of leather 4" wide by 46" long. Allow for two $\frac{1}{2}$" hems when drawing the designs shown in the sketch to the left.

When drawing the designs determine the middle of the belt and work to either side, properly spacing the designs.

An embroidery hoop is helpful.

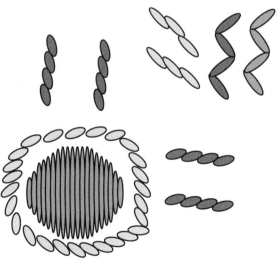

Pictured above are stitches the actual size of those used on the belt.

The designs on the belt are symbols of the sun, thunder, lightning, and rain. All of these symbols are sacred and have power.

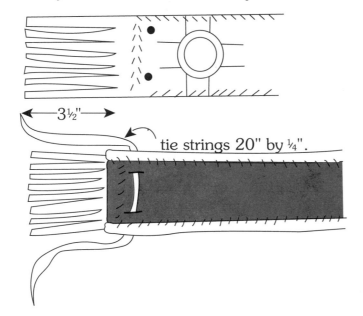

Holes are punched on each end of the belt, as shown in the sketch to the left.

A 3" wide piece of red flannel lines the back. The edges of the leather are turned back over the flannel and whip-stitched into place, as shown in the above sketch. Your belt should now be ready to wear.

In this photo the embroidery work on the belt can be seen in progress on the hoop.

156

THE WAMPUM BELT

In the old days the Cherokee made belts of great worth, honor, and meaning. These belts sealed friendships, agreements, and even signified war between two Native American nations. Such belts were not worn, but presented to one's foe or to friends when peace was agreed upon. So sacred were wampum belts that events and information could be brought back to memory by looking at the designs.

If you choose to make a wampum belt, it can be made on a loom using pony beads or small tubular beads. The old type wampum is difficult to get these days. To make wampum requires a great deal of time, so that may not be feasible.

White wampum beads stood for peace and the purple wampum meant warfare. Black beads are for death. Red beads are also a symbol for war and bloodshed.

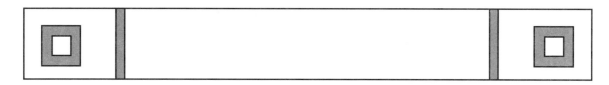

This belt seems to show that hard feelings, hatred and war are blocking the two sides or nations from walking the white path of peace.

The white path of peace is depicted in this belt. On this belt nothing is blocking peace.

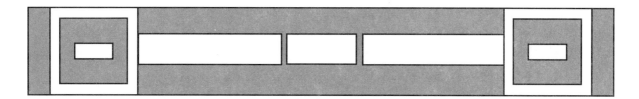

On this belt, one might read that the two sides or nations want peace. Although the road to peace is broken and not yet complete, there is still hope.

This is a black belt of death and war. The hearts of each side or of allied nations are still black as hatred for the enemy rages. Peace is no where to be found.

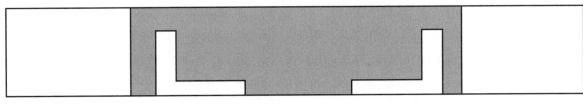

Here the belt portrays two nations at war with each other but desiring peace. They need to smoke the pipe of peace.

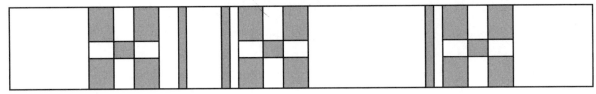

This belt depicts three nations at war. The road to peace is blocked, but there is hope.

A solid black or red belt is an open declaration of war and death to the enemy.

The interpretations I have given to the wampum belts are my own. When you make wampum belts, look for appropriate symbols and designs to represent the meanings you wish to ascribe to your belts.

DRESS STYLES OF THE WOMEN

The dress customs among the Cherokee women varied, as it did in the other tribes of the Southeast. Women of Native American cultures liked to dress in beautiful and attractive ways. Husbands wanted their wives to dress up and in some cases did not want to out dress their spouses, because they were so proud of their wives.

Before cloth and trade blankets became available to make the women's dresses, deerskin was the primary material used for clothing. To begin with, let us consider the under clothes of a woman.

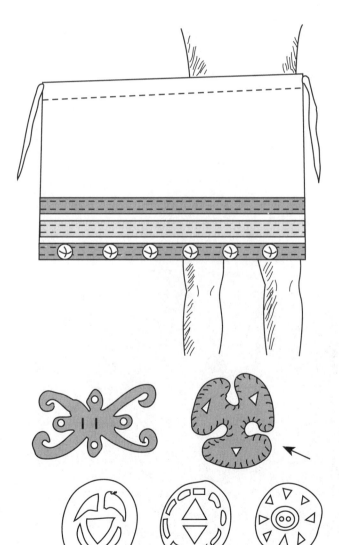

They wore wrap-around slips underneath their dresses. The slips were made of deerskin in early times, but later were made of cloth, such as yellow calico or other materials.

This wrap-around slip was tied at the waist and usually reached down to the top of the knees.

The everyday wrap-around slip, worn while doing chores, was most often plain. When it was worn for her husband, the wrap-around slip was decorated with ribbon-work of red, blue and yellow. To make it fancier, silver brooches, beads, quillwork or embroidery were used.

copper brooches

 silver brooches

THE WRAP-AROUND SKIRT

In the old days during warm weather, the women wore a wrap-around skirt over their petticoat or slip. This wrap-around skirt was usually knee length, but at times was worn longer. Older women, tending to be more modest, liked the longer skirts.

The bottom of the skirt was sometimes fringed for important events. A skirt could also be decorated with quillwork, embroidery or beadwork.

As you can see in the sketch to the left, the wrap-around skirt was often worn without a top. Warm weather and the chores had a lot to do with this custom. When a top was needed, a vest or jacket was added. It was usually fringed and had decorations.

tie strings

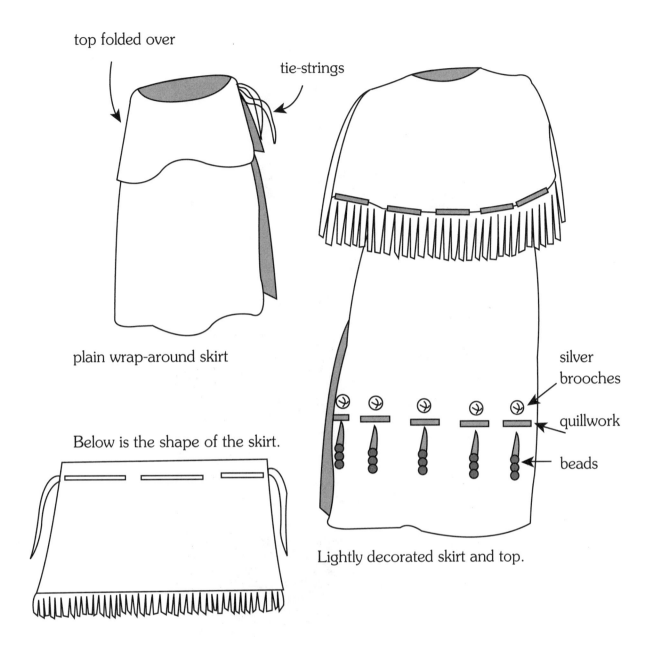

top folded over

tie-strings

plain wrap-around skirt

Below is the shape of the skirt.

silver brooches

quillwork

beads

Lightly decorated skirt and top.

If deerskin or leather can not be obtained to make the skirt and top, use imitation leather or cloth that is suitable. Types of decorations and designs are almost unlimited. The women used various things to make a skirt or dress look beautiful.

The size and length of the skirt and top had a lot to do with one's own personal taste and status.

TWO PIECE WRAP-AROUND DRESS

Above the author's wife, Mable, models a two-
piece dress composed of a wrap-around skirt
and jacket.

The two-piece dress was worn by Cherokee women during the warm part of the year.
It could be worn with or without a top or jacket, since it was not considered shameful for
the upper body to be exposed.

On the following pages, I will show how the above dress was made.

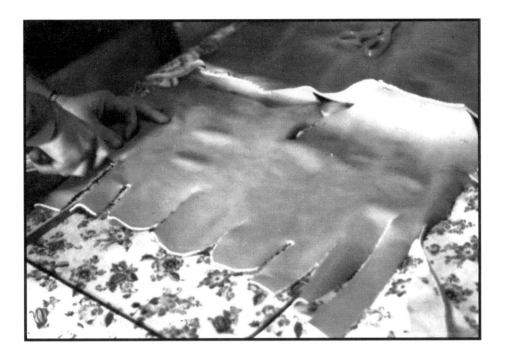

The top or jacket shown above is made of soft white leather. Lay your own blouse on the leather and mark the shape of it onto the leather with a pencil.

If leather cannot be obtained, use dyed flannel, felt or imitation leather cloth. Soft deerskin is the best material to use for an authentic outfit.

When using a utility knife to cut leather on a table, always put a piece of glass or plywood underneath the material.

The front and back pieces of the top are cut the same size and are stitched together at the shoulders. Turn the top right side out when all stitching is finished. There are no sleeves to this kind of top, but leather strings can be put through the front and back at the armpit area to help hold the top in place. Refer to the sketch on the next page.

TOP OR JACKET TO THE WRAP-AROUND SKIRT

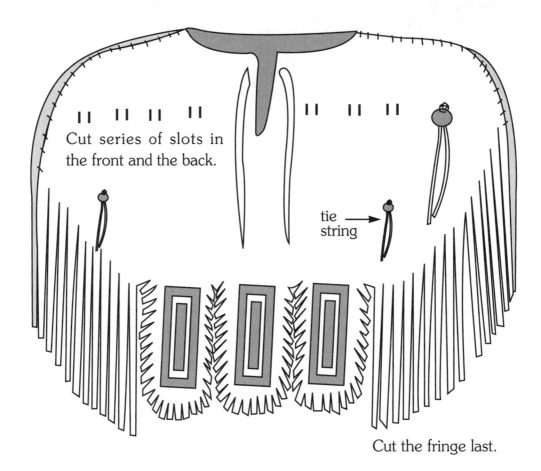

Cut series of slots in the front and the back.

tie → string

Cut the fringe last.

The sketch above shows a jacket like that on the previous page. It is sewn together at the shoulders, fringed and beaded. Orange and black seed beads are used to make the front designs. A loom can be used to do the beadwork. The fringe goes all around.

The sketch to the left shows how string decorations using large beads are made and attached to clothes. The string is $1/4$ inch wide and 18 inches long. Double it in half, lace each end through a slot and then both ends through the large bead.

BROWN LEATHER WRAP-AROUND SKIRT

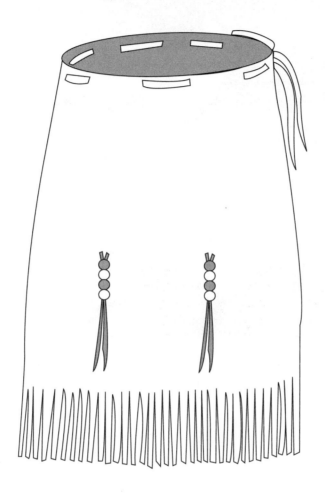

The wrap around skirt shown in the sketch above is the same one shown in the photograph on page 162. It reaches below the knees and is fringed at the bottom. The leather tassels on the skirt are the same length as the ones on the jacket. To get the proper shape of the skirt, use a long skirt of your own as a pattern. Lay your pattern skirt on top of the leather or material and mark the pattern with a pencil.

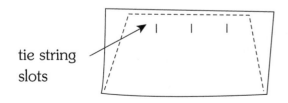

tie string
slots

Cut the excess leather away, as shown in the sketch at the left.

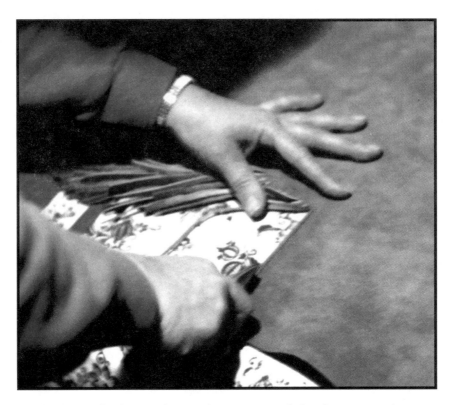

The photograph above shows the cutting of the fringe on the wrap-around skirt. A piece of plated glass can be place underneath to protect your table.

Once the skirt has been cut out to your size and fringed at the bottom, cut a series of slots at the top of the skirt as shown in the sketch below. Now cut a leather belt and insert it into the belt slots. A finger-woven belt can also be used. The belt should be long enough to hang down at the side.

You may want to use other decorations on the skirt you make. This same skirt can be made of cloth, using leather for the fringe.

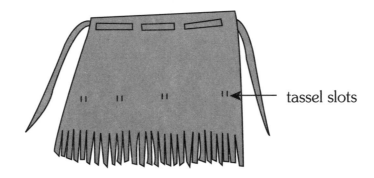

tassel slots

THE ONE-PIECE DRESS

Shown in this photograph is a one-piece dress. Since no deerskin was available, tan colored cloth was used. Cloth is easier to work with, but leather is more outstanding in effect.

This dress can be worn during ceremonies because of the many decorations of beadwork and fringe. Seed beads are used to form the designs, although embroidery or quillwork could be used.

Old time deerskin dresses were very soft as well as beautiful. If they got wet, the leather had to be resoftened by a rubbing process.

Some Cherokee women liked to use tin cones, bells, jinglers, ribbon-work, and other things to decorate their dresses. Even painted designs were used.

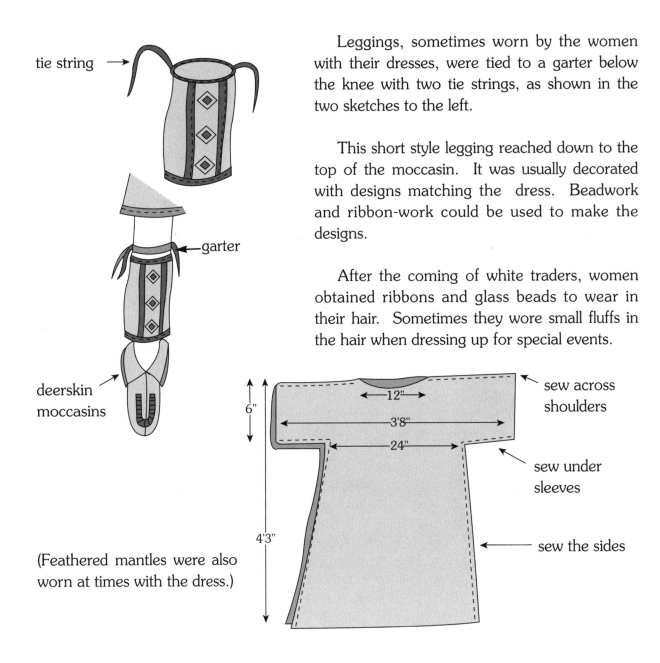

tie string →

garter

deerskin
moccasins

Leggings, sometimes worn by the women with their dresses, were tied to a garter below the knee with two tie strings, as shown in the two sketches to the left.

This short style legging reached down to the top of the moccasin. It was usually decorated with designs matching the dress. Beadwork and ribbon-work could be used to make the designs.

After the coming of white traders, women obtained ribbons and glass beads to wear in their hair. Sometimes they wore small fluffs in the hair when dressing up for special events.

sew across
shoulders

12"

6"

3'8"

24"

sew under
sleeves

4'3"

sew the sides

(Feathered mantles were also worn at times with the dress.)

The above sketch of the dress shows how it was cut out and sewn together, like the one in the preceding photograph. You must cut the front and back of the dress from doubled material, trimming out the front and back neckline. Use a loose fitting dress of your own, laying it on the material and marking the outline of the dress. A long gown can be used as a pattern for this dress.

Refer to other dresses in this book, especially the patchwork dress on pages 175 to 180, to get a better understanding of basic methods.

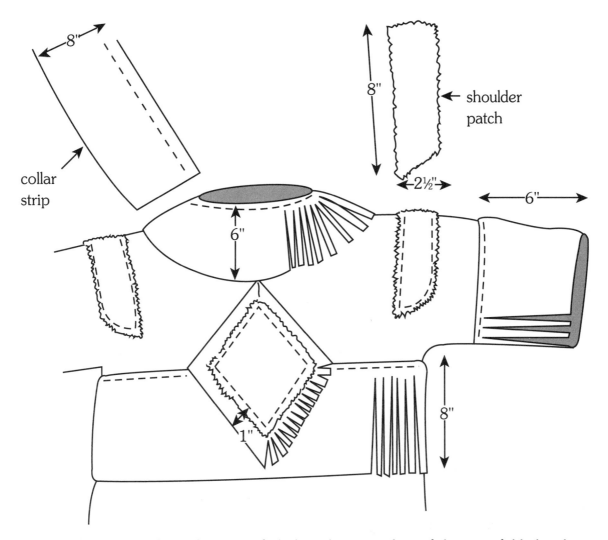

The collar is an eight inch piece of cloth with two inches of the strip folded to hem it as it is sewn into place. This strip of cloth should reach all around the collar. Cut the collar strip into fringe later, as shown above.

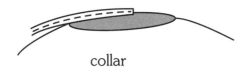

collar

When hemming the collar, turn the material under, as it is sewed on.

Then cut two 2¹/₂" by 8" strips for the patches on the shoulders, using pinking shears to get a jagged edge. Sew a patch on each shoulder as shown in the above sketch. Sew a six-inch wide strip of cloth around each sleeve. Fringe the sleeves after all beadwork is finished.

Now you are ready to sew an eight-inch wide strip of cloth all around the dress just below the armpits, horizontally. Fringe this strip of cloth after all beadwork is finished. Finally, cut a diamond-shape piece of cloth to be sewn into place at the chest area as shown in the sketch above.

To make a pattern for the diamond-shaped cloth patches, fold and cut a sheet of typing paper as shown in the sketch below. Lay your pattern onto the material, marking it in pencil.

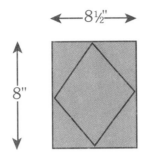

With the pinking shears, cut out two diamond-shape patches. Once you have the two diamond-shaped patches cut, mark two more diamonds, making them one inch larger all around.

Center the smaller diamond on top of the larger diamond, then pin them in place on the center of the eight inch strip of cloth sewn across the chest area of the dress. It is wise, as I have stressed before, not to cut the cloth into fringe until all beading is finished. This prevents tangling of the fringe.

Once the diamond patches have been sewn into place, you can mark the designs on them and on the shoulder patches. I will show the designs on the next pages.

Cut patches the shape of those shown in the sketches below. Sew the smaller patch on top of larger patch to the dress. After the above patches are cut and sewn into place, they are ready to be marked with designs and beaded.

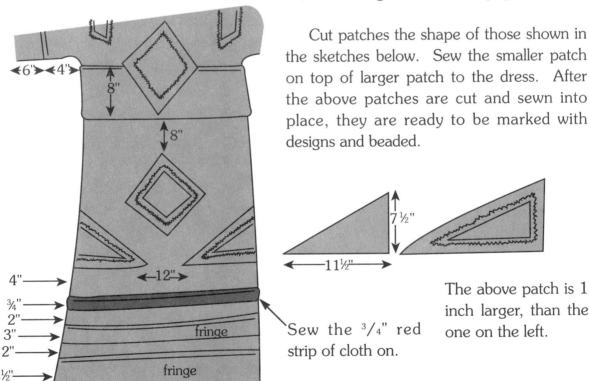

Sew the ³/₄" red strip of cloth on.

The above patch is 1 inch larger, than the one on the left.

The above measurements are the ones I used. Alter measurements to fit your size.

The above photograph shows the beadwork in detail. Designs were drawn onto the patches and strips across the bottom of the dress. Your freehand designs may vary. The number of beads you use when filling in the designs may also vary.

Beadwork on the dress can be done best by putting the dress on an embroidery hoop. A quilting hoop on a stand is also good when doing large areas of beadwork.

It takes a lot of patience and several days work to make this dress.

You may wish to refer to books on methods of doing beadwork (check with your book supplier or library). I used spot-beading, lazy-stitch beading and rosette methods on this dress.

Below are the actual pencil patterns I drew on the diamond patch for the chest patch.

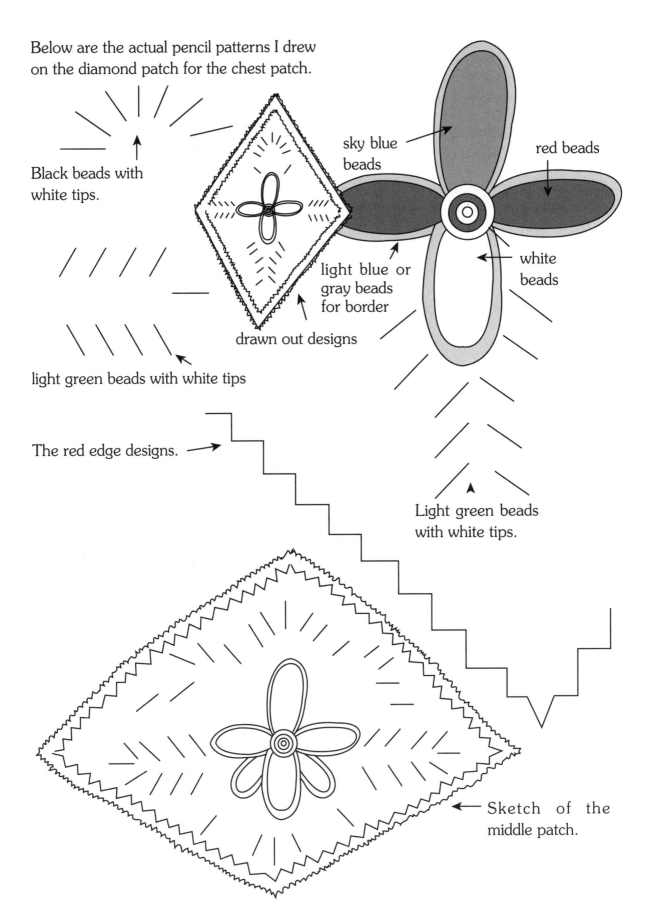

Black beads with white tips.

light green beads with white tips

The red edge designs.

sky blue beads

red beads

light blue or gray beads for border

drawn out designs

white beads

Light green beads with white tips.

Sketch of the middle patch.

This sketch shows the designs for the shoulder patches.

Remember that the left shoulder patch shape is reversed when it is made and sewn to the dress.

Below are sketches showing the sequence of designs going around the bottom of the dress.

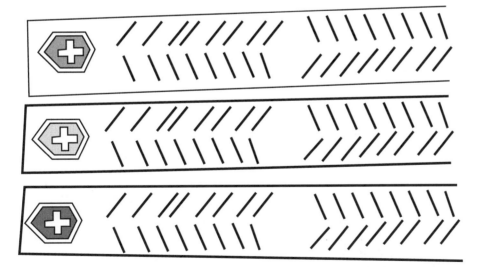

Each of the diagonal line of beads are tipped with a white bead. Continue the beaded band until it is completed all around.

The above photograph shows the detailed designs on the side of the dress.

This sketch shows the designs
of the side patches

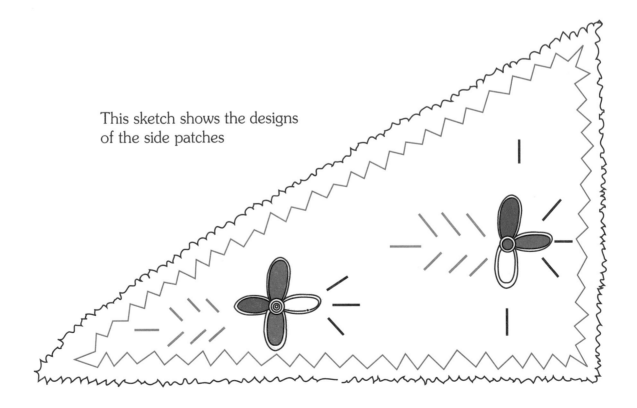

PATCHWORK DRESS

This dress is one piece. Deerskin would have been the primary material, and the designs would have been made of dyed deerskin. After women obtained cloth from the traders, dresses and patchwork designs were made of cloth.

This particular style dress was suitable for special occasions, such as ceremonies, festivals, ballplays, etc. Since this dress was so colorful, it was eye-catching. Basket designs are used to decorate the dress.

On the next few pages, I will show how this dress is made. Select other Cherokee designs according to your own taste.

Nora Sizemore, author's mother, models the patchwork dress in the above photograph.

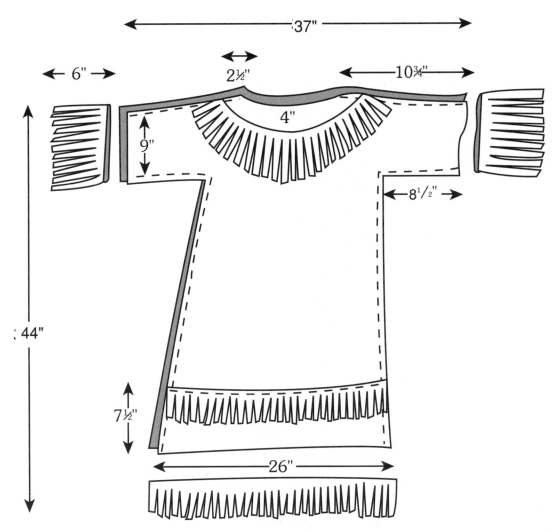

To make the above dress, cut two pieces of tan colored material to the above measurements or that of your own. Always allow from $1/4$" - $1/2$" extra in the measurements for the seams when sewing the dress together. Add double stitching at the arm-pits so the dress will not rip out when worn.

Round the neck opening on the front a little more that on the back. The neck opening, the sleeves and bottom of the dress should be hemmed before adding the fringe. Cut the fringe strips the proper size, as shown. The fringe strips should go all around the dress from front to back.

In order to get your own size measurements, it is best to use a loose fitting gown as a pattern to mark the material.

Use thick cloth for the patchwork designs. The yellow and red wooden beads can be purchased from a craft store. Be sure you use beads that have an opening or hole large enough for the leather string to pass through when making the tassels.

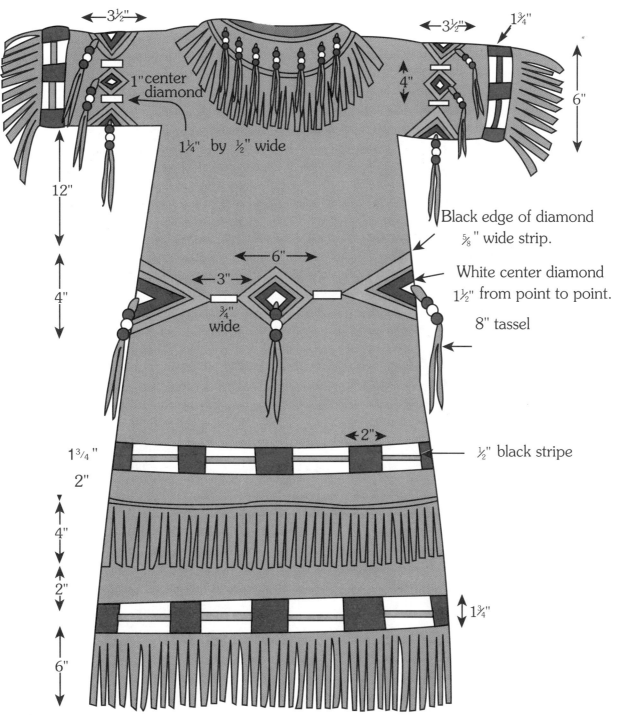

←3½"→ ←3½"→ 1¾"

1"center diamond

4"

6"

1¼" by ½" wide

12"

4"

Black edge of diamond ⅝" wide strip.

←6"→

←3"→

¾" wide

White center diamond 1½" from point to point.

8" tassel

←2"→

½" black stripe

1¾"

2"

4"

2"

1¾"

6"

If the dress is made of leather, instead of cloth, the red, white, and black designs look best if done in quillwork. Since I had no deerskin, I used cloth for the entire dress. In ancient times, Cherokee used deerskin dyed red or black to make designs, etc.

NOTE: Please be aware that the diamonds and other designs in the illustration above show position placement only and are not in correct size proportion. Use text descriptions for sizes of all designs.

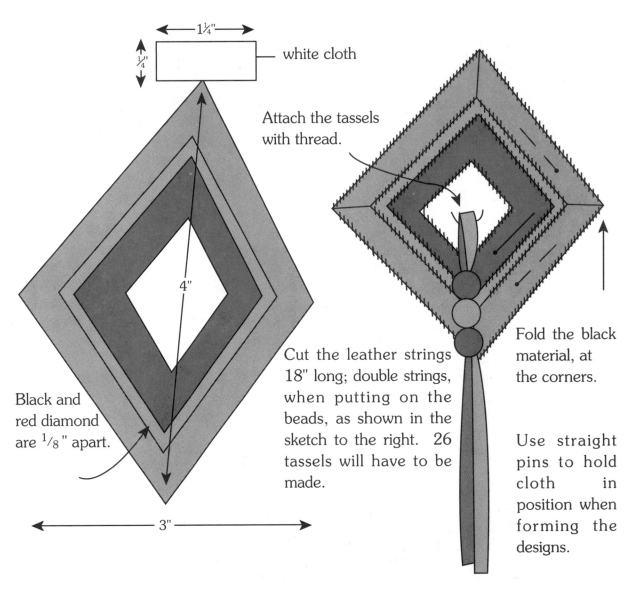

1¼"

¼"

white cloth

Attach the tassels with thread.

4"

Black and red diamond are ⅛" apart.

Cut the leather strings 18" long; double strings, when putting on the beads, as shown in the sketch to the right. 26 tassels will have to be made.

3"

Fold the black material, at the corners.

Use straight pins to hold cloth in position when forming the designs.

Cut a paper pattern about the same size as the ones in the sketches above. When the red material is cut to form, as seen above, turn the edges under and sew down using a whip-stitch. The red diamond then becomes about the size as in drawing on the right.

Next cut black strips of cloth 1" wide, turning under the edges as you whip-stitch them in place. Separate the black and red diamond, allowing the material underneath to show between. The black strip narrows down to 3/8" wide.

Sew the white diamond in place, centering it in the middle of the red diamond.

When all patchwork is finished on the sleeves, do the other designs on the rest of the dress the same way.

This sketch shows the actual size of the large diamonds at the middle of the dress.

When cutting the large red diamonds, cut them ¼" larger than the sketch on this page.

Center the red diamonds on the dress and sew in place.

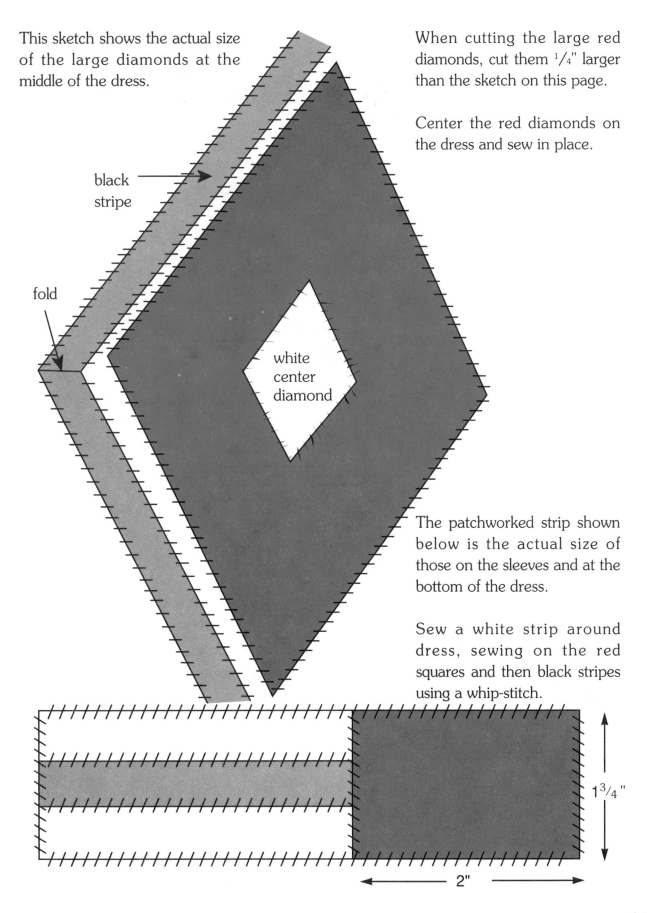

black stripe

fold

white center diamond

The patchworked strip shown below is the actual size of those on the sleeves and at the bottom of the dress.

Sew a white strip around dress, sewing on the red squares and then black stripes using a whip-stitch.

1³/₄"

2"

Shown above is the completed dress made from tan corduroy. The diamonds signify the diamonds on the sacred rattlesnake. Designs formed by the bands of squares and stripes represent long and dangerous paths that we sometimes have to take in life.

The patchwork dress should now be finished, and though it took a great deal of time to make, it can be worn with pride to any ceremony or occasion dealing with the Cherokee Native American.

Try making other Cherokee dresses using other designs and decorations now that you have the basics. On the next page, I have sketched two other dresses that you may want to make.

Two more variations for the one-piece dress are shown on this page. Dresses of this type are ideal for cooler weather.

The deerskin dress above has black and red-dyed leather stripes sewn on it. Mussel shell disks and white beads form the tassels.

Embroidery work forms the designs on the white band around the dress above.

Finger-woven sashes or leather belts can be used to gather the dresses at the waist.

CHEROKEE MOCCASINS

The moccasin was a very important part of the Cherokee dress. Moccasins worn during the daily chores were rather plain with few decorations. Footwear worn during ceremonies and special times were decorated with such things as quillwork, embroidery, fringe, red dyed hair, tin jinglers, seed beads, small bells, turkey spurs, etc.

Moccasins became easily soaked during the rainy seasons, but this was remedied by rubbing bear grease, or some other kind of animal fat, into the leather to make it water resistant.

Warm weather moccasins or boots were of plain leather. Those worn during cold weather had fur on the inside. The Cherokee adapted their footwear to the weather conditions.

The moccasins shown in the photograph are patterned from a pair made by modern Cherokees. The designs are imitation quillwork painted onto the moccasins. In ancient times, Cherokees wore the center-seam moccasin which I will later describe.

First, when making moccasins, select a split cowhide that is about $^1/_8$th of an inch thick. Colors of tan, gold, or brown are good to use. The measurements given in my instructions are for a man's size 10. You may have to alter the measurements I have given to fit your own foot size.

Use a pencil or pen to mark the parts on the leather. Make a paper pattern first. Once the parts to the moccasins are clearly marked, use a utility knife or scissors to do the cutting. (I put a piece of glass underneath the leather on the table to protect my work area.) The first sole you cut can be turned over on the leather and used as a pattern for the other sole.

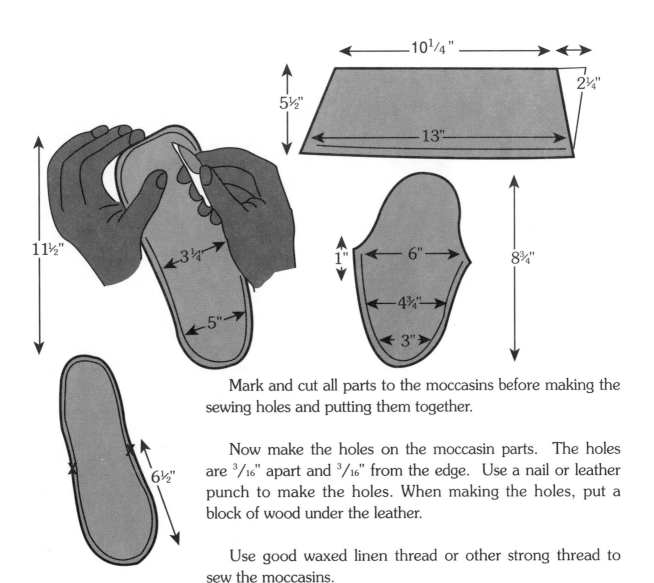

Mark and cut all parts to the moccasins before making the sewing holes and putting them together.

Now make the holes on the moccasin parts. The holes are $^3/_{16}$" apart and $^3/_{16}$" from the edge. Use a nail or leather punch to make the holes. When making the holes, put a block of wood under the leather.

Use good waxed linen thread or other strong thread to sew the moccasins.

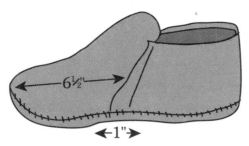

Make a pencil mark on the sole part of the moccasin at the instep on each side, $6^1/_2$" from the toe to the instep, as in the sketch above. While holding the toe part in place with the instep mark, overlap the ankle part of the moccasin one inch. Begin your stitching at the instep, while holding the parts in place. Continue stitching all around the moccasin.

If it is easier for you, stitch the two upper parts of the moccasin with prior holding stitches before you start sewing on the sole.

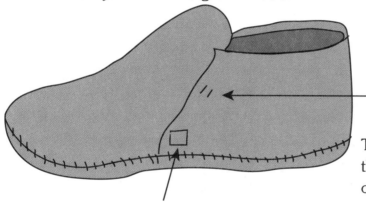

Slots are $^3/_{16}$"

The ankle slots are on both sides of the moccasin and are cut on angles of 2" - 2 $^1/_2$" from the bottom seam. Cut first slot $^1/_2$" back from the edge.

Holding stitches are used primarily to add strength to the instep.

The tie strings are 14" long and $^5/_{16}$" wide. One end of the tie string is knotted and laced through the pair of slots.

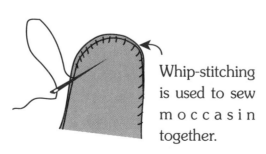

Whip-stitching is used to sew moccasin together.

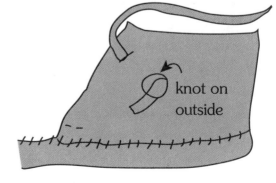

knot on outside

184

The ankle part of the moccasin can be left up or turned down when worn. If you plan to leave it turned down, you might like to fringe it as shown below.

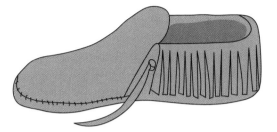

Cherokees used many designs to decorate the toe and sides of the moccasins. Try to use matching designs which have special meaning to you.

Long ago a person could be recognized as a Cherokee by the designs on his moccasins. Even the enemy knew when he encountered a Cherokee, because his dress was distinctive to his tribe.

Deerskin was the primary leather for moccasin making, but sometimes other kinds of leather were used. Sinew was used for thread.

While on the warpath or on long journeys, more than one pair of moccasins was taken along.

The photograph below shows embroidered patches for moccasins done on an embroidery hoop.

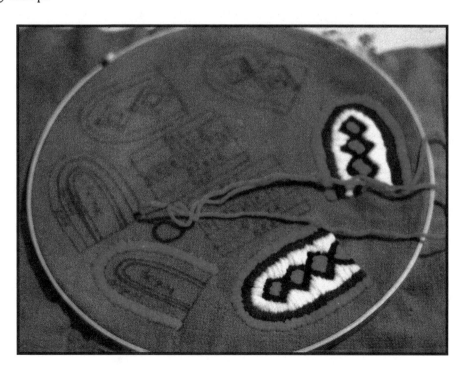

To sew the emoroidered patches to the moccasin toe use the sketches below. Cut extra cloth around the patch to be turned underneath when the patch is sewn onto the moccasin.

It is a good idea to punch holes in the toe of the moccasin in a pattern, as shown in the sketch below, to make it easier to sew on the patch. If you plan carefully you can punch the holes for the patch before assembling the moccasin.

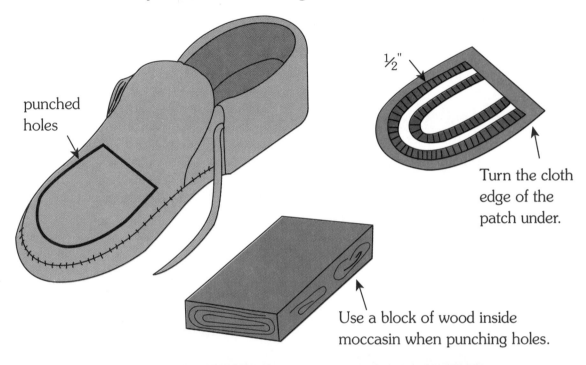

punched holes

½"

Turn the cloth edge of the patch under.

Use a block of wood inside moccasin when punching holes.

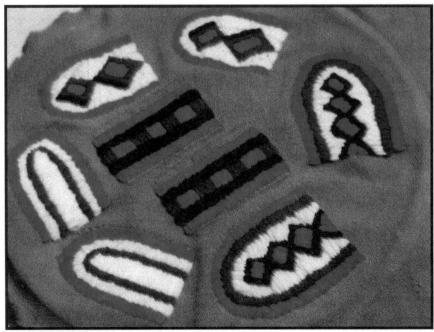

Embroidered patches

If you wish, the designs can be done with enamel paint. While the paint is still wet use a tooth pick to rake out straight lines. This is a short-cut form of imitation quillwork.

Other designs can be made with seed beads. Some Cherokee used red earth stains to add color to their moccasins.

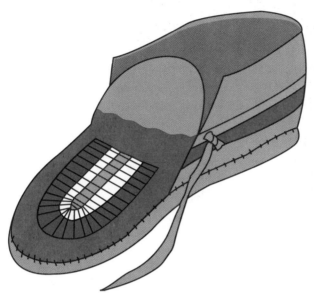

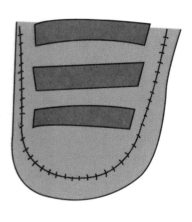

The above moccasin has quillwork and painted earth stain with a black stripe.

Red stripes were sometimes painted on moccasins as shown above.

Embroidery work

Beaded designs with tin cone hair tassel

Beaded moccasin

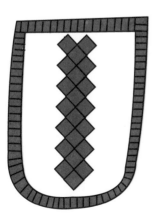

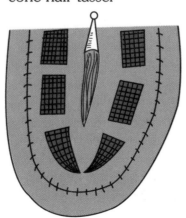

THE CENTER-SEAM MOCCASIN

The center-seam moccasin was also worn by many of the Southeastern tribes, including the Cherokee.

They are seen in paintings of the Cherokees as far back as the 1760's. One of the paintings of Sequoyah shows him wearing the center-seam style of moccasin.

Deerskin was used to make moccasins, but today cowhide is commonly used. The photograph shows a pair of center-seam moccasins of split cowhide.

On the following pages are instructions for making your own center-seam moccasins.

To make the center-seam moccasin, you will need a pattern. First, you will need a 24" by 24" piece of paper. Fold the paper in half to get a center line as shown below.

Place both feet firmly together on the floor with the center line running evenly between the feet, as shown in the sketch below.

Now, without moving the feet on the paper, use a pencil to draw around the feet. Keep your feet in place. Now measure from the bottom of the foot up to the center of the ankle bone. If you get 3 inches, for example, then add 3 inches on the paper on the outside of each foot.

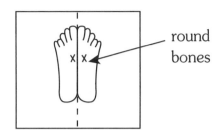

round bones

For the cuff part, add 3 more inches to each side. Refer to the sketches below. At each 3-inch mark on the pattern, draw a broken line.

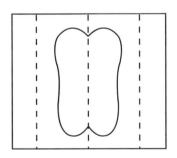
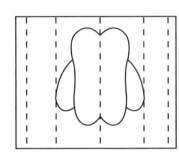

Another way to get the 3" side measurements is to scoot the right heel over and mark around it. Now scoot the left heel over and mark around it, then draw the vertical lines. Add the same measurements beside those vertical lines as shown in the sketches .

Whichever method you chose to get the side line measurements, put your feet back in the original position with the center line.

Locate the round bone on the upper side of each foot above the instep of the foot. Put a mark on each vertical line in alignment with the round bone. Remove the feet and draw a horizontal broken line as seen in the following sketch, using the marks as a guideline. Measure up on the outside vertical lines 2 inches from the horizontal line and put marks, as seen in the sketch on following page.

Next add $1/2$" at the toe part of the pattern, tapering it down to $1/4$ ", then to zero, as you can see in the sketch of the pattern. This forms the toe parts of the moccasins, as well as the curves in this pattern. Do the same kind of tapering on the other end of this curved pattern to where the cuff starts. Add $1/2$" horizontal line behind the heels as seen in the following sketch.

Next, cut out your paper pattern, fold it in half, trim up any unevenness. You will notice a $1/2''$ section which is cut out at the heel of this pattern to form the heel of the moccasin when sewn together.

The instructions given in the drawing of the paper pattern is for a size ten. Using the instructions and common sense, you will be able to make a pattern of your own size.

Before you cut out the leather to form this kind of moccasin, make a pair from cloth to see how they fit. If some part of the cloth moccasins is not right, adjust it until the fit is right. You can now proceed to make the moccasins from leather.

The paper pattern is for both feet (right & left). Each moccasin is made of one piece of leather, thus the designation, "one-piece type."

Un-cut paper pattern

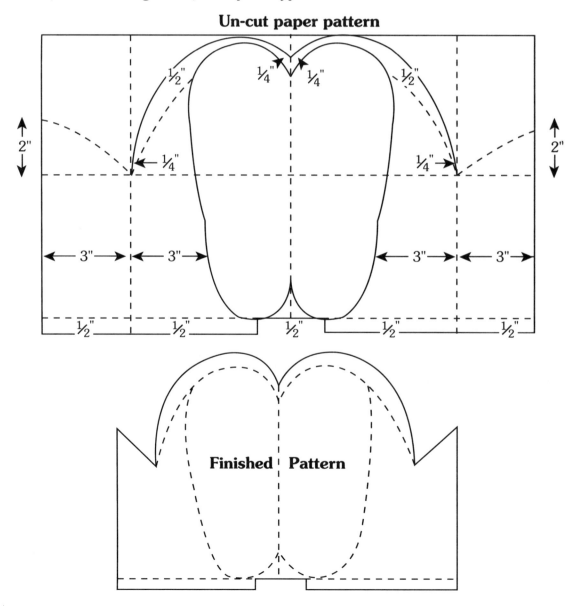

Finished Pattern

Now that the pattern is made, and you have experimented with a cloth pair of moccasins to see if the pattern works, let's use the real thing, leather!

Lay the leather to be used on the floor or a table. The smooth side of the leather should be turned up. This will be the side to be marked. Put the paper pattern on the leather and mark out two identical pieces. A pencil or ink pen is used to do the marking. Scissors or utility knife are used to do the cutting.

Next, fold the moccasin parts in half putting right sides together and using clothes pins to hold them evenly. Now use a punch or nail to make the holes as shown in the sketch below. Be sure to put a board underneath the leather when using a punch. The holes are $3/8$" from the edge and $1/4$" apart. Folding the leather as shown insures that the holes will match on opposite sides of the moccasins.

clothes pins

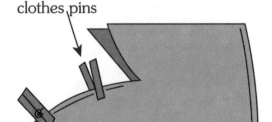

Start stitching at the first set of holes at the toe-fold. Make sure the first stitch is knotted and tied securely. Continue stitching up over the toe-part of the moccasin, stopping 2" from the front part of the cuff.

add double stitches

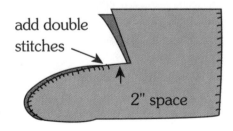

2" space

Punch the holes.

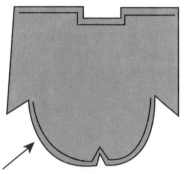

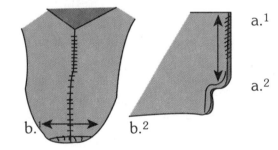

Stitch at the top of the cuff at the back of the moccasin from a.¹ to a.², as shown in the sketch above.

Next, push the bottom of the heel up and stitch to b.¹, then to b.².

You now have the finished pair of center-seam moccasins and are ready to decorate the moccasins with quillwork, embroidery or beadwork on the toe seam of the moccasins.

Once all the sewing is done on each moccasin, turn the moccasins right side out. Press the seams where you have stitched as you turn the moccasin. Turning the moccasins right side out will take effort.

Keep the cuff turned up as you put the moccasins on, as you would a boot. The cuff can be left up or turned down. Both ways were used among the Cherokee. When taking the moccasins off of your feet the cuff has to be up. This style of moccasins was meant to fit tight, so tie strings did not have to be used. When they are worn for the first time, they will cramp the toes and feel uncomfortable. For this first wearing, soak both moccasins in water. Wear the moccasins until they are dry. The moccasins will now feel comfortable and will be molded to the shape of your feet.

Center-seam moccasins were decorated in the same ways as other moccasins, by sewing embroidered, beaded or quilled patches or strips up the seam and along the cuffs.

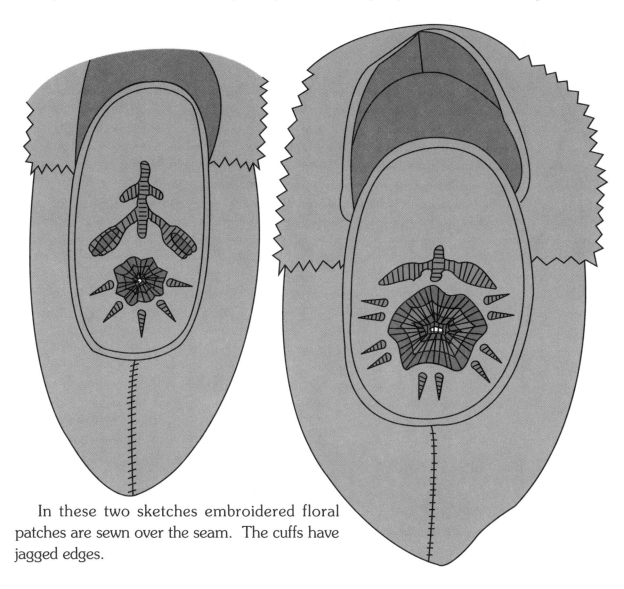

In these two sketches embroidered floral patches are sewn over the seam. The cuffs have jagged edges.

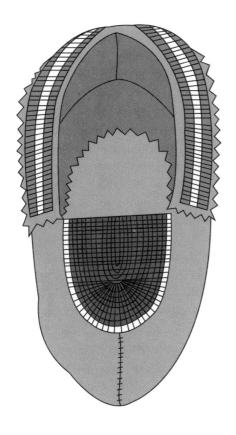

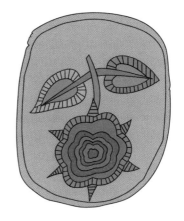

The toe-patch of the above moccasin is done in red, blue and white seed beads and represents an animal track. Along the cuffs are rows of green and white seed beads.

Floral designs were also common among tribes of the Southeast. Such patterns came from observation of wild flowers. Spring beauties, violets and a great variety of other flowers were abundant.

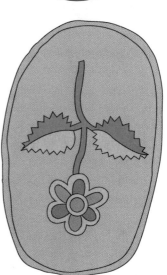

THE CHEROKEE BOOT

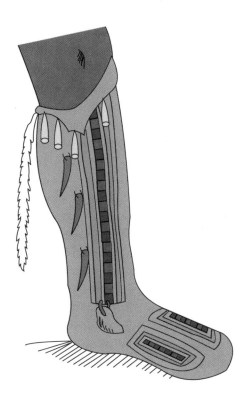

The Cherokee wore another kind of footwear, which was common in the Southeast - the boot. It was made of deerskin, although bear hide was sometimes used as another source. Cowhide is suitable and easier to obtain.

Boots were ideal for rough terrain when traveling or hunting. In colder weather, the boot was worn for warmth and protection from the elements. The fur could be left on the leather of boot material and turned inside to help keep the feet and legs from getting frost bite.

Decorations for boots, especially ceremonial boots were as numerous as they were for moccasins. The boots shown above are the center seam style. You may want to decorate the boots with beaded or embroidered patches shown on previous pages. Quillwork, fur tassels, beadwork, feathers, paint, embroidery, tin cones, turkey spurs, deer hoofs, or patchworks of cloth may be used on your boots to add to their beauty. Try to stay true to the Cherokee ways of decorating the boots, while making them personally your own.

THE THREE-PIECE AND ONE-PIECE BOOT

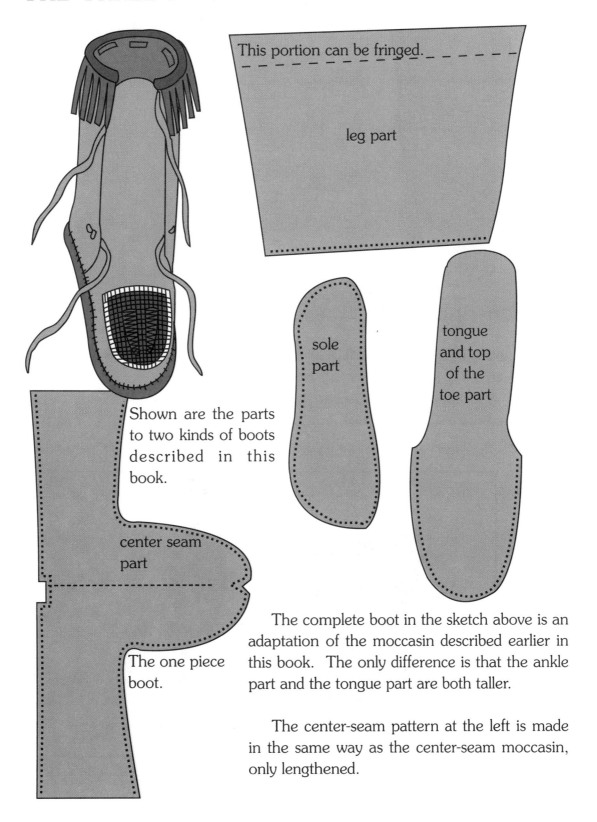

This portion can be fringed.

leg part

sole part

tongue and top of the toe part

Shown are the parts to two kinds of boots described in this book.

center seam part

The one piece boot.

The complete boot in the sketch above is an adaptation of the moccasin described earlier in this book. The only difference is that the ankle part and the tongue part are both taller.

The center-seam pattern at the left is made in the same way as the center-seam moccasin, only lengthened.

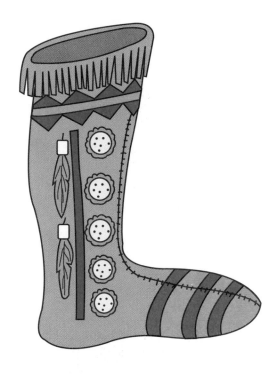

The above boot shows how lacing can be used to hold the front of the boot together and keep it snug on the leg. Lacing the boot also helps to keep out the rain or snow.

Above you can see how using paint, silver brooches and large beads with feather tassels add beauty to a boot.

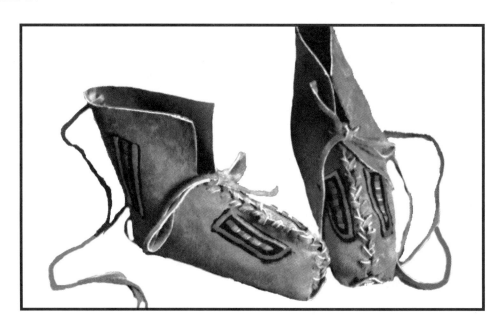

The above center-seam boots were sewn together with lacing.

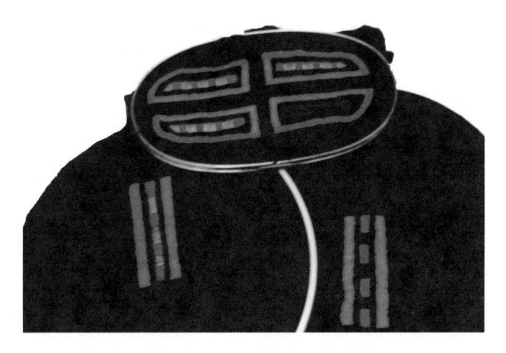

In the photograph above, the designs are shown as they are drawn
on the cloth and embroidered on a hoop.

When doing embroidery designs on the boots, you may want to make a paper pattern in order to get the designs alike on both boots. If the leather is soft enough, embroidery can be done directly on the leather, otherwise the embroidery will have to be done on cloth then transferred to the boots. Allow at least $1/2$" of extra cloth around the outside of the patch to be turned under when the patch is sewn onto the boots.   Use a punch to make holes in the leather where the patch is sewn onto the boot, as shown in the sketch below.

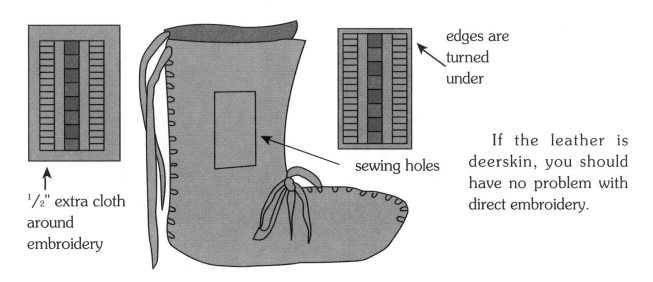

edges are turned under

$1/2$" extra cloth around embroidery

sewing holes

If the leather is deerskin, you should have no problem with direct embroidery.

197

DESIGNS THAT CAN BE USED ON FOOTWEAR

The above floral designs can be embroidered directly on soft leather or on patches. The patches then are transferred to the toe part of moccasins or boots.

Beadwork or quillwork designs, below and on the next page, are good examples of symbols from Cherokee pottery and baskets, which can be used on footwear.

Studying collector's items and museum pieces of the Cherokee is a good way to find designs to use on boots and moccasins. Below are some designs which can be done in beadwork or quillwork to enhance footwear.

HEADDRESSES

Native Americans throughout the Southeast took great pride in wearing various types of head coverings. The construction of a headdress had special meaning, indicating one's rank as chief, medicine man, warrior, or common person.

The turban style was common headdress during the troubled times of the Cherokee as they sought to relate to the white insurgence. It seems to have grown out of a desire to approximate the look of the old style hat. Turban trends were seen throughout the Southeast by artists who captured Native Americans on canvas and the sketch pad.

Pictured is a version of the turban showing its resemblance to the old style head dress.

The above sketch shows the cloth turban which was worn during the last few years of the Cherokee Nation in the Southeast. It was formed by wrapping a cloth around the head. Some tried to keep the Native American look by adding an attachment of feathers to the crown. Other men wore the turban plain.

Perhaps the oldest hat worn by the Cherokee was a fur hat of otter, opossum, rabbit or other animal furs. Sometimes it had an eagle or turkey feather attached to it. This type of hat would have been part of the winter apparel.

To make a fur hat, cut a leather band 1 $\frac{1}{2}$" wide and long enough to go around the head loosely. Sew the ends together like a headband, then make another band the same width. Sew it to the front and the back, as shown in the sketch below. You will need to try on this base for the hat as you sew it together in order to make adjustments to properly fit your head size.

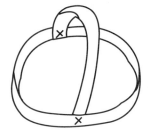 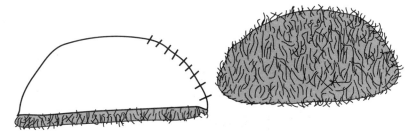

Once you have a base for the hat, cut two pieces of fur the same size, large enough to cover the straps forming the base. Keep the fur on the inside as you whip stitch the two fur halves together. Then it should be turned inside out when sewn onto the frame.

It is a good idea to make a pattern from cloth before cutting the fur for the hat to avoid wasting fur by improper fit. Fur hats can be decorated in a variety of ways or left plain.

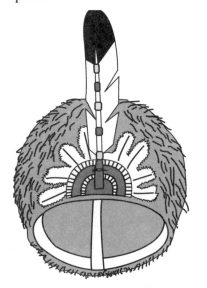

Opossum fur hat dyed red with black fluffs at the top.

Brown fur hat with a red-dyed leather and yellow quilled patch on the front. An eagle feather is standing erect. The bands on the feather can be painted on or quilled.

beaded band

A raven is mounted on this fur hat. The feather used is from a hawk.

Brown fur hat with white tassels hanging loose. White fluffs in a circle with an upright turkey feather mounted to the crown.

The above fur hat has a mounted deer-tail roach. The band is black leather with small mussel shell gorgets attached.

Some fur headdresses were probably made from the heads of deer, wolves, foxes, etc. to denote clans, offices and earned honors. It is known that Native Americans once wore deer heads and deer hide when hunting in order to get close enough to shoot an arrow.

Cherokee wore similar headdresses as part of their dance outfit for personal power during certain animal dances. Feather headdresses were also popular in the Southeast. Below are some examples of the feathered headdress.

The above headdress is made of an otter skin cap and black leather band with sun disks. Black-dyed crane or heron feathers, and red and black fluffs adorn the hat. This is the hat of the war chief. A peace chief wore a hat made the same way except in white.

Above is a hat made of yellow-dyed crane or heron feathers. It was worn during the Chief's Dance held every seven years. His whole outfit was yellow.

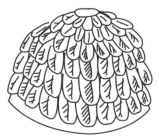

Some Cherokee men of great rank were seen wearing hats of white fluffs. The sketch above depicts a hat made of soft white feathers.

The Beloved Woman's hat was made of layered brown turkey feathers. The band could be red for war times or white for peace times. A yellow band was used for the initiation ceremony.

Layered turkey feathers adorn the hat above. Wing feathers are mounted on the top.

Above is another version of the Beloved Women's hat. Red feathers would have been for war.

The long wing or tail feathers seen on hats were held in place by using a hollow bone fastened into place on a leather strap, as shown in the sketch above.

To make the bone attachment, you will need a bone or a 3" piece of river cane. It should be hollowed out as shown in the above sketch. One end is funnel shaped tapering down on the inside. A hole is bored straight through the bone for the leather string which ties the bone to the leather strap on the underside of the hat.

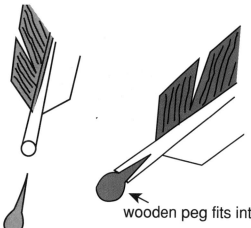

Now carve a wooden peg like the one shown in the sketch. The feather to be used is cut off at the pointed end leaving enough of the quill for the peg to be inserted.

wooden peg fits into the cut off end of the feather

To assemble the feather to the bone, put a string of leather through the two holes of the bone shaft. Tie it into place on the hat base where desired. Stick the end of the feather all the way through or far enough into the bone shaft while you push the wooden peg inside the bone into the end of the quill. A drop or two of glue on the end of the peg will secure it to the quill.

Next cut the covering for the hat the same way you did for the fur hat, except this time instead of using fur, use cloth or soft leather. You can use an old felt hat by cutting the brim off. A row of feathers is glued or sewn all around the lower part of the hat. Move up a row and glue on another row, all around the hat.

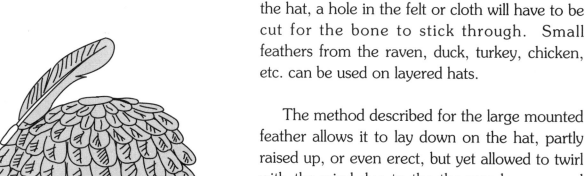

Put glue on the underside of the feather.

Keep gluing on rows of feathers until the hat is completely covered and the top feathers are glued into place.

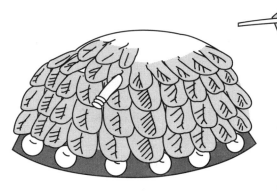

No matter what kind of covering is used for the hat, a hole in the felt or cloth will have to be cut for the bone to stick through. Small feathers from the raven, duck, turkey, chicken, etc. can be used on layered hats.

The method described for the large mounted feather allows it to lay down on the hat, partly raised up, or even erect, but yet allowed to twirl with the wind due to the the wooden peg and bone shaft.

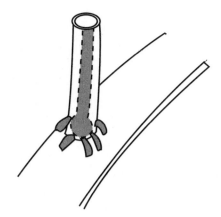

If you want a feather to stand upright on the top of the hat, bore small holes around the base of the bone, as shown in the sketch to the left.

Fix your feather and peg, as instructed before, then with a leather string or twine, fasten it to the hat base strap.

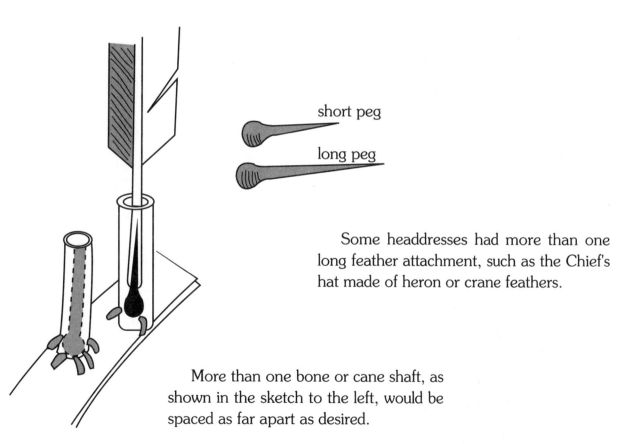

short peg

long peg

Some headdresses had more than one long feather attachment, such as the Chief's hat made of heron or crane feathers.

More than one bone or cane shaft, as shown in the sketch to the left, would be spaced as far apart as desired.

THE DEER TAIL HEADDRESS

The type of headdress shown here was worn throughout the Southeast by many tribes. Paintings of Cherokees indicate that they, too, wore this style of headdress.

Deer tails used for such a head dress were dyed red, and black fur was fixed to the base of it. The base was made of stiff leather in the form of a disk.

The bone is pulled out of the deer tail with a pair of pliers. Then, with a utility knife, the deer tail is cut into long thin strips. These strips of fur are then sewn around the disk and dyed red. Black fur is then added as shown on the following page.

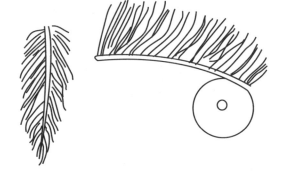

A hole was put in the center of the disk so that, when the headdress was worn, a portion of the scalp lock was plaited and inserted through the hole. Refer to the sketch.

A bone or wooden pin was pushed through the plait to hold the head dress in place. The rest of the scalp lock was free from the holding plait.

The deer tail headdress was worn by warriors who had achieved great honors in war. In some tribes the deer tail headdress was dyed red after earning a first war honor for striking or killing an enemy. War honors varied from tribe to tribe.

If deer tails can not be obtained from hunters, the headdress can be made from unraveled hemp or grass rope. Use commercial dyes or red ink to make the fibers red. Since the scalplock is no longer worn to hold the headdress in place on the crown of the head, a harness of leather straps and headband can be used.

original
type of
deer tail
headdress

Times have changed, and deer tails may be difficult to get. I will show you how to make one using a piece of felt or leather to make a base of layered disks.

Cut out four or five disks, four inches across. To get perfectly round disks use a can, cup or bowl 4" in diameter to mark around to form a disk.

Stack the disks on top of each other, whip stitching them together around the edges.

disks marked on felt

You may want to cut out the center holes out in the disks before sewing the disks together. If using a leather disk, punch holes around the edge, as shown below. This makes sewing easier. If the leather is stiff enough, only one layer of a disk is needed.

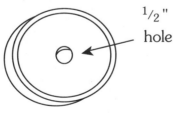

$1/2$"
hole

layered felt disk

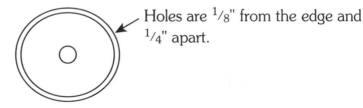

Holes are $1/8$" from the edge and $1/4$" apart.

single leather disk

When making an imitation of the deer tail headdress, use grass fibers unraveled from bailing twine (the type of string farmers use to bail hay). It is a good idea to dye the grass rope after the fibers have been cut in lengths, straightened and fastened into place. Below is shown the method used to fasten the rope fibers to the cord (a shoestring or strong twine):

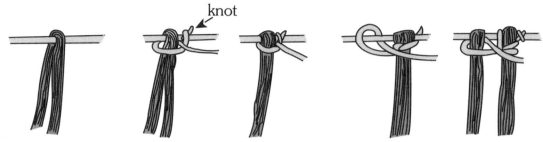

knot

Cut the fibers 20 inches long. Fold in half over a stretched cord.

Circle the thread around the fibers and pull tight.

Make a half stitch and pull the string tight. Continue the same process over and over as you tie on other bunches of fibers.

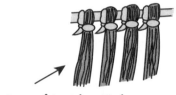

view of inside stitches

When fastening the fibers to the cord, it helps to stretch the cord between the backs of two uprights, such as chairs.

←—————14" - 15"—————→

Trim to 6"

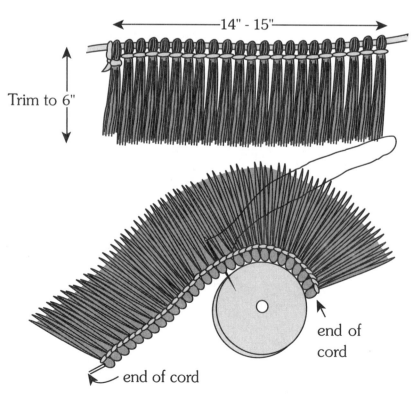

end of cord

end of cord

Sew the completed red roach fibers to the disk using a whip stitch, as shown in the sketch to the left.

Cut off excess. Sew finished ends of the cord of the fibers in place.

Once the red roach part is finished and ready to be used, cut a headband $1\frac{1}{2}$" wide and long enough to go around your head, overlapping the ends a little. Punch holes at the ends of the headband. Stitch the ends together on the band. Make the headband a little loose. Refer to the sketch below.

Next cut two leather strips $\frac{1}{2}$" wide and long enough to reach from the front to the back of the headband.

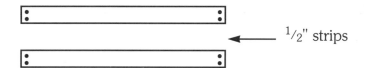

Put the headband on and adjust the criss-crossed strips to fit your size.

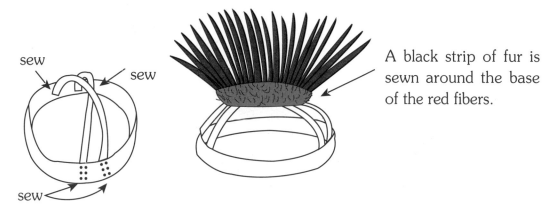

A black strip of fur is sewn around the base of the red fibers.

The two leather strips are sewn where they cross at the top, front and back of the headband. Before sewing the red roach to the straps, sew a black strip of fur around the outside base of the roach, as shown in the sketch above.

When you have sewn the red roach in place, embroider the designs onto the headband. Imitation leather is easier to use for the headband. The designs below can be embroidered with yarn, painted, or beaded onto the material.

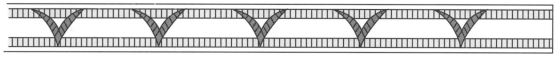

It will help to do the designs on the headband before attaching it to the headdress.

Even though some Native Americans attached a feather or two to the top of this headdress, I have seen no feathers on those of the Cherokee. It is possible, however, that the Cherokee also used feathers to denote extra war honors.

THE ROACH HEADDRESS

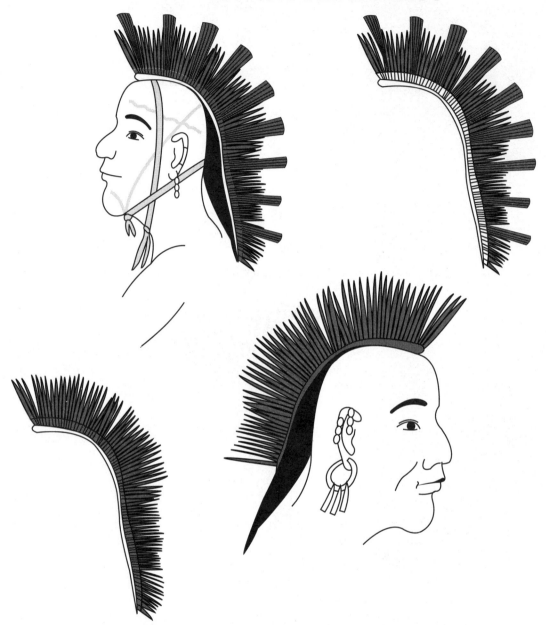

One of the most striking headdresses worn in the Southeast by many tribes, including the Cherokee, was the Roach Headdress. It was worn only after one had earned a war honor. As shown in the sketches above, the styles varied in color, construction, and materials. The styles were due to rank, age, and kind of honors a warrior had earned.

Porcupine guard hair, horse hair, and dyed grass or unraveled rope can be used to make such a headdress. Originally the headdress was held in place by tying it to the scalp lock. Today the roach headdress is held in place on the head by leather tie strings or a leather harness.

Some of the sketches portray roaches with taller bunches of black hair. These black bunches of taller hair were originally of turkey gobblers beard. Dyed fibers or black horse hair may be used as a substitute.

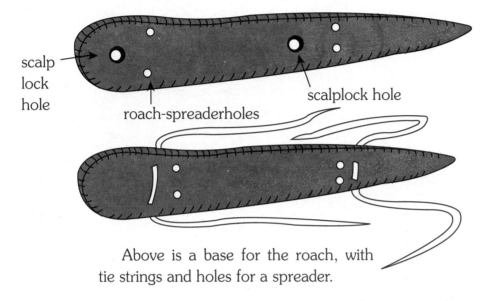

scalp lock hole

roach-spreaderholes

scalplock hole

The original way of making the base used leather. You can use felt layers whip stitched together.

The second sketch shows how the roach is tied on with strings, when not using the scalp lock method.

Above is a base for the roach, with tie strings and holes for a spreader.

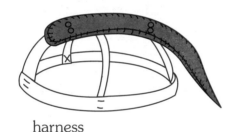

harness

The sketch at left shows the harness method of wearing a roach headdress.

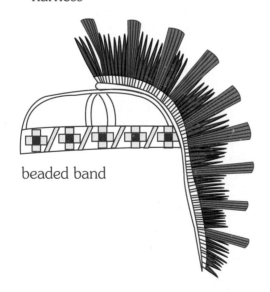

beaded band

When making this headdress, study the directions for making the DeerTail Headdress.
(starts on page 206)

The roach spreader can be seen in the above sketch. It is made a little wider than the roach base to push the fibers outward when it is tied into place. Holes on the spreader are aligned with the holes on the roach base for the strings used in attaching it. A place for feathers is also present.

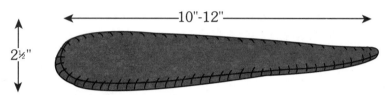

Four layers of felt are used to make the base.

Turkey gobbler beard is shown, spaced equal distances apart, in the above sketch.

12 fibers to a bunch

Shown in the sketch at the left is another method used to make individual bunches of fibers to be laced on a cord.

I prefer to use the method for making the deer tail headdresses when making this kind of roach headdress, since the process is much the same.

If you are interested in the varied meanings of roach headdresses and styles you may want to study Southeastern tribes in further detail.

HEADBANDS

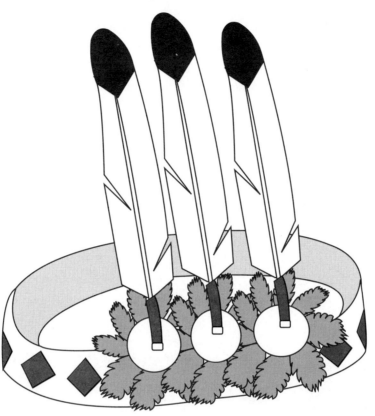

The Cherokee, like many of the Southeastern tribes, sometimes wore a leather or cloth band around the head. This was the custom of both men and women.

A headband served a very practical purpose for those having long hair. It was such a common piece of dress however, that many probably wore a band whether it served any practical purpose or not.

Some headbands were plain, while others were highly decorated. If decorations were used they included quillwork, paint, seed beads, embroidery, shells, and other available items.

Designs followed tribal custom, but personal choice was also used in the make-up of the headband.

When an authentic design is needed for a headband, one can choose designs from Cherokee pottery or baskets.

The headband shown below is made of red cloth with green seed beads forming the designs, and red beads forming the top edge. Leather is used for the backing, with a tie string on either end. This headband was sketched from one worn by a Cherokee woman in an old picture.

A quilled headband is shown below. It has slots cut at each end for a feather to interlock the ends at the back of the head. The slot method of fastening a headband must be adjusted to fit the head size of the individual.

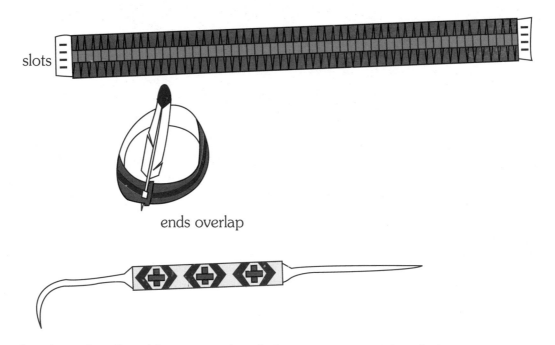

slots

ends overlap

The above headband has tapered ends for tie strings. A beaded strip is sewn onto the cloth or leather backing.

HAIR STYLES AND ORNAMENTS
OF CHEROKEE MEN

A study of Cherokee dress naturally includes Cherokee men's hair styles. Looking at old paintings of both the Cherokee and other Southeastern tribes, one will note great similarity in the way they wore and decorated their hair.

From around 1820, Cherokees began wearing their hair like the white settlers, therefore I will deal little with that era.

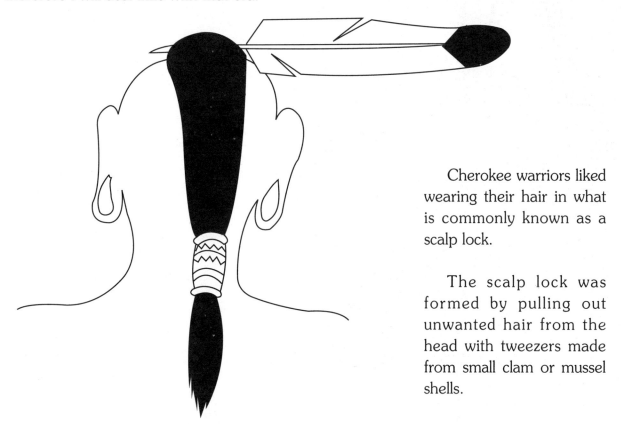

Cherokee warriors liked wearing their hair in what is commonly known as a scalp lock.

The scalp lock was formed by pulling out unwanted hair from the head with tweezers made from small clam or mussel shells.

All the hair was removed, except for a spot on the crown of the head. This spot of hair was usually about 4 to 5" in diameter. It was allowed to grow long. It should be noted that not all Cherokee men cut or plucked out their hair.

Unwanted hair on the head had to be plucked out often to maintain this style. A man's hair was his pride and therefore it was groomed often with bear grease to make it shine. In some way the scalp lock must have represented a person's power, because an enemy or warrior put great value in taking it as a trophy during the scalping process.

The tweezers made from small clam or mussel shells were later made from wire when trade items became available from the white man.

Women often helped their men to pluck out the hair, grease it and put ornaments into their hair. Some say the bear grease lotions for the hair helped to keep away lice, prevent baldness and pacify spirits. Sumac bushes were used as a hair rinse by breaking up the limbs and boiling them in water to make a solution to be applied to the hair.

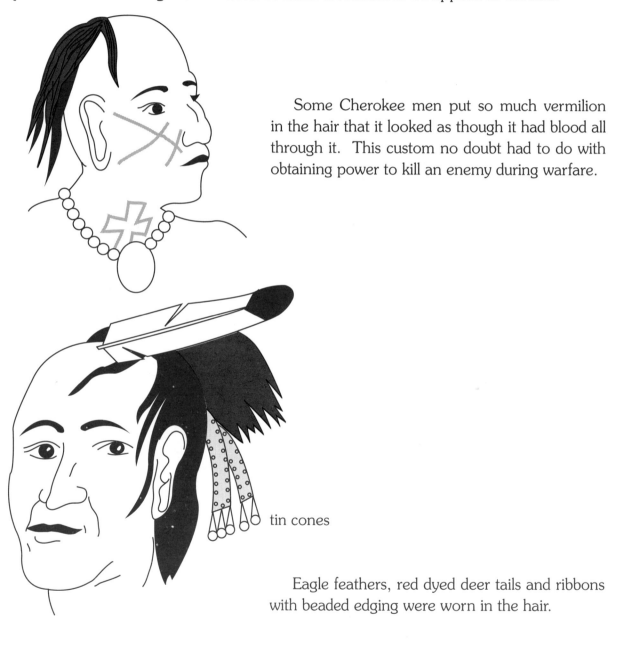

Some Cherokee men put so much vermilion in the hair that it looked as though it had blood all through it. This custom no doubt had to do with obtaining power to kill an enemy during warfare.

tin cones

Eagle feathers, red dyed deer tails and ribbons with beaded edging were worn in the hair.

NOTE: *Many birds are protected by law and the use of their feathers forbidden. Check the laws, both federal and state, before using bird feathers in your projects.*

Some men held the hair in place with a large tubular bone or one made of shell.

The scalp could then be plaited and tied at the bottom of the plait with a leather string or ribbon.

Red braided horse hair string was used by some to tie the hair.

← red fluffs

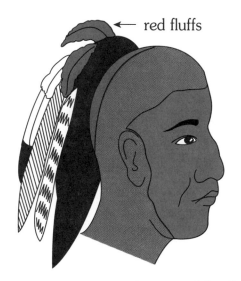

Red-dyed fluffs, turkey feathers or other kinds of feathers were tied into the hair.

Small beads on strings with danglers or cones were also decoration for some men.

Hair ornaments were attached to leather then wrapped around the hair and tied. Cloth wrappings were used later. Such hair wrappings could have danglers of tin.

white fluffs

The quill of the feather could be beaded or decorated as shown in the sketch to the left.

White feathers, in a bunch with tin danglers, were also worn as hair decorations.

In this sketch, the hair is gathered at the top of the head and tied with red-dyed notched feathers. Red feathers were usually worn during times of war.

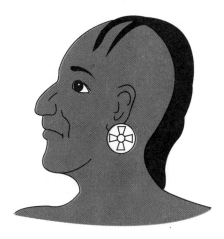

This drawing portrays a side view of a Cherokee man's scalp lock as it hangs loose.

As shown above, some men wore their hair rather plain, colored with vermillion, with the scalp lock loose.

Above, a man is depicted wearing a deer tail headdress. The scalp lock is tied or wrapped with a leather string.

Some of the men, including the Medicine Men, often wore long hair.

One of the clans of the Cherokee people is called the "Long Hair Clan," indicating that long hair was the preference of some. Those who wore their hair long used decorations similar to those who wore the scalp lock.

Each clan most likely had it's own feather and color.

HAIR STYLES AND ORNAMENTS
OF CHEROKEE WOMEN

The women's hair could be worn several ways. Young women often wore their hair loose, while others would put the hair in a long braid at the back of the head. Another style was to wear the hair fixed in a club-like fashion, as shown in the sketch on the next page. Older women, such as the "Beloved Women," liked to fix their hair in wreaths as shown on a following page.

The woman above portrays the single braid style.

A back view is shown in the sketch above. In the old days, braided hair was tied with a leather string. Later, ribbons were used to tie the hair and were often woven into the braid.

During the old days, when a woman folded the braid or her long hair up in the back, to form a club-look, it was wrapped and held in place with ribbons, leather string, or a "hair-tie." The hair-tie was popular among many of the Southeastern tribes, so it is reasonable to believe that the Cherokee women used it also.

To make a hair-tie, cut deerskin or cloth to the shape shown in the sketch below. Cut a piece of stiff leather or cardboard the same shape to go inside. Two pieces of cloth, cut the same, are put on either side of the cardboard or leather to make a front and a back. The sides, top and bottom of the hair-tie are now whip-stitched. Turn the edges of the cloth under as you sew.

Use ribbons or leather strings, as shown in the sketch below, to hold the hair-tie in place on the hair. The size of the hair-tie is a matter of personal preference.

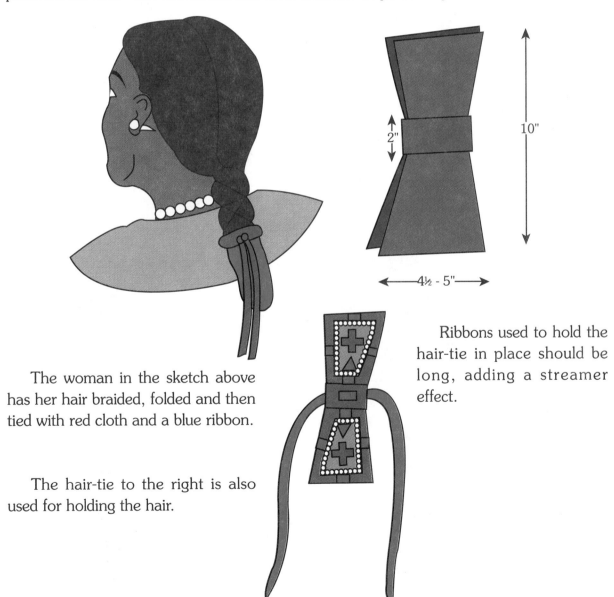

The woman in the sketch above has her hair braided, folded and then tied with red cloth and a blue ribbon.

The hair-tie to the right is also used for holding the hair.

Ribbons used to hold the hair-tie in place should be long, adding a streamer effect.

The hair-tie can be decorated in many beautiful ways. Designs are done with seed beads, quillwork, patch-work, silver broaches, etc. If the hair-tie is made entirely of leather, the designs can be painted on.

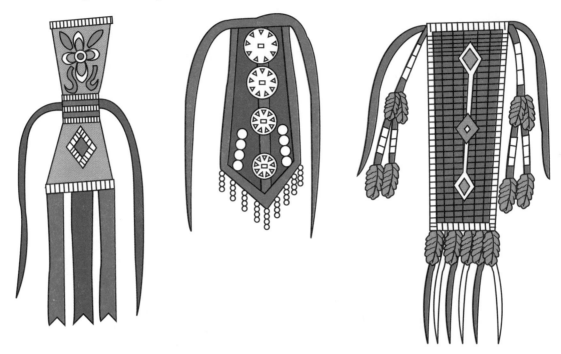

When the Cherokee women bundled the hair up to form a club, they sometimes used a tanned eel skin to tie it, believing the eel skin would cause it to look more beautiful and grow longer. Like the men, they often used bear grease to dress the hair and make it shine.

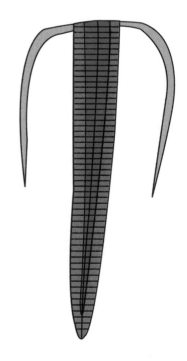

Cherokee women let their hair grow long; they seldom, if ever, cut it. The long hair of older women, such as the "Beloved Women," was sometimes plaited into wreaths as shown below.

The plaits were turned up and fastened on the crown of the head with a silver brooch. Sometimes small beads were woven into these plaits to add to their beauty.

Side view of the wreathed hair style.

Back view of the wreathed hair style.

The wreathed hair style was worn by distinguished women of high status during special times, such as ceremonies, festivals, council meetings, etc.

The hair was sometimes worn loose as shown in the sketch to the left. A headband and small fluffs or ribbons could be worn in the hair.

Hair styles among children and young people were simple but gradually evolved into that of the adults. The ways of the adults were taught from childhood. The youth learned from the elders how to groom the hair and keep it clean in traditional ways.

Children were taught that hair had a power or essence about it. We can see that hair was very important by how the Native American placed value on taking scalps, decorating their clothes with hair tassels, casting hair to "Grandfather Fire" to be kept for the person in the hereafter, not going to bed with wet hair, washing a dead person's hair before burial and a widow wearing her hair down to show mourning.

Even the way feathers and hair ornaments were worn in the hair was learned from childhood. It was important to teach the customs to the children.

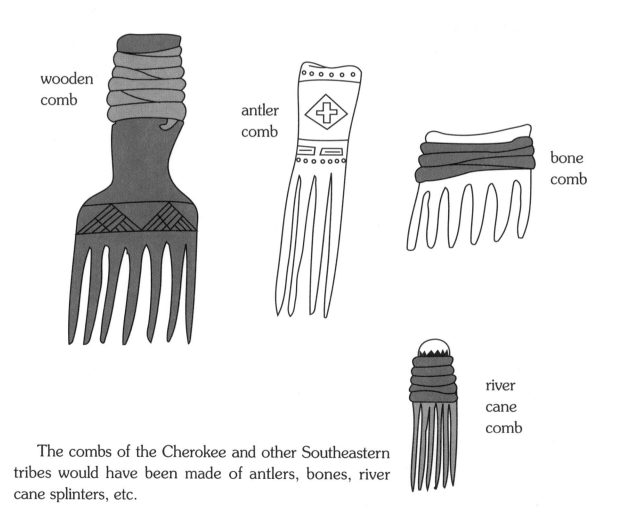

wooden comb

antler comb

bone comb

river cane comb

The combs of the Cherokee and other Southeastern tribes would have been made of antlers, bones, river cane splinters, etc.

QUILLED HAIR ORNAMENT

The beautiful hair piece above is done using basket designs. Since quills are hard to get, yarn was used to give a quill effect.

Hair ornaments of this style were worn throughout the Southeast after the trading influenced the blending of clothing and ornament styles over many tribes.

A hair piece like the above was tied at the back of the head after the hair had been fashioned into a braided club. If a club-look hair style is not worn, then the hair piece can be attached to a head band by a loop on the back of the hair piece.

Directions follow for making the hair piece in the photo above.

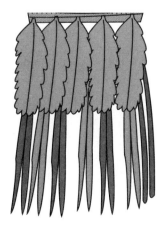

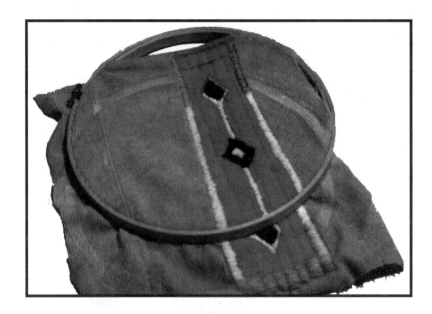

How the embroidery looks on the hoop.

First choose a suitable material like leather, or a good substitute like tan corduroy. Imitation leather or chamois skin are also good to use. Once the material has been selected, make the shape on the material by measuring the sizes with a ruler.

Mark the outline of the designs, then place the whole piece of cloth on an embroidery hoop, as shown in the above photograph. Allow enough extra cloth to remain for the embroidery hoop to hold the cloth in place.

Red, white, and black yarns are used to make the parallel embroidery stitches. Glue will also be needed for the black fluffs and the yarn wrapping on the leather projections.

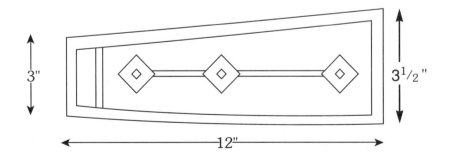

Draw the designs as shown in the sketch to the left.

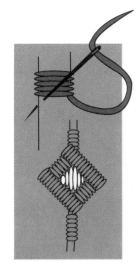

Do the embroidery work in rows, as shown in the sketch to the left. All of the stitches are done the same way.

The sketches to the left show the stitches on the diamond designs.

Once all of the embroidery work is finished, remove the whole thing from the hoop. Fold the excess cloth over the back side of the hair piece. Do some trim work, so the cloth will fold properly on the back. Stitch up the middle part and sew up the sides, as depicted in the sketch to the left.

back view

Yarn tassels go at the bottom of the hair ornament. The strands of yarn are cut 12" long and then folded in half. Alternate the colors as they are attached to the bottom of the back side of the hair piece, as shown in the sketch to the left.

The points of the black fluffs are glued and inserted between the two layers of cloth on the front side at the bottom.

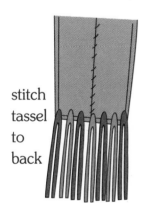

stitch
tassel
to
back

In the sketch below is shown one of the 6" projection parts made of leather. Yarn is wrapped around the projection.

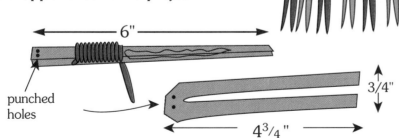

punched
holes

Cut the two forked projections, as shown in the sketch to the left.

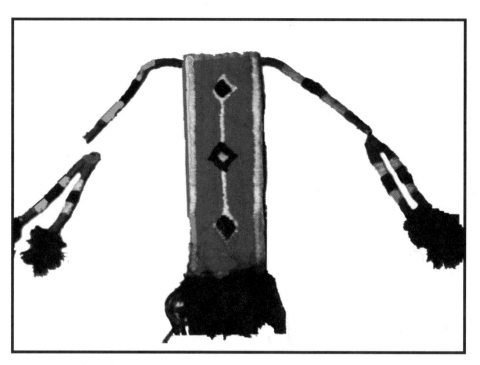

In the above photograph the hair ornament assembly
is almost completed.

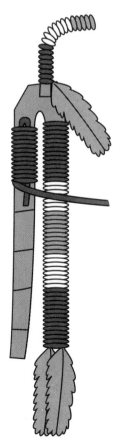

Sew forked projection to straight projection.

Mark the color pattern on the projections. Wrap the yarn, using glue, indicated in the sketch to the left, keeping the ends of the yarn concealed as you change colors.

Put glue on the points of each fluff and insert under the yarn wrapping as shown.

Sew on a loop for head band attachment. This is optional.

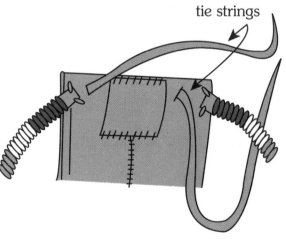

tie strings

back of hair piece

(Cut tie string 24" long and insert, as shown in above sketch.)

FEATHER WEARING

All Native American tribes were fond of wearing feathers. This custom may have started from watching birds in their freedom of flight empowered by the Great Man Above. Wearing feathers was thought to indue one with the mystical power of the bird.

Feathers of all kinds were worn in the hair and on clothing for power, as well as beauty. Some feathers had to be earned before they could be worn. The eagle feather, for example, was obtained only through a professional "Eagle Killer." He had to follow strict rules, taboos, and rituals before killing an eagle for its feathers. There were special prayers to be said before killing an eagle, or the spirit of the eagle would be offended. Other feathers of lesser powers could be obtained after one had a dream or vision.

Feather positions, whether upright, down, leaning to the left or right, or horizontal on the head, had a specific meaning. The way feathers were adorned with paint, dye, quills, hair, notches, etc., meant something special to the Cherokee as it did to the other Southeastern tribes.

Some Cherokee men chose to wear wings of small birds such as red birds or blue jays. Others even wore the entire preserved bird head as power symbols. According to the old people among the Cherokee, who still know the old bird lore, certain birds had meanings as follows:

Owl -   Something bad, such as death, was going to happen. Owl feathers were
                 worn by Medicine Men and had to do with mystical powers.

Dove -   The call of the dove meant someone had suddenly died, and the dove
                 was grieving for the person.

Kingfisher -   Its feathers were worn by the Medicine Man to help remove sickness
                 from his patients.

Redbird -   It had power in its call to foretell that a gift, money, good fortune
                 or something else you have needed, was on its way.

Blackbird -   The blackbird feathers had to do with war.

Crane, Heron -   Feathers were worn by the chiefs for leadership, authority, etc.

Blue Jay -   These feathers had to do with happiness, or a sign that something good
                 was to come.

Eagle -   Eagle feathers symbolized peace, and were used during the friendship dance and on the eagle wand. Eagle feathers had great power and were worn by many warriors to shown achievements, status and honor.

Whippoorwill -   Its call told you that you would have a good sleep or perhaps a dream that meant something good.

Peacock -   Its feathers or fluffs are worn by Cherokee as depicted in old paintings. They were probably just for looks; perhaps sometimes worn for peace and goodwill.

Hawk -   Its feathers had to do with power, strength.

Joe Ree -   You were going to have good health for a time, with nothing to worry about regarding illness. (Also known as a Towhee)

Turkey Buzzard -   Its feathers were worn in the hair of the Medicine Men to help bring healing to the sick.

Turkey -   Feathers would have to do with the warrior, war, power, etc., since the call of the turkey sounded like the "war cry."

Many birds, their feathers, calls, symbols, etc. had special meanings to those who wore feathers in the hair. I suggest that you study old legends of the Cherokee or listen to a native story teller to get even more understanding about feather wearing. Look at shell gorgets with carvings of birds on them, and maybe you will discover more hidden meanings about birds and feather wearing.

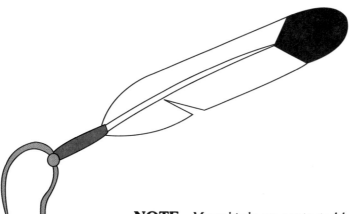

Feathers, one or more, could be tied to the hair with a leather string. This method allowed the feather to move with the breeze.

NOTE: *Many birds are protected by law and the use of their feathers forbidden. Check the laws, both federal and state ,before using bird feathers in your projects.*

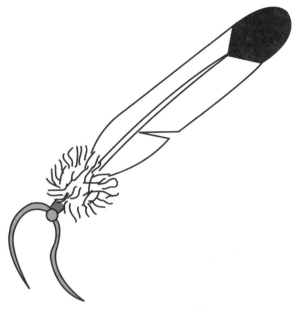

Some hair feathers, such as an eagle feather as shown above, had several white fluffs at the base. This type of decoration was tied to the hair on the scalp lock.

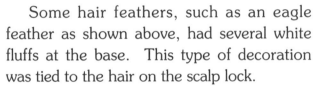

Many Native Americans used a tapered wooden peg, split and wrapped, with the feather stuck in it. More than one feather could be used in this manner. Upright feathers or angled feathers in a stationary position can be fixed like this. It is stuck into the hair or tied in place.

There were set rules among the "Warrior Societies" which were followed closely when feathers were worn. Each warrior knew what he could wear and not wear on the scalp lock.

leather or rawhide wrapping

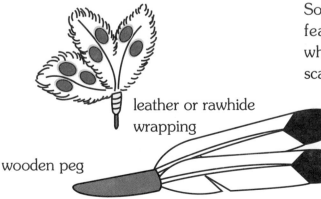

wooden peg

231

METHODS OF CUTTING, PIERCING, AND ORNAMENTING THE EAR

In the old days, some Cherokee men cut the outer portion of their ears. Warriors practiced this custom with zeal, probably to show they could withstand pain.

When this operation took place, it took weeks to heal, and infection was always a danger. Such cuttings were done with a sharp piece of flint. The Medicine Man probably did most of these operations because of his knowledge of healing herbs.

Since cotton was not in use, a ball of hair from the mountain buffalo was soaked in bear grease and put in place at the incision to absorb blood and drainage until the ear was healed.

After the healing process was finished, wire from the white traders was encircled around and around the detached part to stretch it even more. The wire also made the ear hang outward.

The practice of cutting the ear went out of style during the historic period. Some men got this cut portion of the ear torn off from bushes, fights, and frost-bite.

On the next page are sketches of this ear style with decorations.

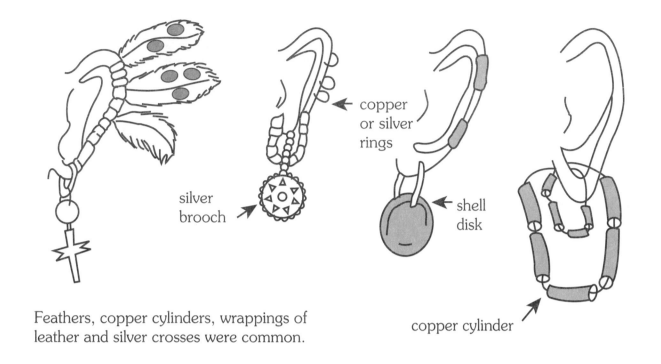

copper
or silver
rings

silver
brooch

shell
disk

copper cylinder

Feathers, copper cylinders, wrappings of
leather and silver crosses were common.

Cherokee people wearing earspools are dipicted on shell gorgets in museums. To
wear a spool, a slit or cut had to be made in the ear lobe to make a hole for the spool to
be inserted. The incision would have been treated medically the same way as the
procedure for cutting the outer part of the ear. This style of wearing ear spools was
practiced by the men. Women seemed to favor ear pins.

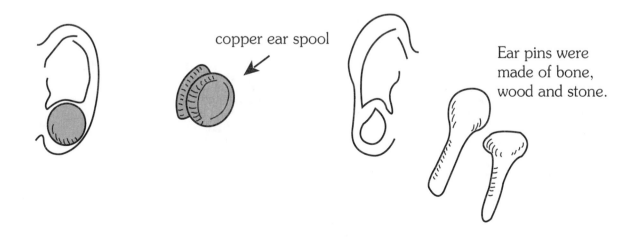

copper ear spool

Ear pins were
made of bone,
wood and stone.

Piercing the ears became more popular during the historic period when glass beads and silver brooches came to the Native American. To pierce the ear, a sharp bone, metal or wooden needle was used. Even a metal punch obtained from the white man was sometimes used.

In the sketches below are ways in which the Cherokee and other Southeastern tribes decorated pierced ears.

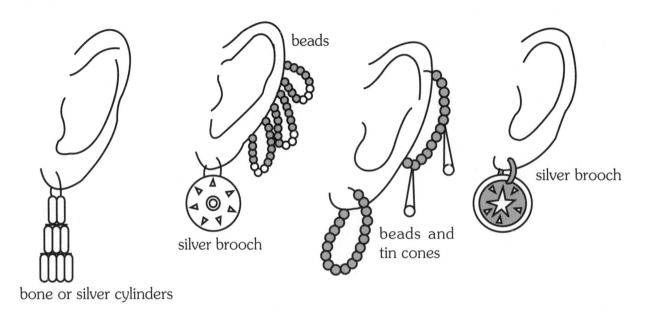

beads

silver brooch

silver brooch

beads and
tin cones

bone or silver cylinders

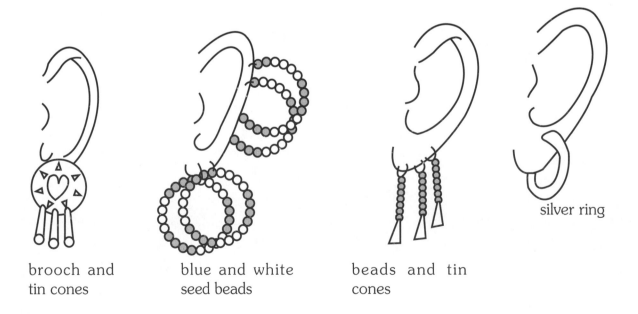

silver ring

brooch and
tin cones

blue and white
seed beads

beads and tin
cones

TATTOOING

From ancient times the Cherokee were fond of decorating their clothes, ceremonial objects, and practically everything they made. The designs they used had great meaning, even protective and religious powers, as well as helping them to remember events of importance from the past.

A long time ago someone discovered a way to put designs on the skin that would not come off. Many tribes of Native Americans in the Southeast practiced this custom, even in historic times. It gradually declined from a well developed art form to a less respected custom.

I have studied old paintings and sketches of the Cherokee, as well as other Southeastern tribes, for many years and have been fascinated by the many tattooed designs on their faces, necks, arms, chests, and legs. It seemed most of their bodies were tattooed with circles, sun symbols, four direction symbols, "X" shaped designs, lines, snake designs, dots, half moons, stars, animal designs, etc.

Warriors, Chiefs, and women had tattoos which they wore with great pride. It appears that the designs recorded events or achievements earned through one's life. The very young received simple tattoos which were enhanced as they grew older until most of the body was covered.

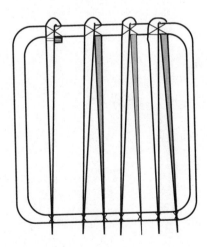

The custom of "scratching," as it is called, may have been a reflection of the old tattooing custom. When a person was "scratched" for a ritual, it was done on the arms, chest, back or legs. A person being "scratched" did not show sign of pain, or he would be shamed. This custom is still practiced today by those who keep old Cherokee customs.

A scratching comb can be made of turkey quills or river cane splinters as shown in the drawing on this page. Thin quills or splinters are sharpened, then doubled over the top of the frame and held in place at the top and bottom by thread or string.

The Medicine Man used the comb for this ritual of "scratching" and always kept it among his sacred possessions. This one shows one leg of one quill missing. This leaves seven teeth on the comb (the sacred number).

A design to be tattooed onto the body was first drawn on the skin. Charcoal, made from poplar bark, ground or mashed up into powder was used as a coloring agent.

The tool used to make the tattoo was a small sharpened stick having one or more prongs. Sometimes teeth of the garfish were used to make the tattoo.

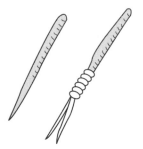

When the design had been selected, the skin was pricked until the blood came out. Powdered charcoal was put on the pricked area and left to heal. The coloring agent was trapped underneath the healed skin of the design.

Designs usually turned out with a bluish color. Red designs were made by using red sulfur. Gun powder was used as a dark coloring agent during the historic period after the Cherokee began trading with the white man.

Below are three sketches illustrating how facial designs looked when tattoos were used by the Cherokee and other Southeastern tribes.

In the sketches below, face and chest designs are shown tattooed on the bodies of Southeastern Native Americans. The Cherokee used similar designs to decorate their bodies.

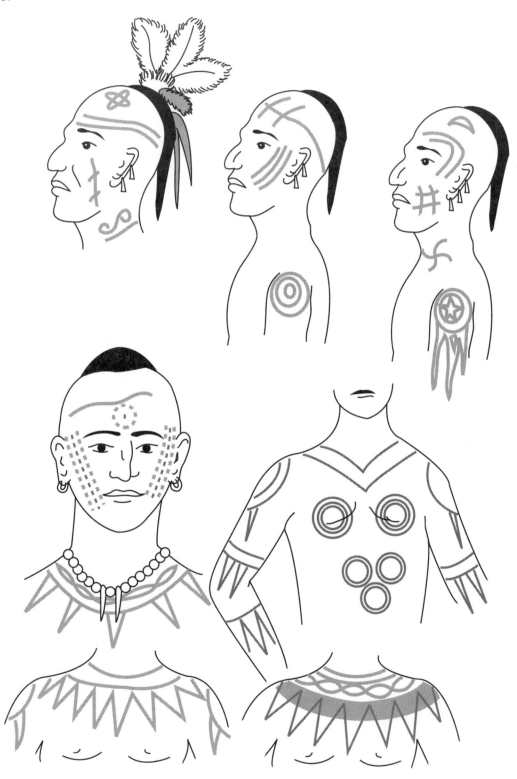

The sketches below show how the complete chest, sides, arms, and legs were tattooed. Designs match and are spaced apart in series of bands or rows. Usually there are two rows of designs above and below the bend of the arms and legs. Although the legs were tattooed with designs similar to those of the arms, more designs could be put on the leg area if a person so desired.

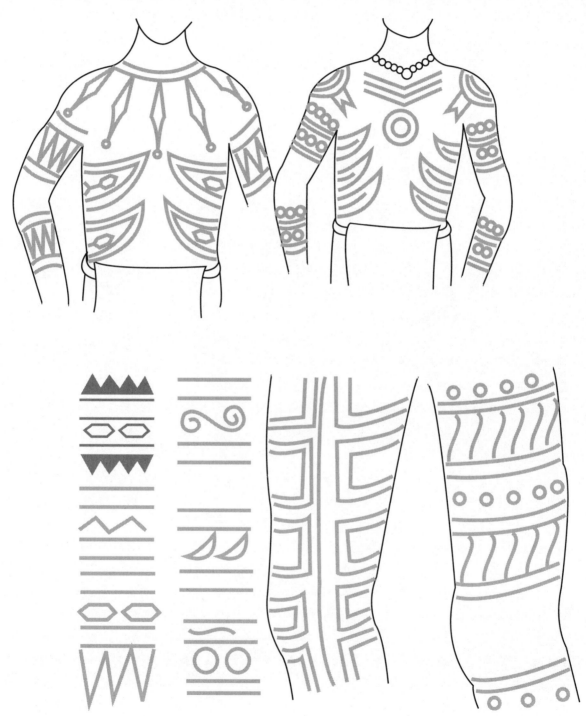

THE USE OF BODY PAINT

Native paint was used among the Cherokee to decorate the body from birth until death in one form or another. The Cherokee thought it very important to "paint-up" whether it was for personal beauty or one of the many ceremonies. Paint was used also for times of war and death.

Early in life the skin was protected from the sun, weather, and insects by applying a red ointment on the skin made from bloodroot and bear grease. This ointment acted as a skin screen giving a red tone to the skin.

In the old days, red ocher, a clay containing iron ore, was mixed with bear grease to produce a body paint. When the white man came, vermillion was used by the Cherokee. Men colored their hair with it on occasions, as shown in the sketch below. Women liked putting vermillion at the hair line or a spot of it under one eye on the cheek or in front of the ears.

The everyday use of paint by the Cherokee for decorative purposes made smooth skin desirable.

Since men had trouble with unwanted hair, they used tweezers to pluck it out. Tweezers were usually made of small mussel shells or of a piece of wire. A small leather pouch was carried on the belt at all times to carry such things as tweezers, paint, tobacco, bear grease, and other items.

239

tobacco pouch

mussel shell
tweezers

wire tweezers

Above are some of the contents of a personal pouch. The mussel shell tweezers had sharpened edges. Wire tweezers, used after white trader influence, were of brass or heavy wire bent to the above shape with flat sharpened ends.

For powdered paint containers, small cups were made of soapstone and other materials. When the paint was to be used, paint powder of the desired color was mixed with bear grease as needed. It was then stored in the pouch ready to use.

Lids for paint cups could be made with a piece of leather and string or a wooden stopper. When a substance was ground for paint powder, a small shallow dish and grinder was used, as shown in the sketches below.

paint containers

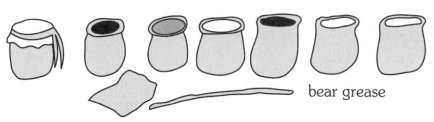

bear grease

wooden mixing
board

leather cloth and string tie

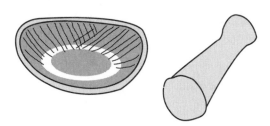

The mortar and pestle could be made from wood or stone, carved and shaped for grinding.

To make the different colors of powdered paint, the Cherokee would have used the following substances:

Red   - from clay containing iron ore; red sulfur

White   - from white clay

Black   - from charcoal

Blue   - from a bluish clay

Green   - from copper scrapings

Yellow   - from yellow sulfur or ocher

Vermillion - from trade with the whites

Paint and dyes of all kinds were later obtained from the white traders. Bright colors became available and largely replaced the milder colors of the old days.

Colors held great meaning to the Cherokee, especially when used in harmony with designs done with body paint. Some of the meanings of colors were as follows:

Red   - for the east, beginning, blood

Black   - for the west, night, the "darkened land," and death

Blue   - for the north, grief, sadness

White   - for the south, peace

Yellow   - for happiness

Sometimes Cherokee men, when going on the warpath, would paint their faces red, adding a black circle above one eye and a white circle around the other eye. The red signified war, the black circle for seeing the enemy and killing him, and the white circle for good sight in spotting the enemy.

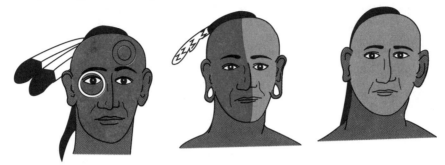

Some warriors painted half of the face red for war and the other half of the face black, as shown in the above sketch. The black meant death to the enemy. Other warriors painted the whole face black signifying death to the enemy.

Cherokee warriors also put stripes of paint on their faces. These stripes were red and black, indicating their hope of killing an enemy. This style was worn by junior warriors, out to kill their first enemy or trying to get war honors.

When studying Native Americans, one learns that there were Warrior Societies which governed how each rank of warrior painted the face and body during warfare. Each warrior had to paint a certain way to show his status. Black and red were the war colors and could be used in many ways to help a warrior have power and protection from the enemy.

Around 1800-12, Cherokee warriors on the warpath against the Creeks must have changed war colors a little. They were wearing red, white, and yellow slashes on their faces and chest. This might indicate that the customs were changing as the Cherokee became allies with the whites. Each warrior wore a headband with a deer tail hanging down at the back of the head, so the white soldiers would not get Cherokees mixed up with Creek warriors during the battle.

Cherokees had certain designs painted on the body for dances. The sketch below shows how an "Eagle Dancer" would have looked. On his body were painted red circles, spirals in blue, and white hand prints.

The blue spirals would have been made by dipping a finger into paint and making the design. Circles and stripes were made by using one or more of the fingers to spread the paint. Large areas of the body were painted by putting the paint on the palm of the hand and pressing it to the body. Hand prints are simply done by wetting the whole palm with paint and pressing the paint onto the body. No brush was used.

A sharpened stick, a piece of leather, or some other porous material was used to paint designs on objects other than the body, such as robes, moccasins clothing, etc.

Body painting was a sacred thing which had a power about it to aid the Native American in his daily life, religious ceremonies, dances, festivals, war, etc.

Even at death, paint was used to color the corpse's face red for the after-world.

When wearing Cherokee clothing, stay in harmony with the occasion by using appropriate colors and designs of body paint.

NECKLACES

The Cherokees of the past did not consider themselves well dressed without a necklace of some kind to wear with their clothing. Necklaces were worn for their beauty, but, more importantly, for the powers they contained to help the ones who wore them. Men, women, and children all wore necklaces of some type.

They made their necklaces from a variety of things, such as, bearclaws, eagleclaws, animal teeth, animal bones, shells, copper, and other items of power. Seashells were turned into beads, such as wampum, which they prized very highly. There must have been a trading system with coastal tribes to obtain the shells. Later, after the Cherokee began trading with the white man, glass beads were used for necklaces.

Necklaces from fresh water mussel shells made into gorgets were especially appealing because of the designs engraved on them.

Cherokee Medicine Men wore a large gorget breast-plate. It had two holes bored in the middle of it. Buttons made from the horns of the male deer were attached at these center holes with an otter string. Designs of half moons, stars, and circles were engraved around it.

This breast plate gorget was 6" or 7" inches wide like the kind Native Americans in Florida wore. It was made from a univalve seashell or a very large mussel shell.

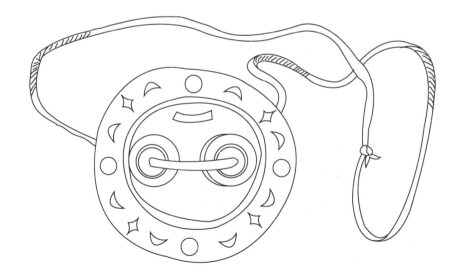

Smaller gorgets, about 4" wide, were worn by the Cherokee. Two holes were usually bored at the top of a gorget for the tie string. A pump drill was used to bore the holes. These necklaces hung down just in front of the neck or even lower on the chest. The leather string had beads strung on it.

Making a shell gorget from a mussel shell took considerable time. A sandstone was used to grind the shell to the round shape.

To make the designs, a sharp piece of flint was used to engrave them on the concave side of the shell. The back of the shell gorget was also smoothed down to a nice finish.

You can find instructions elswhere in this book for making a shell gorget using modern methods to speed up the process. Mussel shells can be found along shoals and rocky places at the banks of rivers where the water is shallow.

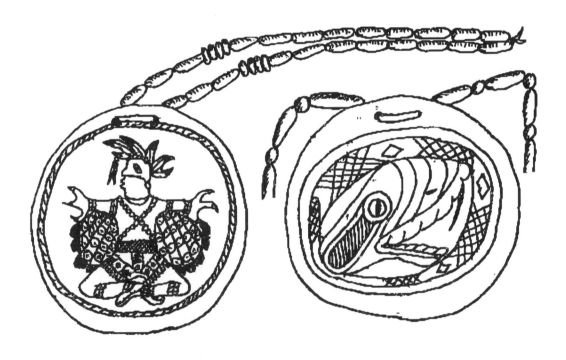

The sketch above depicts a man dressed in a ceremonial bird-dance costume.

The likeness of the rattlesnake can be seen in the gorget shown above.

The shell gorget above has a pendant of round beads and copper danglers hanging from the middle of the four direction design. White shell beads can be substituted with crow beads or other plastic and glass beads which look similar.

Museum collections are good sources for gorget designs.

Gorgets contain many of the old picture writing symbols of the Cherokee.

Face gorget

Woodpecker gorget

STONE NECKLACES

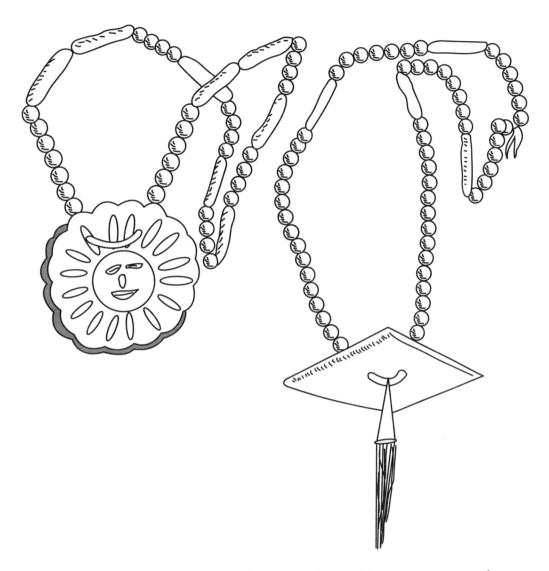

Another material, used by the Cherokee to make necklace parts, was soft stone which could be carved to the desired shape. After the stone was shaped it was polished smooth by rubbing it with a sandstone rock. Designs were cut into the stone with a sharp piece of flint. Holes were bored with a pump drill.

The sun disk necklace, as shown in the sketch above, was sketched from one owned by a lady in Virginia. It is Cherokee. Diamond-shaped stone necklaces, as shown in the other sketch above, were also made in the Southeast.

Numerous shapes of stone necklaces have been found by collectors.

SHELL COLLAR NECKLACE

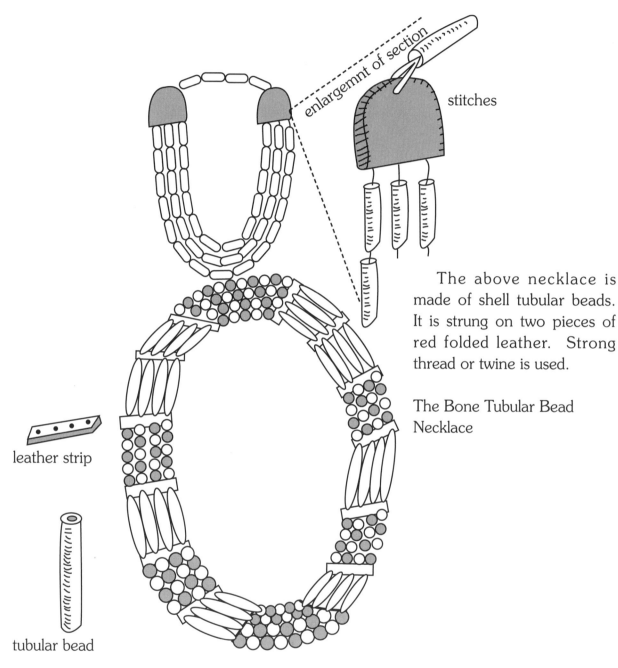

enlargemnt of section

stitches

leather strip

tubular bead

The above necklace is made of shell tubular beads. It is strung on two pieces of red folded leather. Strong thread or twine is used.

The Bone Tubular Bead Necklace

The above two necklaces are made of similar construction. As shown, bones and large beads are used to make this necklace.

Tubular beads can be made of river cane, or the leg and wing bones of the chicken or turkey. Use a hacksaw to cut bones or cane to length. Cut strips of leather and punch holes in the strips, as shown. White and red wooden beads can be used on this necklace.

FEATHERED COLLAR NECKLACE

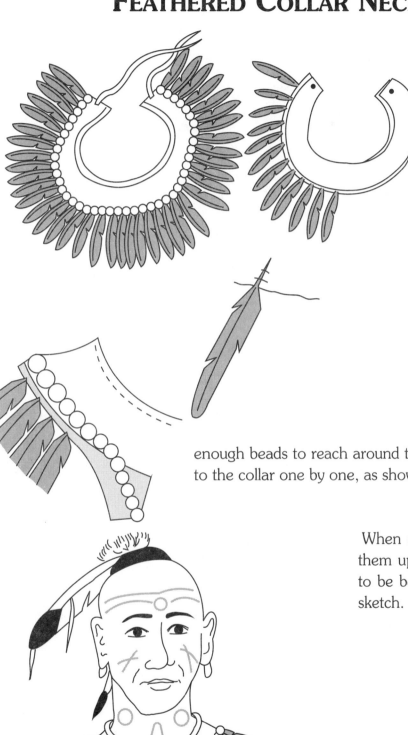

Two identical layers of 3"-4" wide rounded leather are the base for the necklace, as shown in the sketch.

Red cardinal feathers or any small bird wing or tail feathers can be used. The feathers are spaced a proper distance apart and sewn or glued on the upper side of the bottom layer of leather.

The upper layer of leather is now sewn on top of the bottom layer of leather. String enough beads to reach around the collar, then sew the beads to the collar one by one, as shown in the sketch.

When sewing the beads down, line them up so the feathers will appear to be between each bead. Refer to sketch.

NOTE: *Many birds are protected by law and the use of their feathers forbidden. Check the laws, both federal and state, before using bird feathers in your projects.*

FRINGED AND BEADED NECKLACE

The above is my reproduction of a Cherokee necklace.   The original necklace was in a personal house-museum belonging to a man everyone called Mr. Edds. He and I talked for hours about his collection. Upon learning about my work on this book , he allowed me to photograph some of his Cherokee collection. Mr. Edds has since passed away.

The necklace used as a pattern for the one above was over one hundred years old and had been passed down through generations of a Cherokee family before becoming a part of Mr. Edds collection.

Private collections of art and artifacts are another invaluable resource for authentic Cherokee designs and patterns.

On the next page, there are instructions for making the necklace shown above.

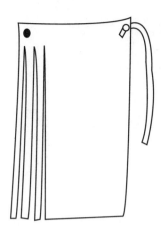

Cut a piece of deerskin or chamois skin 6" wide and 13 $\frac{3}{4}$" long. It is a good idea to lay the leather on a protected surface when using a utility knife to cut the fringe. Scissors can be used.

This necklace has sixteen fringes. The beads are yellow $\frac{1}{2}$" wooden beads. The blue tubular beads are $\frac{3}{8}$". I cut the fringe $\frac{1}{4}$" wide and the neck portion of the necklace is $1\frac{1}{4}$" wide.

Two holes are cut at the top edge of this necklace. Tie strings are then put through the slots. Cut the tie strings 15" long and $\frac{3}{8}$" wide. One end of the tie string is knotted before inserting it through the slot or hole, as shown in the sketch above.

Start stringing the beads on the left side of the fringes. If you have trouble stringing the beads, tie a thread and needle to the end of each fringe. Then use the needle and thread to pull the fringe through the beads.

Refer to the photograph for the proper order of stringing the beads. As each order of beads are strung on a fringe, make a knot at the end of the last bead, as shown in the sketch below. The beads are seven to a fringe and are spaced equal distances apart.

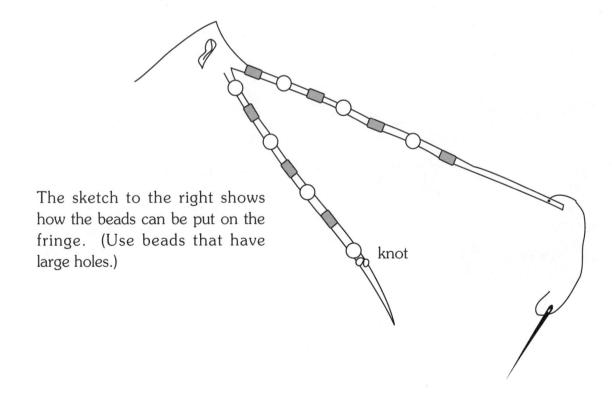

The sketch to the right shows how the beads can be put on the fringe. (Use beads that have large holes.)

knot

BEARCLAW, TEETH AND BONE NECKLACES

Imitation bear claw and wooden bead necklace. The long tubular bead is made from a piece of river cane to imitate a bone bead.

The sketch to the left shows how bear claws can be strung between copper tubular beads.

If you have trouble getting animal teeth, claws, and bones, try whittling them from wood using a pocket knife. River cane can be cut and sanded into long tubular imitation bones. Use a drill for any holes needed. Tubular bones can also be made from chicken or turkey wing and leg bones. A hacksaw is used to cut bones into the desired lengths.

The large round beads can be obtained from a craft store. Round wooden beads are a good substitute for shell beads.

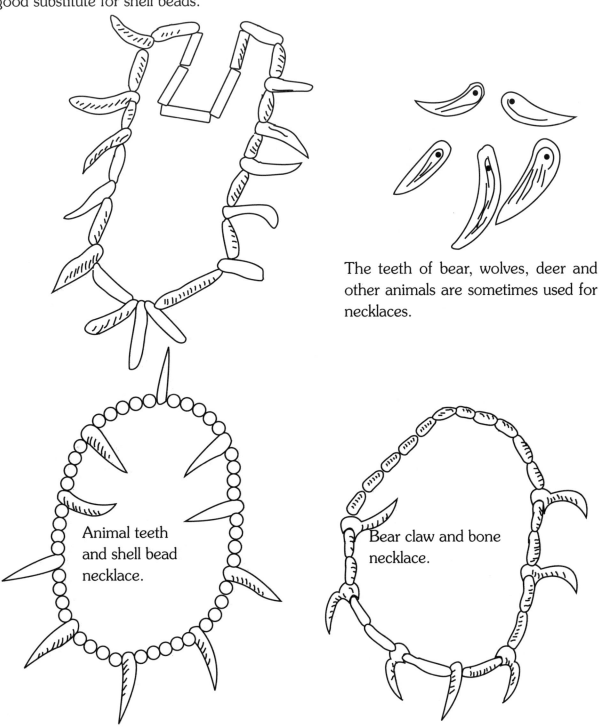

The teeth of bear, wolves, deer and other animals are sometimes used for necklaces.

Animal teeth and shell bead necklace.

Bear claw and bone necklace.

MEDICINE MAN'S BEARCLAW NECKLACE

The Medicine Man of the Cherokees sometimes wore a necklace made of the claws of the bear. It took great courage to kill a bear for its claws and hide. The claws were removed from the paws, cleaned and a hole bored through each claw to make a necklace.

In the above photograph, a bear claw necklace is shown. There are two paws as well as individual claws on the necklace. Round wooden beads and long tubular beads are used on the necklace.

Seeing a Medicine Man wearing such a necklace would impress one that he had great power and wisdom.

There is an old story among the Cherokee that long ago a part of the tribe got tired of living as humans, so they went into the forest to live and became what was known as the "Bear Clan." Perhaps that is why the Cherokee give such great attention and importance to the bear.

The above necklace is patterned after one seen at "The Museum of the Cherokee Indian" in Cherokee, North Carolina.

If possible, find river cane which has turned a light brown. Cut the cane into 32 pieces about 1½" long by ³/₈" wide. Refer to the sketch below.

You can use a coping saw or hacksaw to cut the river cane into long tubular beads. Since river cane is already hollow inside, it makes very good beads. A wire can be run through each bead if needed to get any inside residue out. Sometimes the wire will have to be heated to burn out the cork in each bead. When each bead has been cut to size, file the ends into a tapered shape, as shown below. An electric grinding machine is ideal to sand wooden tubular beads.

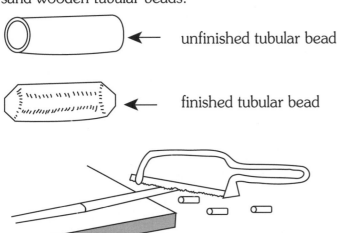

← unfinished tubular bead

← finished tubular bead

Shown above is how a hacksaw is used to cut each tubular bead.

At the left is a wooden bead used in the place of shell beads. Wooden beads can be obtained at craft stores. Use uncolored beads. You will need 31 wooden beads, ³/₈" wide. The two largest wood beads are ½" wide.

Imitation bear claws can be marked out on a pine board ½" thick, then cut out with a coping saw. Next the claws are whittled to the shape seen in the sketch to the left. Plastic bear claws can be bought at a leather craft store.

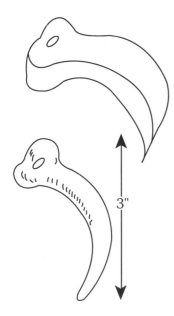

Once each claw has been whittled, sanded and painted with either brown or black paint, bore a hole through each claw. You will need 18 claws.

Another way to color each claw is to hold the claw above the flame of a candle. Darken all parts of the claws, then polish them with grease or varnish. Some Native Americans, when making an ordinary bear claw necklace, paint the joint end of the claw red, white, or yellow.

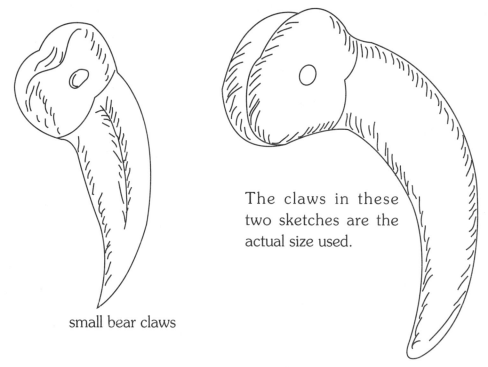

small bear claws

The claws in these two sketches are the actual size used.

Select five bear claws and use a piece of wire to lace the claws together in a circular fashion as shown in the sketch below. Use more wire, twisting it around each claw to hold it in position. The ends of the wire should be at the back of the bear paw.

Try to get the three front claws to stay in position as shown in the sketch to the left.

You may have to look at a picture of a bear to get a good idea of how the paw is to look.

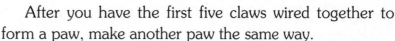
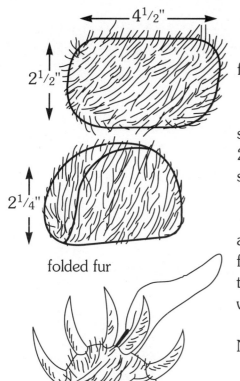

folded fur

stitching the fur

large flat bead

After you have the first five claws wired together to form a paw, make another paw the same way.

Cut two pieces of imitation black fur like the shape seen in the sketch to the left. It should be about 4 $^1/_2$" by 2$^1/_2$" or larger. Your measurements may have to vary somewhat, since these are handmade bear claws.

Fold the piece of fur in half, as shown in the sketch above left. Insert the bear claw part inside of the folded fur. Use black thread and a needle to stitch the fur hems together between each claw. Do the other claw the same way. Rough the fur up to hide the stitches.

Note: The fur should flow toward the claws.

The large flat-like bead at the bottom can be made of bone, wood or plastic.

An imitation bone can be made by cutting pieces of plastic from a clorox jug (or similar white plastic). Place the pieces of plastic in a heap in a metal lid. Next, put the lid on a gas burner.

NOTE: *Be careful not to breath fumes from plastic. They might be dangerous to your health.*

When it is all melted together use a case knife to paddle it in shape of the above flat bead. Do not allow the plastic to melt all the way. When you have the rough shape of the bead, $^3/_8$" thick, $^3/_4$" wide, and 1 $^1/_2$" long, remove it from the stove. Use a pot holder or glove when moving the lid from the stove. You can run cold water over the bead to speed up the cooling process.

Bottom hole goes straight through.

Use a drill to bore a hole all the way through the bead in two places. You can use a heated end of a wire to push the holes through the bead, as shown in the sketch at the left.

Now that *every part* to the necklace is ready, it can be put together in the order shown in the sketch below. Use a very strong piece of twine about 5 $\frac{1}{2}$' long to string the necklace parts. Any excess string can be cut off when finished. Tie the ends of the string together with three knots.

Perhaps as you wear this Medicine Man's necklace you will be able to feel its power!

Cut a leather string $\frac{1}{4}$" wide by 10" long and lace through the flat bead at the bottom. Use a 1 $\frac{1}{2}$" bead on the string tassel.

SILVER CRESCENT GORGET NECKLACES

Another type of necklace the Cherokees wore was the half-moon or crescent silver gorget. It was worn both before and after the removal period. Gorgets of this kind were given to the Cherokee by the white man as medals of honor. Some of the gorget medals had inscriptions or symbols, while others were plain.

No doubt, native silver smiths, such as Sequoyah, made silver gorgets for their people in imitation of the ones the white man gave to important men of the tribe.

Most of the old crescent gorgets were made of "German Silver." Some were made of brass or copper. Today, gorgets can be made from 14-gauge aluminum. Chrome might be used if available. A coping saw can be used to cut out the form.

To get the convex bend of the gorget, it will have to be hammered out on a block of wood that has a hollowed out mold. My sketch below should make this process clear. A vise may have to be used to hold the metal as you are cutting it out and filing rough edges to a smooth finish. A drill can be used to make any holes needed for the tie ribbons.

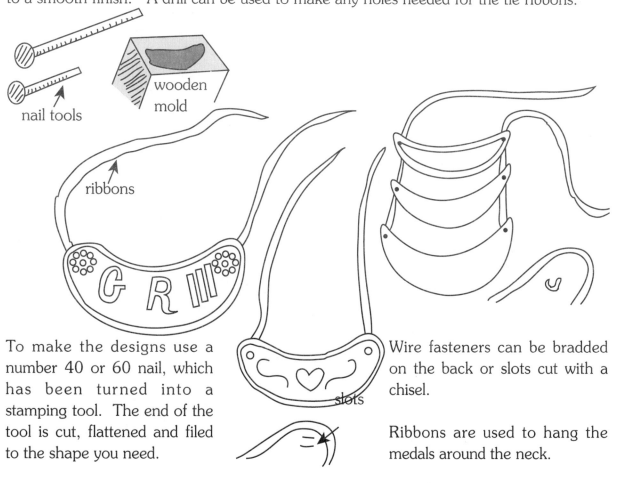

nail tools

wooden mold

ribbons

slots

To make the designs use a number 40 or 60 nail, which has been turned into a stamping tool. The end of the tool is cut, flattened and filed to the shape you need.

Wire fasteners can be bradded on the back or slots cut with a chisel.

Ribbons are used to hang the medals around the neck.

WRIST AND ARM BANDS

The Cherokee, like most of the Southeastern tribes, wore wrist and arm bands. Early arm and wrist bands would have been made of leather, woven material or shell beads. Later on, in the historic period, German Silver was used. Some arm bands were made of copper.

Arm and wrist bands made of metal seen in early drawings and paintings were given to the Cherokee by white traders. Later, Cherokees made their own arm bands of metal.

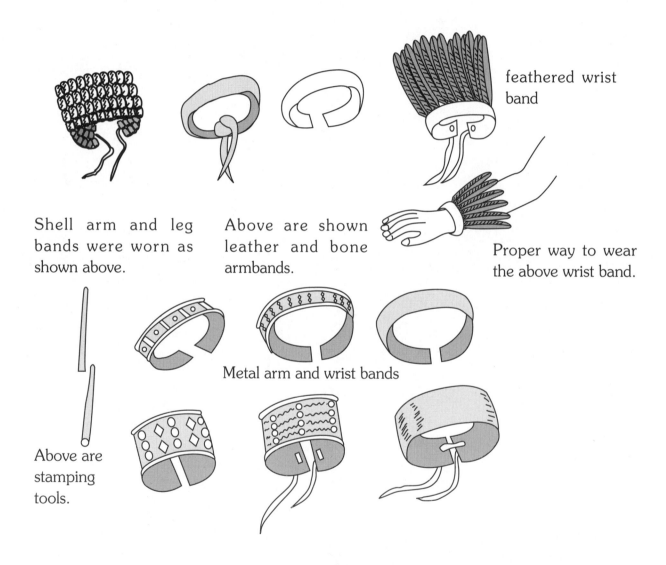

feathered wrist band

Shell arm and leg bands were worn as shown above.

Above are shown leather and bone armbands.

Proper way to wear the above wrist band.

Above are stamping tools.

Metal arm and wrist bands

The designs on metal arm and wrist bands are stamped with similar tools in the above sketch. A hack saw is used to cut the length and width of the metal.

Use a file to smooth down the rough edges. A small chisel-pointed tool makes straight lines, diamonds and mountain designs. To make the circles, a tool as shown below can be used.

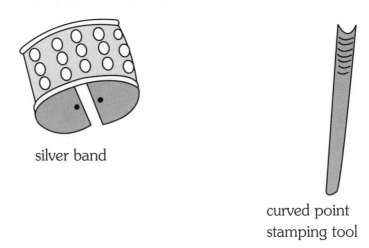

silver band

curved point
stamping tool

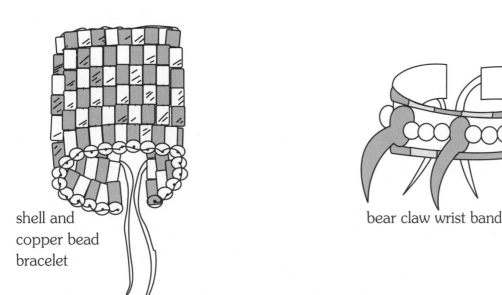

shell and
copper bead
bracelet

bear claw wrist band

Some bracelets were made on a loom of mixed shell and copper beads . The pattern could be an alternating design.

The bear claw wrist band was probably worn by a medicine man or high ranking warrior. A leather band can be used for the base. Quill or seed beads can be used to form the designs. Plastic bear claws strung with large white beads are sewn to the band. Leather strings are used for the tie-strings.

POUCHES AND SHOULDER BAGS

The Cherokee had no pockets on their clothing for carrying fire-making tools, personal items, paint, food, etc.

Larger items were carried in shoulder bags having a finger-woven carrying strap. These bags were beautiful when decorated with embroidery, seed beads, tin cones, hair and yarn tassels. The shoulder bag was needed on long trips and worn on special occasions.

Pipe bags were used to store both sacred pipes and personal pipes. These bags were often very colorful and skillfully made.

Bags of various kinds, shown on the following pages, are typical of the Southeast and are decorated with Cherokee pottery and basket designs.

The bags shown can be made of any soft leather, but deerskin is suggested. Cloth or imitation leather can be used as a substitute. Fringe for cloth bags can be made of chamois skin.

 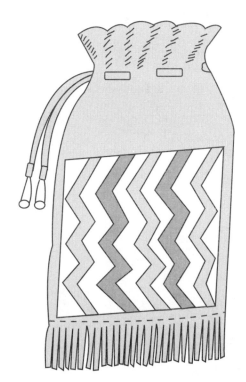

Decorations, choice of colors for designs, even the designs themselves should have a meaning consistent with the purpose of the bag.

EMBROIDERED POUCH

The personal pouch above is made of chamois skin but can be made of deerskin or any other soft leather. It is made of two pieces of leather. The embroidery work on this pouch is done in navy blue, red, purple, and black. Designs on this pouch depict thunder, lightning and the mountains.

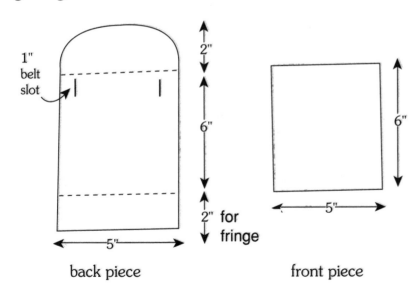

back piece

front piece

First, cut out two pieces of leather using the measurements given in the sketches to the left.

Before the bag parts are sewn together, the designs must be drawn and embroidered on the front piece.

This kind of pouch can be made and decorated in various ways.

Make two one-inch belt slots as shown in the sketch above.

A carrying strap can be attached at the back.

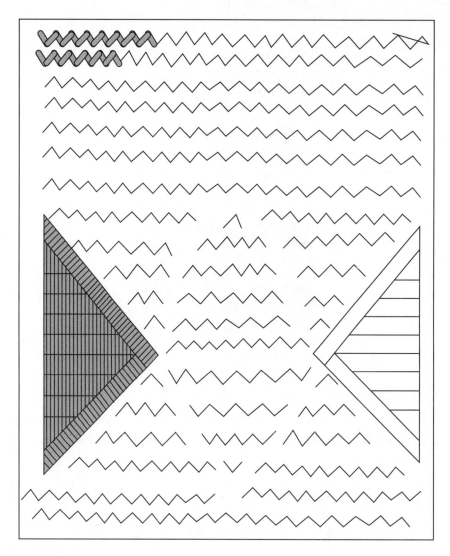

Draw the outline of the design onto the leather of the front piece using a pencil or pen. To start embroidering, knot one end of the embroidery thread. Then come up with the needle from the underside of the leather at the corner of the design.

To make the lightning design, refer to the sketch below to the left. Do all the lightning and thunder designs first, then the mountain designs. The mountain designs are done in a series of parallel stitches.

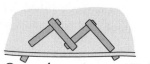

Over-lapping stitches make lightning designs.

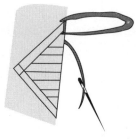

As shown in the sketch to the left, cross over with the thread, go back down into the leather with the needle and back up, repeating the process over and over.

Keep the stitches on the mountain designs close together so the leather underneath will not show. Do not pull the stitches too tight or you will shrink the leather. Use about three strands of thread when doing embroidery.

It may be a good idea to get some help in learning embroidery stitches.

Line the front embroidery piece up with the back piece.

Sew up the sides and the bottom using the in-and-out stitch, as shown in the sketch below. The sewing is about an $1/8$" from the edge.

Using scissors, fringe the bottom of the pouch. Each fringe is $1/4$" wide.

Next cut a slit in the center of the flap. The slit is about $3/8$" from the edge and $1/2$" long. (Refer to the sketch below.)

Open view of pouch

Make a wooden peg from a match stick, small dowel or other suitable piece of wood for the fastener of the pouch. Sew the notched peg to the pouch aligning it with the slit in the flap as shown in the photograph above and sketch below.

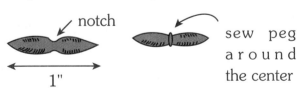

notch

sew peg around the center

1"

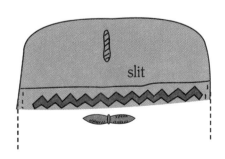

slit

EMBROIDERED TOBACCO POUCH

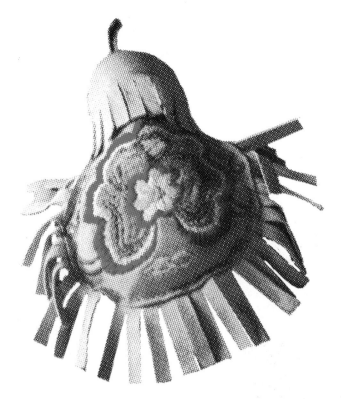

The above tobacco pouch can be made of soft leather such as deerskin or chamois. Floral designs are embroidered with red, light green, and yellow.

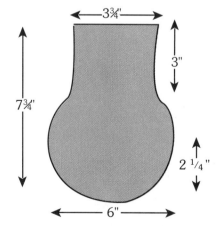

Cut two pieces of leather the same size, as in the sketch to the left; then cut a piece of fringe 14" long by 2 1/4" wide.

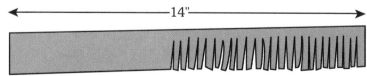

The fringe is sewn between the edges of the bag as shown in the photograph above.

Do all of the embroidery on the front piece before sewing the bag together. Use the in-and-out stitch when sewing the fringe in between the outer seam of the pouch.

Actual size of pouch parts, front and back.

This is an outline of the floral designs and colors.

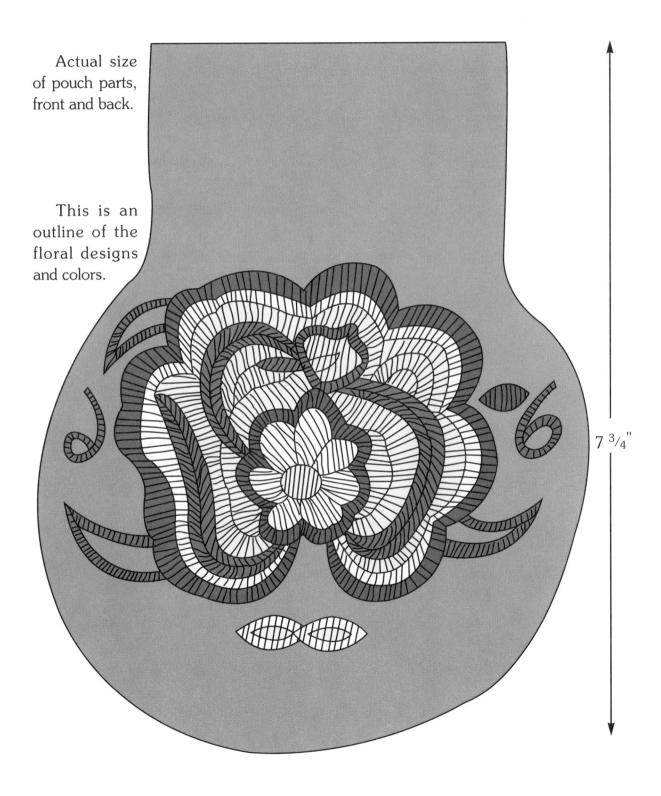

7 $^{3}/_{4}$"

Sew fringe upside down and flip over.

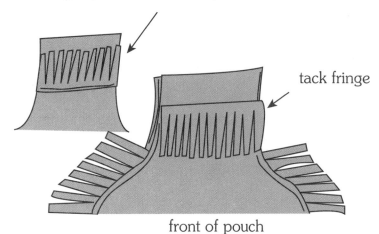

tack fringe

front of pouch

Before you sew the front and back of the pouch together, cut a piece of fringe 2 $1/4$ " wide by 3 $3/4$ " long.

Sew this strip of fringe 1" down from the top of the pouch, on the front, as seen in the sketch to the far left. It is sewn upside down, then flipped over and tacked at each side.

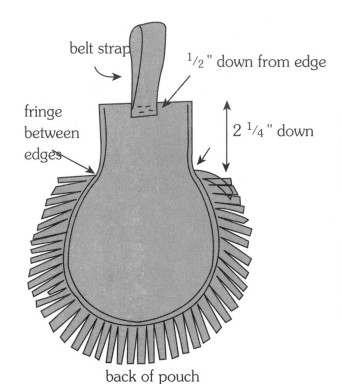

belt strap

$1/2$ " down from edge

fringe between edges

2 $1/4$ " down

back of pouch

Now cut a strap $5/8$ " wide and 6" long. Double this strap and sew it to the top of the back part of pouch, as shown in the sketch.

You are ready now to sew the front and back of the pouch together, inserting the fringed strip between the front and back edges.

The pouch is now finished and can be worn on your belt or sash.

PAINTED POUCH

This pouch is made of two pieces of deerskin. You can use chamois skin or other soft leather.

Two strings made of leather are cut $3/8$" wide and 16" long or longer and used to close the top of the pouch.

Cut slots for carrying strings.

Lace strings in opposite directions and tie ends in a knot.

Place the front piece on the back piece as shown in sketch below, sewing the two parts together, using the in-and-out stitch.

Cut the 6" fringe after all sewing is finished.

back piece

18"

18"

front piece

12"

6"

Mark designs in pencil. Go back over the designs with a soldering gun or wood burning tool with a fine point.

Use red and black enamel paint to color the designs.

BEADED DEERSKIN POUCH 1

The above pouch was made with two pieces of deerskin. The back of the pouch has extra leather for the fringe.

Black and red seed beads are used in the lazy-stitch method to make the designs. Some people call the designs, "the chief's daughters." I prefer to believe the designs are related to the mound builder era and see a likeness to the "forked-eye" design in these symbols. The above symbols are sometimes seen in basket weaves, also.

When earlier Native Americans of the Southeast painted the forked eye design around their eyes, they hoped to receive sight as keen as that of the hawk.

On the following pages are the instructions for making the pouch. Your pouch can be decorated with any kind of design or color of beads to make it personally yours.

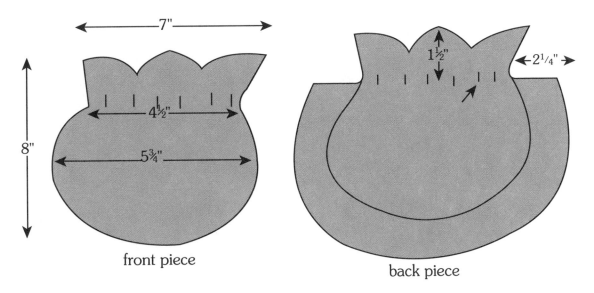

front piece

back piece

In the two sketches above are the measurements of the front and back of the pouch. After you make the front part, lay it on your leather and mark out the back piece $2^{1}/_{4}$" larger around the bottom and sides. The extra is for the fringe.

Before sewing the pouch together, draw the designs on the front piece and do the beading as shown in the photograph above.

Below is a sketch of the actual size of the designs on my pouch.

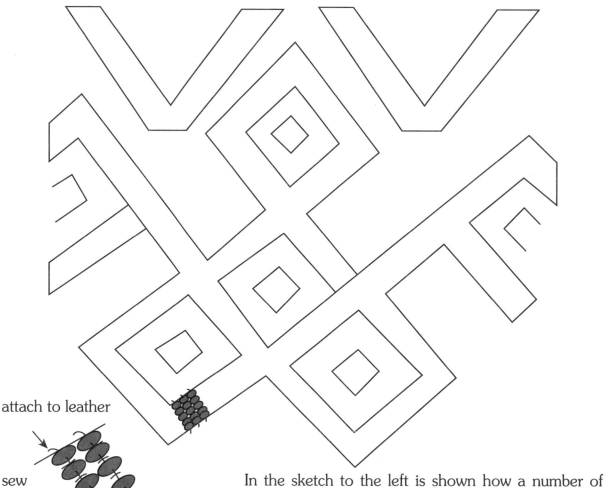

attach to leather

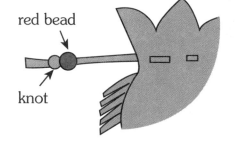

sew
down
between

red bead

knot

In the sketch to the left is shown how a number of beads are put on a thread starting at one side of the design and attaching the other end of the thread to the leather.

Sew down between every one or two beads. Once one row is completed move on to the next row and then the other rows of the design.

When putting the beads on the thread to fill up a space, you will be able to determine how many it takes to fill a row.

After all beading is finished, sew the pouch together, cut the fringe, and make a draw string $1/2$ " by 20". Lace the draw string to the pouch and add a red wooden bead to each string at the end. Make a knot after each red bead.

BEADED DEERSKIN POUCH 2

The deerskin pouch in the photograph is patterned after one seen in the Museum of the Cherokee Indian in Cherokee, North Carolina.

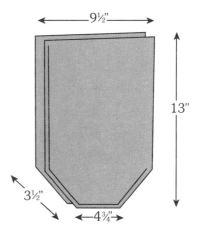

I used the above measurements folding a piece of leather and cutting it to size.

Do not sew the bag together until all the beading is finished.

The following pages illustrate the procedure I used for making this pouch.

Use red flannel cloth for the background of the beadwork. This cloth is 7 $\frac{1}{2}$" by 10".

Draw the designs on the cloth. Then use seed beads to make the designs. The method of spot beading is used. Beading can be started on the "four direction" symbol in the center.

Attach the thread at one side of the design and string on the number of beads it takes to go to the other side. Attach the thread there.

Come back up with the needle, sewing down every two beads. You may want to put the cloth on an embroidery hoop to keep it stretched.

Below is a photograph of the beading in progress.

NOTE: *It might be helpful to use a beadworking book to become familiar with beading techniques. Check with your craft supplier, book store, library or publisher of this book.*

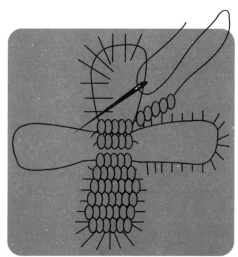

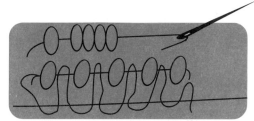

Sew in between each bead.

This sketch shows how to take the thread underneath the cloth and back up with the needle to start a new row of beads. Every one or two beads in a row is sewn down before going on to the next row as shown above.

Seed beads should be separated by color, using shallow dishes or saucers to hold them while beading. I usually check the number of beads on the thread twice to make sure I have enough to make a row. If you have too many beads for a row, just pass the needle back through the eye of the bead. If after sewing a row of beads down, you notice there are too many beads, use a pair of narrow nose pliers to break away the unwanted bead, being careful not to cut the thread

To make a "Rosette" or round design such as a sun, star, or circle symbol, sew down one bead in the center of the circle. With the needle start a circle of beads around the center as shown in the sketch below. It usually takes 7 or 8 beads to encircle the center bead, as shown in the sketch. To complete the circle, pass the needle through the eye of the first bead on the strand.

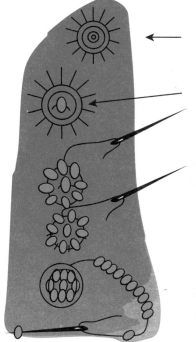

← design

center bead

Pull out the slack, then sew down every bead in a circle, as shown in the sketch to the left.

Lay another circle of beads around the previous row or circle of beads, adding the needed number to complete a circle.

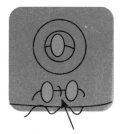

Sew between beads

Connect the ends together, pulling out the slack, proceeding to sew down every one or two beads of that circle. Keep making these rows of beads until the design is the size you want.

Creating straight lines with beads is shown below. Attach the end of the thread on the drawn out line and string on seven or eight beads, pushing them to the end of the thread. Insert the needle into the cloth at the end of the strung beads, as shown, pulling out the slack. Next, bring the needle back up through the cloth and through the eye of the last bead strung on the thread. String on more beads and repeat the process until the line of beads goes all around the pouch and connects as seen in the photograph on page 273.

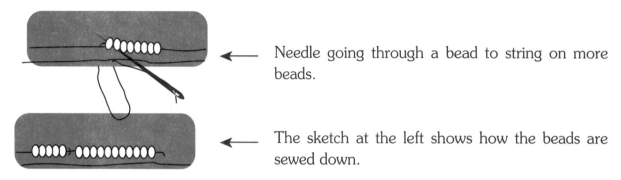

← Needle going through a bead to string on more beads.

← The sketch at the left shows how the beads are sewed down.

When beading the lightning design around the border of the pouch, string 5-6 beads per strand. Insert needle into the cloth and string on the proper number of beads, attaching the thread. Pull out the slack, then go back and sew down the beads, coming back up through the eye of the last bead, as shown below. Now string on more beads and begin the other angle of the design, using the same method. Repeat the process over and over until completed.

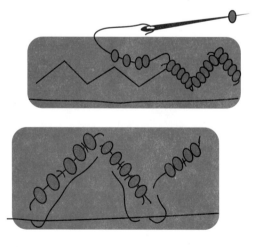

These sketches of the lightening design are given to help further your understanding of beadwork.

The broken lines in the sketch at bottom left is the thread underneath the cloth.

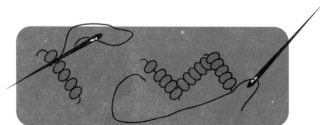

Other books on beadwork can be found at your local bookstore, the library or ordered from the publisher of this book.

After most of the beadwork on the cloth is finished, you may want to take the cloth off the embroidery hoop.

Sew the leather pouch together. Use the in-and-out stitch on the pouch. Then turn the pouch inside out. The rough side of the leather should be the outside of the pouch.

Put the beaded cloth on the pouch as shown in the photographs of the completed pouch. Use a whip-stitch to sew the beaded cloth in place. Keep the edges of the cloth turned under as you sew it into place.

Pinch the cloth together with the leather as you sew. This gives the leather a puckered look.

Once the beaded cloth has been sewn on, do the rest of the bead work.

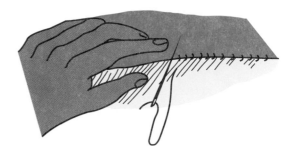

Shown above is the pouch with the beaded cloth sewn in place
and with the final beadwork almost finished.

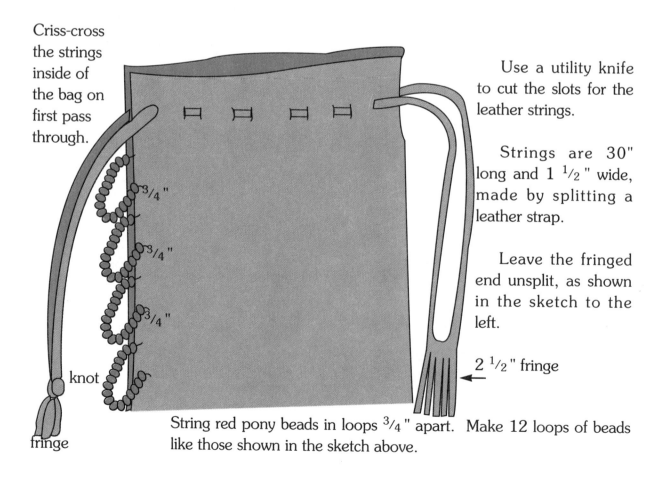

Criss-cross
the strings
inside of
the bag on
first pass
through.

Use a utility knife
to cut the slots for the
leather strings.

Strings are 30"
long and 1 $\frac{1}{2}$ " wide,
made by splitting a
leather strap.

Leave the fringed
end unsplit, as shown
in the sketch to the
left.

2 $\frac{1}{2}$ " fringe

$\frac{3}{4}$ "

$\frac{3}{4}$ "

$\frac{3}{4}$ "

knot

fringe

String red pony beads in loops $\frac{3}{4}$ " apart. Make 12 loops of beads
like those shown in the sketch above.

SMALL CHARM POUCH

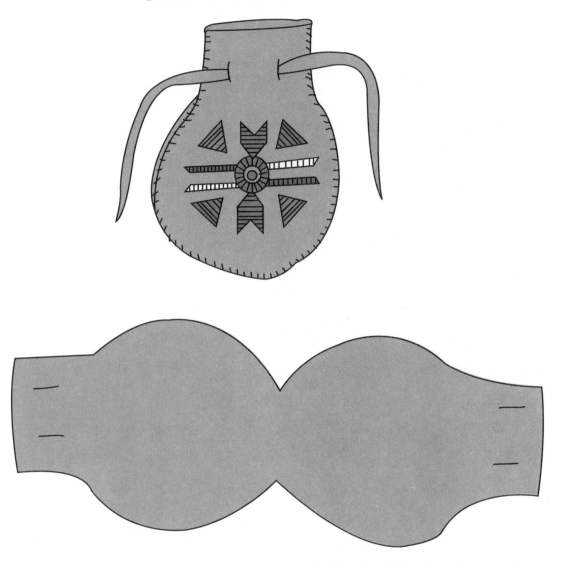

Small pouches, like the one above, were needed by the Cherokee for carrying small items that were used as charms. A charm pouch was usually worn suspended from the neck by a leather string. Most often it was concealed underneath the clothing so it's power could be kept personal.

One of the things often kept in a charm pouch was a crystal. A person keeps his pouch with him most of the time. It is considered important to let no one see the contents of such a sacred pouch, less it's power be weakened.

When making a charm pouch use soft leather such as deerskin, cutting it to the shape shown above. Mark sacred power symbols or designs on it that have spiritual significance for you. Embroider, bead, or paint the designs on the pouch, then sew up the sides, lace on a string, and add your own special items that have a spiritual significance for you.

MEDICINE BAG

The Medicine Bag shown to the left is one I made for myself.

This bag is made of semi-soft leather, and the designs are done with seed beads.

The zig-zag designs on the above bag stand for the thunder and lightning. A sun symbol can be seen in the center, symbolic of "The Great Man Above." I used a seven pointed star to represent the seven clans of the Cherokee. A green plant symbol is used to represent healing herbs. The deer symbol is for the Deer Clan. Included is a rattlesnake symbol for sacredness and power. A bear symbol is for the office of the Medicine Man. The yellow half-moon symbols are for power during the night, and the red sun stands for power during the day.

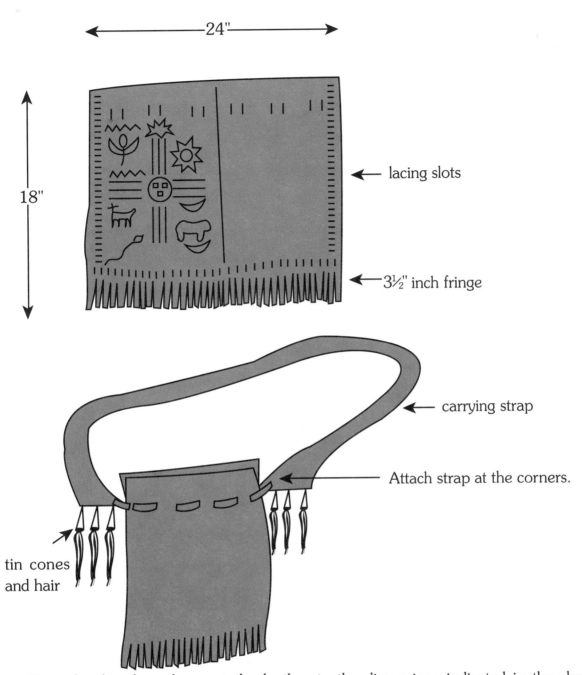

24"

18"

← lacing slots

← 3½" inch fringe

carrying strap

Attach strap at the corners.

tin cones
and hair

To make the above bag, cut the leather to the dimensions indicated in the sketch. Draw the designs on the leather, then spot bead all symbols. Now lace the folded bag along the sides and bottom with leather lacing string.

A carrying strap may be made of leather, or a finger-woven sash can be used. The strap is attached at the end corners as shown above. Decorations for the carrying strap might include tin cones and hair tassels. Beadwork or painted designs can be put on the carrying strap.

Things such as a crow skull, string of red or white beads, etc. were placed in the bag.

QUILLED POUCH

Feathers are looped on the ends so they can be attached to the bag.

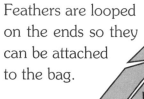

Use 3 or 4 inch feathers.

The above pouch can be made of deerskin with red and black leather or ribbon stripes. Quillwork and seed beads are used for the designs.

A finger-woven sash can be used for a carrying strap.

pattern

MEDICINE POUCH

The above pouch or bag is made of a thick surgical towel which I received after treatment for the loss of my left hand.

Designs on the bag were drawn in a way to portray my tragic accident and how "The Great Man Above" healed me after the doctor had done all he could do for me. You can also see in the designs how I regained courage to make Native American crafts again.

It has embroidery and beadwork. Thin bone-like beads, red cloth, crow beads, wooden beads, and colored feathers are also used.

The bag is simple to make. Fold the towel to the shape shown to the left, then sew up the sides, and add tie strings.

A carrying strap can be added to the bag if desired.

SHOULDER BAG

Many of the Southeastern tribes, including the Cherokee, were carrying shoulder bags during the 1830-40 period. These bags were usually beautifully decorated and had finger-woven sashes attached.

Below is a shoulder bag made totally of yarn. The bag was woven on an upright loom. Designs were done by using the twining method of weaving (see next page). The bag is usually worn on the right hip with the strap crossing the chest and over the left shoulder.

On the following pages are some of the details for making such a woven bag. I prefer to make such bags of cloth or leather because weaving is very time consuming.

an upright loom

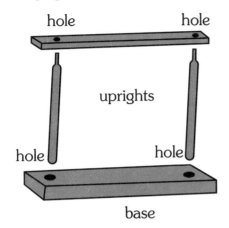

The bag on the preceding page, was made on a loom like the one shown here.

My loom was made using a thin board with drilled holes for the top. The two uprights were made from sections of a broom-stick. (The pointed ends were whittled with a pocket knife.) A 2x4 piece of wood was used for the base.

Tie on a doubled horizontal string, because when all weaving is finished this part of the bag is sewn together and becomes the bottom of the bag.

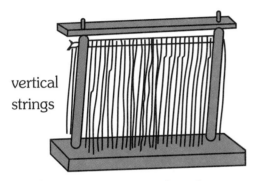

The assembled loom with a horizontal string tied around the upper part of the uprights.

The vertical strings are cut the desired length, then doubled and attached to one of the horizontal strings. Once a vertical string is doubled as shown in the sketch, the top is folded over and the two hanging strings are pulled through the loop (steps 1, 2 & 3 as shown). These strings go all around the horizontal string.

When all vertical strings are in place, the actual weaving can begin. I used two horizontal strings to weave across the vertical strings to make the designs on the bag.

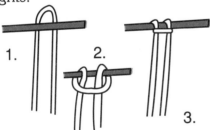

Steps 1, 2 and 3 are used in tying on verticals.

Illustrated above is the weaving of two horizontal strings.

Two red strings will make the red stripes, two blue strings the blue stripes, and two black strings the black stripes. To stop off with one color, tie on the color you want for the design at that particular starting point. Cut off the unwanted color, keeping the splice knot on the inside of the bag.

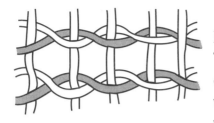

In the sketch to the left is shown white and black horizontal strings being woven across the vertical strings. This method produces the checked designs. Keep the color of yarn you do not want to show on the back side of the vertical strings. It will take several rows of this method of weaving to make the checked designs.

Keep the horizontal weaving pushed up and even to make the designs look right. I won't go into any further details on how to make this bag. You may want to pursue a greater understanding of weaving through other books from your craft supplier or library.

The above shoulder bag is made of leather and is quilled with various designs. Tin cone tassels are attached from two of the diamond designs at the top flap. Instead of black hair tassels, red hair tassels were used on some shoulder bags. Yarn tassels can also be used. Often tassels were put at the edges of the bag, along the sides, bottom and the lower edge of the flap.

Beads of all sizes can be used, especially seed beads on this style of bag. Along with beadwork, you may want to use embroidered designs or ribbon-work.

If using cloth, try to get blanket cloth, velvet, flannel, wool, or other thick cloth. Cloth colors for these bags were most often black, red, or dark blue.

Whatever way you may choose to make one of these bags, stay true to Cherokee designs. The following pages show more examples of shoulder bags.

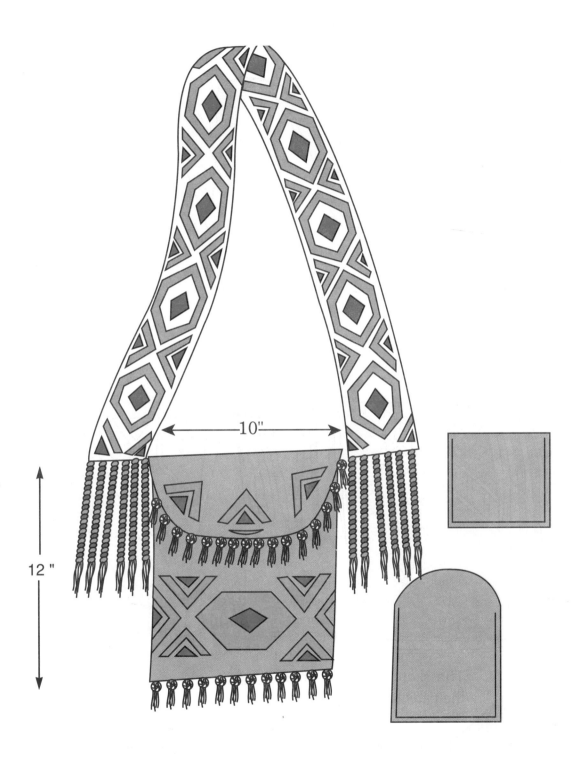

Above is a deerskin beaded shoulder pouch with a finger-woven sash. The front piece is beaded first then sewn to the back piece. You can bead the flap later and add the yarn tassels in the proper positions.

The fastener for the flap can be a string tie, wooden-peg fastener, button, or a snap.

These two shoulder bags are made of cloth such as velvet. Beads can be used to form the designs.

Sashes are 3 - 3 $\frac{1}{2}$" wide and long enough to allow the bag to hang at hip level.

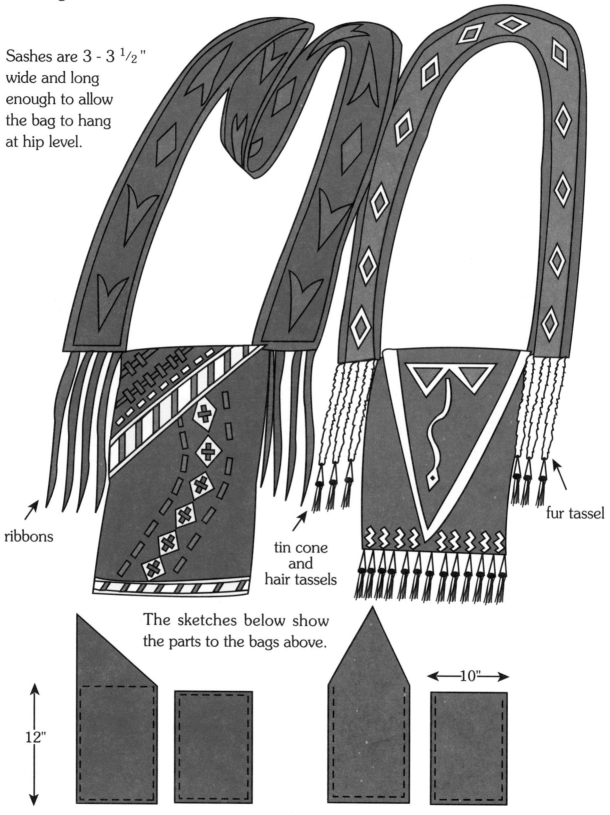

ribbons

tin cone
and
hair tassels

fur tassel

The sketches below show the parts to the bags above.

12"

←——10"——→

An embroidered shoulder bag and a quilled shoulder bag are illustrated below.

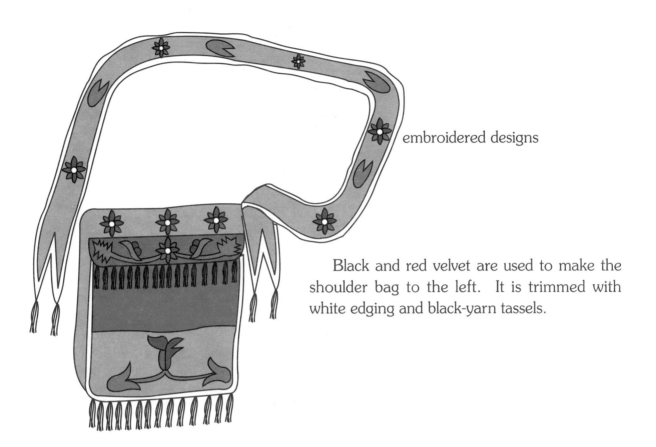

embroidered designs

Black and red velvet are used to make the shoulder bag to the left. It is trimmed with white edging and black-yarn tassels.

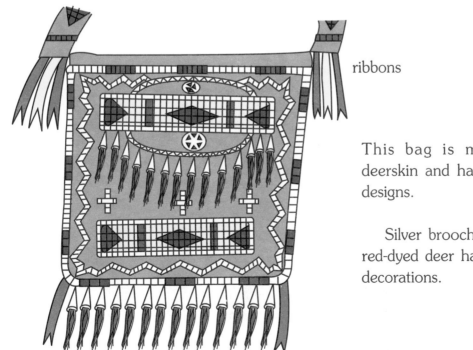

ribbons

This bag is made of black-dyed deerskin and has quillwork or beaded designs.

Silver brooches and tin cones with red-dyed deer hair tassels are used for decorations.

KNIFE HOLSTERS

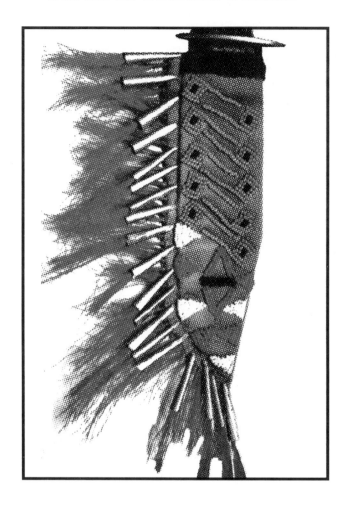

The picture of a Cherokee warrior, or any Cherokee man in the typical clothing of his tribe, would not be complete without the knife and knife holster.

The knife holster was most often very elaborate and beautifully made. Above is an example of a knife holster using tin cones, hair tassels, and seed beads. Imitation leather is used for the holster material.

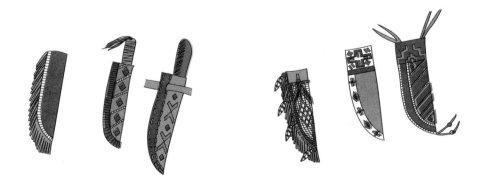

The knife holster itself can be made of rawhide, which was sometimes painted. If leather such as deerskin is used instead of rawhide, then the holster can be quilled or beaded.

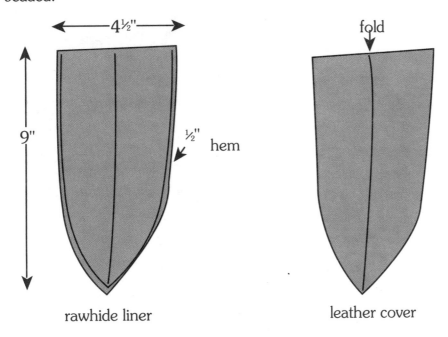

rawhide liner   leather cover

If you are going to use soft leather for a cover to the rawhide inner lining, lay your knife on the rawhide and mark your pattern, as shown in the above sketches. Make both the liner and leather cover at least $1/2$" larger than the knife.

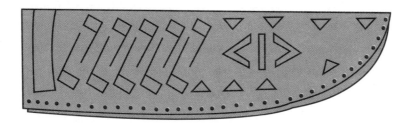

Now that you have the leather cover ready, fold it in half as shown in the above sketch. Mark your designs.

Make the holes for the stitching at the outside edges of the holster. A punch or nail can be used to make the holes. Use strong twine, leather string, or sinew to sew the holster together around the side.

SPOT BEADING AND HAIR TASSELS

Stitch the leather cover over the top of the rawhide liner, stitching around the top and down the side.

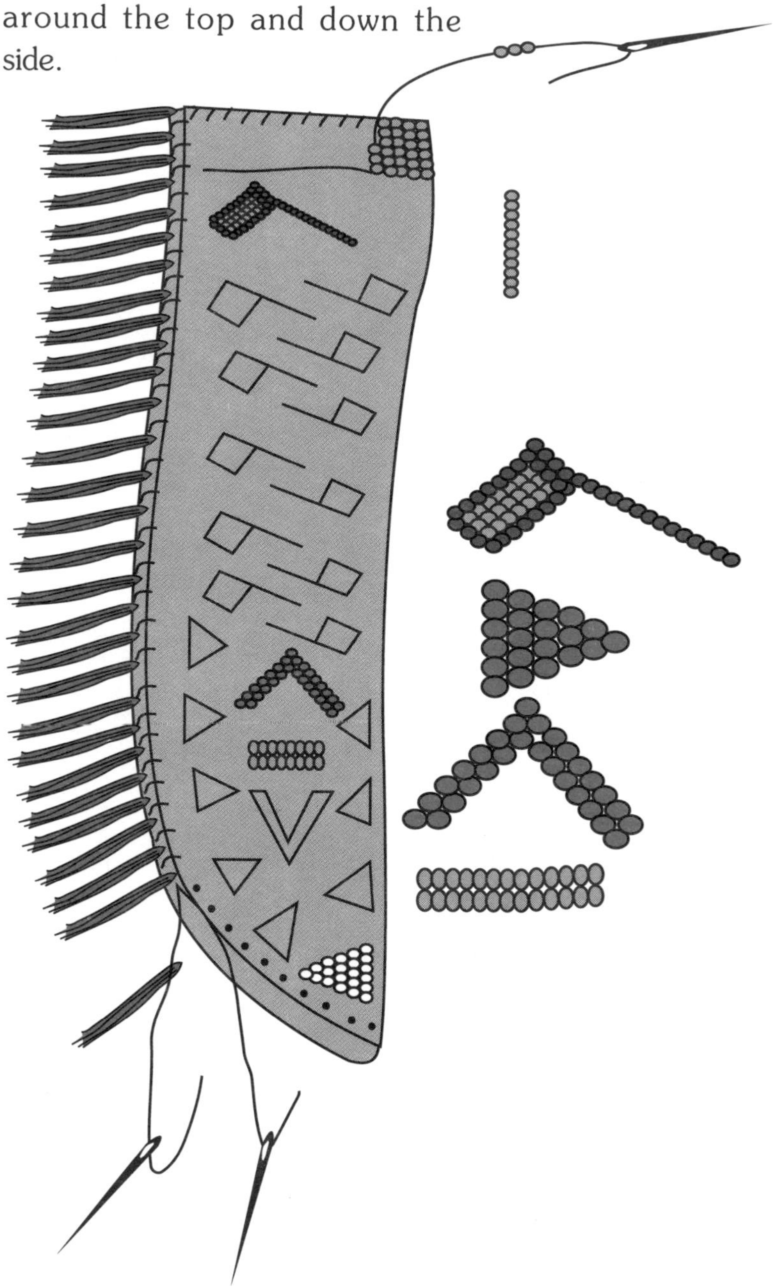

Tack down every two or three beads. I used 8 black beads per row to make the black strip at the top of the holster.

Put the proper number of beads on the thread, then go back, sewing the beads down.

If you have not already mastered the art of beading, consider painting or embroidering the designs onto the leather.

Some examples of beaded designs are shown.

String on each tassel one by one, using needle and thread as shown in the above sketch. Push the tassel's end between the two edges of leather, then use the other needle to form a holding stitch as shown. The second needle sews up the edge of the holster.

Leave space between these tassels to add tin cone tassels if desired (see page #295).

Making The Tassels For The Holster

←——3½"——→

First you will need red-dyed hair or unraveled grass rope.

Use 30 to 40 bristles per tassel.
Good guess work is the trick!

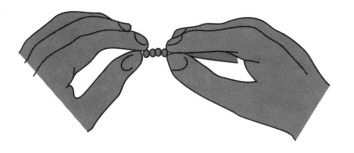

a. Hold one end of the bundle between the thumb and forefinger of the left hand, twisting or rolling it between those fingers. At the same time, hold it firmly with the thumb and forefinger of the right hand.

b. While the tension is still on the fibers, loop part of the end of the fibers back, forming a loop, as shown in the sketch at the left.

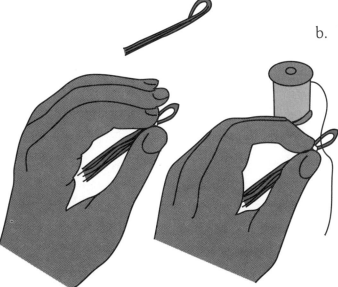

c. Now, while still holding the fibers in place, wrap thread around the neck of the tassel. Wrap several times, and tie the ends of the thread in two or three knots. Cut off the ends of the thread on the tassel as shown below.

Cut ends off.

finished tassel

Make about 65 tassels for this project.

MAKING TIN CONES FOR THE TASSELS

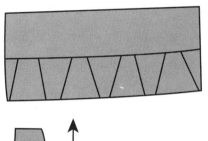

1½"

a. Use a tin can, cutting off the top rim and bottom rim with scissors. When working with tin, be extra careful not to cut yourself.

b. Roll out the tin to make it flat. Mark a pattern on the metal, as shown in the sketch to the left. The use of a paper or cardboard pattern will help in marking the cones on the metal.

c. Cut out the tin parts of the cones, making each part the same.

d. Bend the tin around a tapered paint brush until the tin cone takes on a "U" shape as shown in the sketch.

e. With pliers, finish bending the cone until the middle seam comes together, shown in the sketch at the left.

f. Make 20 tin cones.

finished cone

METHOD OF FASTENING THE CONE TASSELS

a. Tie a knot on one end of the thread, pulling the thread through the leather from the back of the holster to the front.

b. Now that the thread is on the front of the holster, pass the needle through a tin cone. Push the tin cone all the way up on the thread to the edge of the holster.

c. On the same thread, string on a red-hair tassel. Push the tassel all the way up to the tin cone. It should be about $1/2$" up inside of the cone as you start tightening up the thread.

d. Hold the tin cone in place where it is to be positioned. Insert the needle through the cone pulling up the slack.

e. Pull the needle through the cone. Then go down into the leather with the needle beside the first stitch and to the next cone position, repeating the process to completion, as shown in the sketch to the left.

In the sketch below a carrying strap is sewn on the back of the holster.

KNIFE HOLSTER DESIGNS

Red flannel, leather fringe, and beadwork

Black leather with quill work.

Spot beaded with red paint

Below is a quilled holster with large red beads and feather tassels.

Bead work on black cloth

Red-dyed leather with quills and blue cloth.

GLOSSARY

BELOVED WOMAN a title given to certain important Cherokee women who served in the tribal government.

BONE NEEDLE ancient sewing tool made of a slender bone with a hole in the tip for the thread.

BONE PUNCH ancient tool made of a sharp pointed bone used for making holes in leather.

BREECHCLOUT a length of leather or cloth worn suspended from a belt in the front and back of the body in the loin area.

BROOCH ornamental metal disk attached to clothing, similar to a concho.

CHAMOIS a soft leather made of sheep or goat skin, commonly used today to dry automobiles after washing.

COPING SAW a saw with a narrow blade in a U-shaped frame used for cutting curved lines in wood.

CROW BEAD bead which is 6 by 9 mm. in size.

COWRIE SHELL small oval shaped seashell of a certain sea animal.

CORNER KNOT a term coined by the author to describe a very small pointed stitch made at the corner of an embroidery design.

DEW CLAW functionless digit on the foot of some animals, as on the inner side of a dog's hind leg or above the true hoof in deer, cattle, etc.

EMBROIDERY a process using a needle and various colors of thread or yarn to form ornamental designs on cloth or soft leather.

FINGER WEAVE a process using the fingers to weave or braid strands of yarn into sashes or strips.

FLINT KNIFE an ancient knife-like tool made of flint.

FLUFFS the softer and lighter feathers of any bird or foul other than the wing or tail feathers.

FRINGE narrow strips of loose hanging leather used as ornaments on the sleeves and seams of clothing.

GARTERS bands of leather, braided yarn strips or other material worn below the knees

GORGET a large round shell disk worn as an ornament on a necklace.

HACKSAW a saw for cutting metal consisting of a narrow fine-toothed blade held in a frame.

HAIR PIPE/BONE a long tubular bead made of cow bone.

JINGLERS tinkling metal objects hanging loosly as ornaments on a garment, in the hair, etc.

LEGGING a tube shaped covering for the leg.

MANTLE a long sleeveless cloak or cape worn hanging loosely from the shoulders.

MUSSEL SHELL   any of the various bi-valve mollusk shells found in the rivers of the Eastern U.S.

OCHRE   an earthy clay containing iron ore, usually yellow or reddish brown in color (red ochre).

PINKING SHEARS   scissors with notched blades making a jagged edge on material when cut.

PONY BEAD   bead 8 mm in size - a little larger than the seed beed.

PUMP DRILL   an ancient tool consisting of a small bow with string and a wooden shaft with a flint drill bit used in the drilling process.

QUILLS   spines of the porcupine.

QUILLED   designs made of quills on clothing and accessories.

QUILLWORK   a process using flattened quills to make designs on leather clothing.

RAWHIDE   animal hide that has not been tanned.

ROACH   a headdress with a crest made of porcupine guard hair, horsehair, tampico or manila fibers.

ROSETTE   a beaded circular ornament on which the beads radiate from the center.

SEED BEAD   the smallest bead made.

SINEW   animal tendons which have been shredded to form thread or string.

SPOT BEADING   sewing seed beads directly onto leather or cloth allowing some of the material to show as background.

STITCH, HOLDING   a stitch made with thread or twine to tack a portion of material for holding it in place.

STITCH, IN-&-OUT   method of sewing two layers of cloth by going into the cloth with the needle and back up again.

STITCH, LAZY   method of sewing several seed beads (6 or more) at a time onto thread in parallel rows on leather or cloth.

STITCH, OVERCAST   same as whip stitch below.

STITCH, WHIP   a method of sewing which forms a seam by taking each stitch over the edges of two layers of cloth after each pass through the cloth. Also known as the Overcast Stitch.

TASSEL   any loose hanging ornament used on clothing, made of fur, beads, hair, etc.

TIN CONES   tapered cylinders of rolled metal used as decorations on clothing.

TUBULAR BEAD   beads of various sizes which are tube or barrel shaped.

TWINING   method of weaving in which two strands of yarn are alternated between vertical strands of yarn on a loom.

UPPER WORLD   in Cherokee mythology this region exists above the earth.

VERMILION   a bright red mecuric sulfide, used at one time by Native Americans as a coloring for face and body decoration.

WAMPUM   small beads made of clam, conch, periwinkle and other seashells. Often used by Native Americans as a form of money.

SUGGESTIONS FOR FURTHER STUDY

ADAIR, JAMES
1930   *History of the American Indians.* edited by Samuel Cole Williams, Johnson City, Tennessee.

CATLIN, GEORGE
1973   *Letters and Notes on the Manners, Customs and Conditions of the North American Indians.* New York, New York: Dover Publications, Inc.

FUNDERBURK, EMMA LILA & FOREMAN, MARY D., EDS.
1957   *Sun Circles and Human Hands.* Laverne, Alabama: The Southeastern Indians Art and Industry.

HORAN, JAMES
1975   *North American Indian Portraits.* New York, New York: Crown Publishing, Inc.

HUDSON, CHARLES
1976   *The Southeastern Indians.* Knoxville, Tennessee: The University of Tennessee Press.

JORDAN, JAN
1973   *Give Me the Wind.* Engle Cliffs, New Jersey: Prentice-Hall, Inc.

KING, DUANE
1979   *The Cherokee Indian Nation.* Knoxville, Tennessee: University of Tennessee Press.

LEFTWICH, RODNEY
1970   *Arts and Crafts of the Cherokee.* Cherokee, North Carolina: Cherokee Publications.

LEWIS, T.M.N. AND KNEBERG, MADELINE
1958   *Tribes That Slumber.* Knoxville, Tennessee: University of Tennessee Press.

MAUER, EVAN
1977   *The Native American Heritage.* Chicago, Illinois: Institute of Chicago.

MOONEY, JAMES
1900   *History, Myths and Sacred Formulas of the Cherokees.* Cherokee, North Carolina: reprinted by Cherokee Publications, 1992.

PHILLIPPE, LOUIS
1977   *Diary of My Travels In America, Louis Phillippe, King of France 1830-1848.* New York, New York: Delacorte Press.

SATZ, RONALD N.
1979   *Tennessee's Indian Peoples.* Knoxville, Tennessee: University of Tennessee Press.

RIGHTS, DOUGLAS L.
1988   *The American Indian in North Carolina.* Winston Salem, North Carolina: John F. Blair, Publisher.

SHARPE, J. ED
1970   *The Cherokees Past and Present - An Authentic Guide to the Cherokee People.* Cherokee, North Carolina: Cherokee Publications.

SPECK, FRANK G. AND BROOM, LEONARD
1983   *Cherokee Dance and Drama.* Norman, Oklahoma: University of Oklahoma Press.

STEELE, WILLIAM O.
1917   *The Cherokee Crown of Tannassy.* Reproduced in 1977, Charlottee, North Carolina: Heritage Printers.

STRICKLAND, RENNARD
1975   *Fire and Spirits - Cherokee Law from Clan to Court.* Norman Oklahoma: University of Oklahoma Press.

WOODWARD, GRACE STEELE
1963   *The Cherokees,* Norman Oklahoma: University of Oklahoma Press.

APPENDIX

1. The examples of clothing in this book, designated as **Cherokee**, are based on descriptions of earlier writers such as James Adair, James Mooney and others. Dress styles of the early/late eighteenth century are mainly what I am concerned with in this book. During this time period in history, Cherokee dress had already been greatly changed in appearance by the use of trade items such as cloth and glass beads. An old print in the British Museum, the New York Library and the University of Georgia shows Ostenaco and two other Cherokees in London in 1762. They are wearing a mixture of clothing influenced by white man's trade items, such as wool blankets, long cloth shirts with ruffled sleeves, metal gorgets, etc. The native look can also be seen in their costume, center-seam leggings, moccasins, and even the hair styles and ornaments.

   The Cherokee during the eighteenth century, who dressed like their Euroamerican neighbors, as reflected in the drawing of Seven Cherokees in London in 1730, which can be seen in the British Museum, are not dealt with in this book. As you scan through this book, you can see illustrations of clothing made of leather as well as cloth, which can be worn in a mixture of ways, as Cherokee did during the eighteenth century. The all leather look which was still in style during the early eighteenth century can also be seen in this book.

   Since we know of few pieces of Cherokee clothing from the eighteenth and early nineteenth century that exist today, many items in this book reflect twentieth century copies or renditions, which can be seen in such places as Oconaluftee Indian Village, Museum of the Cherokee Indian, the outdoor drama - "Unto These Hills," and the Cherokee Cyclorama Wax Museum all in Cherokee, North Carolina. Versions of my own are also used in this book.

   We must also understand, when trying to make Cherokee clothing of the eighteenth century, that many of the Southeastern tribes wore very similar clothing . Even designs, such as floral designs, were borrowed from others and exchanged among tribes.

   The largely stereotyped dress of the early nineteenth century, when cloth turbans, cloth coats, trousers, and white man's shoes were worn, is not dealt with to any great extent in this book.

2. On page 12 of this book, in paragraph two, I stated, "Long ago, before cloth and wool blankets...," This period in history was the pre-contact/early contact aboriginal time of dress among the Cherokee. Such a period in history is not well documented, even by the early Spanish chronicles, that is why I used a brief description on how to make leather. It is best to study other books on how to make leather, since there are many good books dealing with the subject. Check with your craft supplier or contact the publisher of this book.

3. The hunting shirt on page 17 in the sketch, is a version of my own, worn during the late eighteenth century by many people at that time, Indians included. This shirt style shows a lot of influence from the Euroamerican contact.

4. Yarn garters on page 18 are only examples based on those made by Cherokees today, in North Carolina, which reflect the late eighteenth century style garters. They were also worn by some traditional Cherokees in the early nineteenth century, as can be seen in the painting of "Sequoyah" in the Library of Congress.

   The belt, moccasin, and boot on page 18 are examples I drew to depict items worn during the early eighteenth century, based on descriptions by Adair, modern renditions of such items from drawings or paintings from that period, and a touch of my own.

5. Page 19 shows two Cherokees, I drew from descriptions found in James Adair's *History of American Indians,* Charles Hudson's, *The Southeastern Indians,* etc. These styles of men's dress would be eighteenth century. The shirt on this same page is based on a drawing of "Tuchee," called "Dutch" by George Catlin, in the Thomas Gilcrease Institute and the drawing combined with the shirt or coat from the sketch of the Cherokee mode of dress by George Catlin in the Library of Congress. From the mentioned pictures of the early 19th century, I created an 18th century shirt, which is conjecture on my part.

6. The leather outfits on page 20, are of early 18th century clothing, based on those seen in the "Cherokee Cyclorama Wax Museum" in Cherokee, North Carolina.

7. The shirt on page 26 is based on the one worn in a photograph of Will West Long in the early 20th century in Cherokee Dance and Drama by Speck and Broom. It has been noted by some writers that some shirts had open sleeves and that is what I tried to show in this rendition. Instead of using small feathers, as in the Will West Long shirt, I used hawk feathers. Please remember, it is against the law to kill hawks, eagles and other protected birds. The feathers for this shirt came from a dead hawk found along the roadside which my father brought to me a number of years ago.

8. The making of the shirt shown on page 28, is based on the information related in number 5 of the Appendix.

9. A rendition of the hunting shirt, changed to a war shirt, is seen on page 37. This is conjecture on my part.

10. The cloth shirts at the top of page 40, are based on a sketch from an old English newspaper, which can be seen in the Cumberland Gap Historical Museum, Middlesboro, Kentucky. It probably is a sketch of Iroquois, but holds true to the style of cloth shirts worn also by the Cherokee of the 18th century.

   The leather shirt on the same page 40 is based on shirts depicted at the Cyclorama Wax Museum, Cherokee, North Carolina. Such a decorated shirt, is a rendition of the 18th century.

11. The Chief's cloak on pages 41-47 is based on the ones which are presented to the public at the "Unto These Hills" outdoor drama, Oconaluftee Indian Village, and Museum of the Cherokee Indian, Cherokee, North Carolina. Such items, represent those of the 18th century as described by early writers.

12. Feather skirts worn by the Beloved Women of the Cherokees, as seen on page 48 of this book, are based on an example shown to the public at the Oconaluftee Indian Village, Cherokee, North Carolina.

13. Capes were worn by Native Americans in the Great Lakes area by such tribes as the Sauk and Fox etc., as you can see in the book North American Indian Portraits by James D. Horan, on pages 29, 30, 37, 39. In the Northeast, tribes such as the Iroquois wore capes; see page 3 of the same book. The Shawnees to the South wore such capes; see page 24 and 25. Even George Catlin painted a portrait of The Prophet, a Shawnee who was wearing a fur cape as can be seen in the book, Letters and Notes on the North American Indians, edited by Michael M. Mooney. Even the Seminole Indians, as far south as Florida, liked wearing the cape, as shown in the same book of James D. Horan's on pages 68, 70, 72, 73, 74, 75. See also, Diary of My Travels in America, by Louis Philippe, page 96. He describes a Cherokee cape.

Since many of the tribes, North and South of the Cherokees wore such capes or variations of it at a time when most Southeastern tribes dressed much the same way, then why would the Cherokee not wear capes, too? If you look close at paintings by George Catlin, of "Tahchee" or of "Dutch" and Spring Frog from McKenney and Hall's in the book, North American Indian Portraits by James Horan, pages 79, 82, you can see a resemblance of such capes, grafted into the make-up and structure of their cloth shirts of the early 19th century period, reflecting the cape pattern of the prior century. Perhaps all of this is conjecture on my part but I think the Cherokees, sometimes wore capes, too. Pages 49-56 are examples in my book, on how such capes may have looked.

14. The embroidered vest on page 68 shows floral designs. Such designs were used by The Great Lake Indians in the north, tribes in the Northeast, and then tribes to the South such as the Cherokee began using the designs. Such floral designs are believed to be borrowed from the whites. At any rate, Indians began using them through the late 19th century and present times. A Cherokee "coat with floral designs" can be seen in the book, The Native American Heritage by Evan M. Maurer, published by The Art Institute of Chicago, 1977, pages 78, 79. This particular coat was made in 1854. Since the use of floral designs did not just happen over night, they would have had to be in use to some degree in the late 18th century. Mr. Edds, who owned the vest shown on page 68 of my book told me, "The Cherokee man who sold me the vest was nearly a hundred years old. He got the vest from his father." I talked to Mr. Edds around 1979. It is my guess that the vest is early 19th century.

15. On page 87, the breechclouts in the upper right corner and middle left are based on a James Mooney photograph of the late 19th century. Such breechclouts reflect the 18th century dress. The other examples are renditions of the breechclouts which are portrayed in the outdoor drama in Cherokee, North Carolina today, representing the 18th century. Other examples of breechclouts in this book are similar to ones worn by modern Cherokee men who dress up for tourists. A reflection of the breechclout of their ancestors can be seen in the construction.

16. The war chief's hat on page 98, 98, 100 is based on the ones I saw in the outdoor drama and at the Oconaluftee Indian Village, Cherokee, North Carolina. The meanings I gave to different elements of the hat are my own interpretation. A "swan headdress" is described in James Adair's book on page 427.

17. The sleeveless shirt on page 106, in my book is based on the description in James Adair's book, History of the American Indian, page 87.

18. When I refer to the phrase in my book "The War Chief," it means the war chief or chiefs during the 18th century. There are no modern-day war chiefs in North Carolina or Oklahoma, only those dressed up for the tourist trade. If you wish to see how a War Chief of the Cherokee used to dress, you will have to see the outdoor drama, "Unto These Hills," at Cherokee, North Carolina.

19. Designs from pottery, which can be used on clothing, can be obtained from Early Pisgah to the Late Etowah period fragments, which is from 1250 to 1450 a.d. Qualla Complicated Stamped Pottery from 1880-1900 can be used. Even early Lamar to late Lamar, 1650 a.d.-1838 a.d. can be studied to obtain designs. Duane H. King's book, The Cherokee Nation, pages 14, 18, 25, 26 and 27 show examples of such pottery. Other Cherokee pottery designs, as well as basket designs are shown in a 1920 Bulletin, "Decorative Art and Basketry" by Frank G. Speck at the Milwaukee Public Museum.

20. Center seam leggings can be seen in a print at the British Museum, the New York Public Library and the University of Georgia, showing Ostenaco and two other Cherokees in London in 1762. The leggings on page 126 are based on an illustration of some Cherokees from a British Music Sheet at the Thomas Gilcrease Institute. Side seam leggings in my book on page 134 were also worn by some Cherokees up to the removal period, as shown in the painting of Sequoyah in the Library of Congress.

21. The wampum belts in my book are based on a photograph of the traditional Cherokee Keetoowah, Oklahoma Historical Society, Oklahoma City, Oklahoma. The meanings which I gave to each belt are my own, although the real meaning of the belts are known only by the Keetoowahs.

22. The wrap-around skirts and tops I drew from descriptions of early writers of the 18th century. The one-piece dress on page 167 is based on the one at the "Cyclorama Wax Museum," Cherokee, North Carolina. There are several differences in the dress I made, such as the bead work, etc., but the structure is almost the same. The patchwork dress is based on dresses you may see in photographs in the book, Cherokee Dance and Drama by Speck and Broom.

23. Boots on page 194, 195 and 196, are renditions of my own, going by descriptions of the 18th century. Louis Phillippe, King of France, 1797, contains a drawing in his diary of a Cherokee man wearing boots reaching nearly to the knees. Since Cherokees wore center seam moccasins, their boots were probably made the same way, only higher.

24. The fur hats on pages 200-203 are based on the fur hat mentioned in William O. Steele's book, The Cherokee Crown of Tannassy. The feathered hats are based on descriptions given by James Adair, History of the American Indians, page 89 and 176.

25. The shell gorget necklace on page 244 is based on one James Adair described in his book, on page 88.

26. Necklaces on page 248 are based on such drawings of "Ostenaco and the two Cherokees" as seen in a print at the University of Georgia, Athens, Georgia.

27. Feathered collars, as seen on page 249 were worn as far north as the Iroquois (shown in a print at The Cumberland Gap Museum at Middlesboro, Kentucky) and as far south at the Chickasaw (described by James Adair, History of the American Indian page 426.)

28. The bear claw necklace on page 254 is based on one I saw in the Museum of the Cherokee Indian, Cherokee, North Carolina.

29. Pouches on pages 262-265 are renditions of my own based on pouch construction of Native Americans using Cherokee designs. The pouch on 266 is based on the one Mr. Edds showed me at his home in Virginia. The painted pouch on page 269 is based on the one seen in The American Indian in North Carolina by Douglas L. Rights, page 258. The other pouches and shoulder bags are renditions of my own based on the painting of the Indian Council of 1843 by John Mix Stanley, and on paintings in North American Indian Portraits by James D. Horan, and a painting by George Catlin of the mode of Cherokee dress during the removal period.

30. The knife holsters in this book are based on general construction of a knife holster by Indians using common methods. These renditions are my own.

ABOUT THE AUTHOR - DONALD SIZEMORE

Donald Sizemore was born March 17, 1950, in the small mountain community of Poff Hill, near Pineville, Kentucky. His parents, Camie and Nora Baker Sizemore, had moved their belongings by wagon to this isolated area in the 1930's. Before 1949, there was no electricity or water in their home, and Donald's older sisters washed their clothing by the banks of the Cumberland River. By the time Donald and his twin sister Carol were born, things were a little easier on the homeplace. They now had electricity, a telephone, and a jeep for transportation. The once huge fields of crops his siblings had helped raise had shrunken to a small garden.

Donald started school at the old Moss Chapel Grade School at the age of seven. At that time, children walked off the mountain, down the railroad, and across the Wasiota swinging bridge to catch the bus for school.

As the twelfth child in the family and with most of his brothers and sisters gone from home, Donald had plenty of time to listen to the stories his father (and other relatives) told about their Cherokee ancestry. Reading, drawing, and making American Indian crafts became a part of his life as he tried to recapture some of his Indian heritage. He says, "I made my first war bonnet from cardboard and chicken feathers, which I thought was really something!" Using scraps and various items he had found, he continued to construct objects relating to the Indian culture, and, as he learned more and more, his work took on a more authentic look.

Donald graduated from the Bell County High School in 1968 and was called to the Army in 1970. In the service, he served as a medic in Germany. While abroad, he was able to visit eleven countries in Europe and the Middle East. Upon his return to Pineville, he worked at Pineville Community Hospital as a Physical Therapist Assistant and later was employed in a local nursing home. It was there he met Mabel Ramey, the woman who would become his wife and who would encourage him to continue with his research of Native American culture.

The Sizemores moved in 1983 to a one-room log cabin located near the old family homestead. There they lived the "old-fashioned way" with kerosene lamps, cooking over a fireplace, growing their own foodstuffs, and having "a very happy way of life." Visitors who admired the Indian crafts hanging on the walls of the cabin were taken to see a crude council house Donald had built several years earlier. There he had the opportunity to explain the uses and history behind the items they found there. "Many were the times I went to the council house to think and to talk to the Great Man Above," Sizemore says, "and believe me, I felt His presence just the same as I had often felt it in the white man's church."

After losing his father, moving into his aging mother's home to care for her, and undergoing the loss of his left hand in a tragic accident, Donald fought off bouts of depression and came to realize he could share his knowledge of the crafts of the Cherokee. Because of the loyal support of his wife, and the overwhelming interest in his work by Ed Sharpe (of Cherokee Publications), Donald was inspired to collect his notes and drawings, his creations and re-creations, for this volume. He had found the purpose of his life.

SOURCES FOR PROJECT MATERIALS & SUPPLIES

Tandy Leather Company
1400 Everman Parkway
Fort Worth TX 76140
(Tandy has stores in major cities
- check yellow pages or write for
location in your area.)

Winona Trading Post
PO Box 324
SANTA Fe, NM 87501

Northeast Bead Trading Co.
12 Depot Street
Kennebunk, ME 04043

Walmart Stores
(in most areas - check your
yellow pages)

Grey Owl Indian Craft
150-02 Beaver Road
Jamaica, Queens, NY 11433

Navajo Gallery
577 Main Street
Hamilton, OH 45013

Walco Products, Inc.
1200 Zerega Avenue
Bronx, NY 10462

Progress Feather Company
657 W. Lake Street
Chicago, IL 60606

Albert Constantine & Son, Inc.
(woodcarving tools)
2050 Eastchester Road
Bronx, NY 10461

Medicine Man Craft Shop
(beads, feathers, leather, etc.)
PO Box 124
Cherokee, NC 28719

NOTE: These are sources used by the author. Check for craft shops in your area carrying appropriate materials and supplies for your clothing projects